MW01603047

Music Appreciation
a Millennium of Music

Roderick MacDonald
Associate Professor of Music
State University of New York

An overview of western music history
with it's creators, artists, & patrons.

Copyright © 2019 Tone Art Media

Library of Congress Control Number: 2019909140

Library of Congress
US Programs, Law, and Literature Division
Cataloging in Publication Program
101 Independence Avenue, S.E.
Washington, DC 20540-4283

Printed in the United States of America 2019

Copyright © 2019 by Roderick MacDonald

Publisher's Cataloging-in-Publication data:

7905 N Crescent Blvd
Pennsauken, NJ 08110
www.bookbaby.com

Music Appreciation: an overview of western music history with it's creators, artists, & patrons.

ISBN 978-0-69215-828-9

1. The main category of the book —Music —Other category. 2.History —From one perspective. 3. An Appreciation of Music

First Edition

14 13 12 11 10 / 10 9 8 7 6 5 4 3 2 1

TABLE OF CONTENTS

The Origin

Millennia passed and "the waters of the land had not yet receded" as the earths form was not yet finished. Waves broke against the rocks, winds howled in the branches, and streams rushed over the rocks. Eventually, living creatures on the earth would croak, bark, peep and growl. That was the Earth's language. Birds chirped at dawn, but still no music.

It was people alone with their knowledge of the world around them that spawned the language of melody, harmony, and their inner movements. Music as a human definition is intelligently designed language perceived as sound.

What brought people to "invent" music and how did they reveal that this play of sound may be a reflection of their inner thoughts and movements? We may now ponder, how long has there been music? Is it possible as long as there have been words and language?

Since primitive humans sought language for a purpose, could you not think that the magical nature of music may also have a purpose? Music of gods in mythology, music is a gift from the gods, where they expressed themselves in legends and fairy tales.

The Greeks revered Hermes as the patron of music. Being the god of commerce and merchants, he was quite far from music, he was also a messenger of the gods. His parents, Zeus and his mistress Maja, sent him out as he walked along the shores of the Mediterranean, finding a turtle shell and stretching gut strings over it, which he had stolen from his brother Apollo. Legend has it that the first musical instrument invented was the lyre or simple harp. The lute is related to this instrument. The origin may still be recognized in its name, al-ud, the original word of the lute. This means not only wood, but also turtle, according to an Arabic-Latin dictionary.

The Chinese had music for a long time before this. Four and a half thousand years ago, the mighty Emperor Haong-ti had ordered music. The jubilation of the birds and the sound of a river became the model for this form of music. In Japan, once the sun goddess plodded back into her cave, it was known that there was nothing better than to lure her out again with a series of sounds, the goddess wrestling in the cave was the poetic symbol of a solar eclipse. In Japan, ancient sages and songs are still being sung during a solar eclipse.

In North America, a tribe believed that their god Tezcathipoca had given the music to them. He built a bridge of whales and turtles, through which one could reach the sun while playing and singing. To the Abyssinians appeared a dove of God, He first taught them to read and write and then gave them the music.

In the Germanic saga, Heimdall, the sky-guard, had a giant horn buried under the world ash and earth. It should be played when the twilight of the gods began. Wotan protected all singers and musicians because he was a heroic singer.

Most primitive cultures interweave the genesis and continuance of their music with their legends. In the Middle Ages, it was believed that it had been invented by Jubal, a son of Cain.

Because music came from the gods, one could speak to the gods through music. With music, the evil spirits could be warded off, death and sickness expelled, the storm and the disastrous fires banished, and rain and fertility brought back. This magic of sound has basically been handed down from many cultures. Nevertheless, in the early spring, people at an early stage of evolution sing songs that seek the fertility of fields and cattle. The grazing cows carry bells for this purpose. Today's people fulfill religious feelings of God's nearness when the little bells ring in the altar at the Catholic service.

Now in the age of science do we by no means despise the old legends and fairy tales, but rather elevate ourselves through their deep and beautiful meanings? Of course, we are not content with such simple allegorical interpretations and strive deeper for the origin of music.

Did music form by way of language? When people were attentive and solemn, they raised their voices and gave the sound's duration. This is not a big leap of faith as the speech of our actors and politicians often resembles a kind of song. In worship, we experience all sorts of effects in a congregation of many voices. The preacher speaks a simple language, but in the liturgical formulas, we experience the transition from the elevated chant to pure singing. First, the raising and lowering of the speech sound is avoided, and the voice stops at a specific pitch. Stepping from one to the other is like singing.

Indigenous cultures might have done the same when worshiping gods. The solemnity of the hour and the force of inner agitation compelled people to utter something that could not be said in words. However, not all of the magical meanings of the music were allowed but reserved for the priests, shamans, and medicine men. Certain melodies were only allowed, and only specified instruments could play them. Ordinary people were forbidden to touch these instruments, and the women were even punished if they only saw them. Indeed, ambition and power strived in music. The priests sought to obtain and maintain their position through privileges. Music, as a ceremony was presented to the gods as a gift, was also a struggle for power and supremacy.

So, maybe, music was born out of language. The hither and thither of the high and low of sounds had changed into a succession of steady highs and lows. This view was presented in a series of scientific doctrines, notably Jean Jacques Rousseau, Johann Gottfried Herder, and Herbert Spencer.

"Why are the birds singing?" Their singing is a solicitation and ultimately serves for its reproduction. Music not only provided worship to the gods but also out of love for one another. The folk songs of the Middle Ages are as folksy as any of our modern times popular songs are, all being the language of love. Once again, these songs promote favor concealed in the words and meanings.

Rhythm & Work

When prehistoric men felled a tree, carried away a heavy load, or buried a stake, they realized that it would be easier if they planned a specific sequence of time or a certain rhythm. Uniform rhythmic action in groups controls unproductive impulse independence. We feel chained into an energy saving sequence. This too is no different today than it used to be. When the acres of wheat, still threshed by hand, the threshing-scythe oscillates in a certain rhythm through the air. If stones are cut and split in a quarry, the people of our day are no different from the primitive human thousands of years ago.

In work, the rhythm gradually developed to the most essential elements of music. The first calls, which will not have sounded much different than our "Haul-push!", were gradually perfected. When the sower waved his arms, wrestling with linen, sowed fields, and as with every action in groups, short, repetitive, rhythmic songs were invented. Karl Bücher, who worked out this theory of the genesis of music, published an extensive series of such methods in his book Work and Rhythm.

Simply said, what gift music from the gods is all about when the deities gave travelers a sense of rhythm for their long trek. When they made their pilgrimage through the desolate land, or they listened to their footsteps, or the steps of their pack animals. To this rhythm, they adapted words that came to their lips, and over time, little songs developed to help them through the loneliness. Because early merchants were the most traveled at that time, it is understandable why Hermes, the god of merchants, according to legend, contributed decisively to the discovery of music. Incidentally, it is no coincidence that in Arabic, all fourteen meters were derived from the gaits of the camels and named after them.

Early on, people noticed that the harmony of some sounds was better than others. Some sound combinations were perceived as unsatisfactory, unpleasant, and even tormenting. We would say today: consonance and dissonance were developed into our early conscience. Shepherds or hunters called a signal over long distances, and the others answered. Depending on the answer, the result may have been a soothing or distressing message.

Which theory about the genesis of music may come closest to the truth? Let's leave the argument to the scholars, as it's likely that all these theories are approximately correct, one thing leads to another, and no steps were missing in between so that music could emerge.

Music of the old world

What did music of the Old World sound like? We do not know, as there are no records of original music notation. Drawings on rocks, tools, foundation walls of dwellings, jewelry and other daily objects ancient people created, have been preserved. The old tunes have all fallen silent, leaving no trace. Their sounds have dissolved like clouds at sunset.

There are two ways one may attempt to give an understanding of the first music. First is through watching cultures that are still at early stages of development mirroring what we have all passed through. We will need to expedite this work because these few isolated cultures and their old songs are in rapid extinction. A large branch of musicology examines these melodies and tries to draw conclusions from them. This is called "comparative music science," and the researchers work on recording and notating an unknown culture's music and it's meaning.

This music simply seems counter to our rhythms. It is sometimes challenging to notate this music in a form for it to be repeated.

Logically the music of the Tierra del Fuego, Busch Hunter, or the Eskimos is unrelated to the ancient Germanic tribes or even the original inhabitants of Europe. They have all developed their own music independently. Still, the Old World remains silent for us.

The second way to track down the singing of the early cultures where the trail has also gone cold, many of their instruments have survived. We can elicit sound from them and draw conclusions about the nature of their old music. Of course, nothing of the very oldest "instruments" made of clay and bone remain.

Drums and rattles pounding on objects is also music. Because it was often too soft to hear well, a soundboard was added for loudness when drumming a beat or rhythm. Dance boards have been found in large numbers. It has not died out yet, because what are the plates on which our tap dancers perform their rhythmic routines? In some cases, a drum could be wooden beams, taut dried animal skins, stones, bowls, etc. Most agree that the history of the instruments the drum was one of the earliest. They might have been used in magical spells or communication.

Of course, the drums were not the only percussion instrument. That one beats on wooden objects, one can see this in the relief drawing of Agostino di Duccio in 1460. The use of stones and bowls as a sounding body was especially widespread in the East. The gamelan orchestras on Java and the Japanese are based on instruments of this principle.

A step forward was the discovery that the air in a hollow object could produce distinct sounds when vibrating. In other words, the wind instruments were invented. It soon showed that the size of the space could also determine the pitch. The longer the tube; the lower the tone, the shorter the tube; the higher the tone.

First, you bundled several such pipes side by side. This instrument was called a flute or syrinx. We know it from Mozart's the 'Magic Flute'

Opera where the character Papageno plays it for the girl Papagena. Cutting holes in a flute and opening or closing them with their fingers also had the effect of shortening and lengthening the pipe, which would also change the sound's pitch. This is how many flute and shawm styles were created. Some of the flutes were blown across the opening and some lengthwise.

The musical staff is the ancestor and starting point of all our wind and string instruments. You can visualize a line on a parchment and you then have the first representation of a string instrument. You could hit the strung fiber, pluck it or brush it with a bow of animal hair. Soon several such fibers were laid side by side at different lengths providing different tones. This invention is the essential principle of the harp, a piano, and all string instruments.

The sounds produced by the first string instruments were probably small and thin but could be reinforced with a sounding box. If you put the whirring wood or the swinging tendon quickly to your teeth, then our head resonates and makes the sound great. An ancient Sitar from India can have 18 strings with the same length. Different pitches arise from pinching with your finger at the proper location along the string. Of course, you can also use other sound boxes: a shell, a box made of wood, stone, metal or glass. Over the millennia, this has led to an almost endless number of musical instruments.

Lurs from Denmark, of the early Bronze Age, circa 900-600v. Chr. might have been in high bloom. It was a bronze wind instrument similar to a horn. At the time of the old Teutons the Celtic Bards, the Anglo-Saxon Skop, and the Scandinavian skalds professional singers went from court to court reciting ancient heroic songs. Those who distinguished themselves as being accomplished were even celebrated as heros themselves. Hildebrandslied preserved such a heroic style of storytelling. There are 2 surviving documents from around 830 Ad. It is set in the 7th to the 8th century and is composed of legendary conflicts.

As we travel through the new millennia, evidence of music becomes more numerous. The music of the old world probably never went beyond one voice or more voices on one line of music (unison). The bow for brushing the strings was introduced only in the eighth century AD. Arabia was particularly crucial for the development of the music because a string instrument was found here in the Rebab. This is the earliest known bowed instrument and existed in the 8th century and possibly even earlier. Arabia is the home of the horse; the hair provided the best material for the bow.

Above all, the ancient Egyptians possessed wonderfully decorated harps, magnificent wood glittered with gold, silver, and precious stones in exquisite colors. Sometimes these harps had 22 strings. Vases and petroglyphs tell us that the Egyptians also knew flutes, shawms, rattles, and drums.

The earliest known musical instruments are small pipes made of bone. They date from the early Paleolithic period and are about 50,000 years old. Egyptian hand harp, flute from the bone of a jaguar made of painted wood are from the year 3500 BC. These testimonies tell of instruments and sound systems from the Sumerians in Old Babylon. From the year 3000 BC to the beginning of the 3rd century BC, Egyptian music was in its prime, followed by a second one from 1600 to 1100. The development of Chinese music sent from their gods is said to have taken place in the year 2697 B.C. and tells us from 2000 B.C. that a high musical culture existed among the Chaldeans and Hittites. Around 1800 BC, the Indians possessed a series of elaborate cult and sacrificial chants, as the songs of the Rigveda manuscript report.

The musical culture of the Greeks was quite involved as was the study of many of the great names like Pythagorus, Ptolemy, Philodemus, Aristoxenus, Aristides, and Plato. It covers the years around 1200 to 300 BC. Even though their beginning reaches much further, their aftermath goes back to the Middle Ages and into our time. With Orpheus, the legendary singer from 'Thrace', whose tragic fate we know from Gluck's grand opera 'Aristoxenus of Taranto', thought Greek music theory was at the end of its development by 300 BC. The Greeks were very interested in the theory behind music. No nation had until then explored the laws of sound. Many things have been forgotten after the disappearance of Greek dominance and had to be rediscovered in the Middle Ages and in modern times.

The Divided Octave

The theory of sounds is often based on the question of how the octave should be divided into individual distinct notes or pitches. The octave is a universal concept that every advancing culture interested in music will run up against eventually. Physically speaking, we hear tones with twice or half the number of vibrations as the same tones. If one tone is at 440 vibrations per second, we hear a second similar tone with 880. We have just created an octave. The higher and the lower tone are alike but not the same. It is the same kind of sound and merges together with an ever-increasing depth of harmony.

How did the sounds get their names? The convention came about by using the letters of the alphabet with a, b, c, and so on. The lowest tone of the male voices that could be reached repeatedly was about an a, and the result was a ladder or scale ascending of a,b,c,d,e,f, and g. We tune in our orchestras today with the a, which more or less 440 oscillations per second. Some countries did not follow the convention and chose a slightly higher pitch of 442-443 Hz. We tend to tune-up a bit higher because this gives the string instruments more shine. The poor singers have to suffer as now their notes become somewhat higher to sing.

How should the space in-between the octave notes be divided? All kinds of methods were found. Initially, a tone set of three, then five levels seemed enough. One convention had arrived at the pentatonic, the five-step system. The notes between c and c are called: c, d, e, g, a, c.

It is easy to see that there are no halftones here. The black keys are missing on such a keyboard.

With this scale, many early cultures, and some in Asia were content. Even today the pentatonic is not extinct. Children often sing their first songs in the pentatonic key. In this scale, there are no halftones intervals. The half tone is considered to be the smallest interval of western music culture and tradition.

The lack of halftone (semitone) steps or intervals prevents it from coming to a modern satisfy conclusions, as we are used to. In using the semitones, the finality of a melody has more strength.

The Greeks went beyond the pentatonic and developed a much more varied system. They already divided the octave between c and c into the tones c, d, e, f, g, a, h, c, as we do today, though this was not their common tone. However, the

Greeks also knew about the whole and semitone steps. But their scale system was different from ours in that the halftone steps were not always in the same place. Among other things, they knew scales with the following structure:

The sound steps were thus distributed differently for different scales and their effects on a melody. Dorian, Phrygian, Lydian, to name a few.

The Greeks attributed ethical power to their scales. It was no coincidence that they were named after individual tribes. The Dorians had come from the north and were considered brave and morally strict. The scale named after them was therefore credited with virtuous and encouraging qualities. The Greeks heard this melody based on this scale with fighting strength. The exact opposite was the case with the Phrygian scale, which has the semitone step second and was the expression of sensual lust. The Lydian key was perceived as sweet, mild, and gently floating.

One night Pythagoras was looked at the stars and suddenly he heard a noise. He noticed that young men wanted to break into the house of a beautiful actress. A shawmer was playing a melody sounding in the Phrygian key. This just spurred on the interest of the youths. Pythagoras went to the wind player and ordered him to change the key to the Doric.

Immediately the youths were sobered and went home. This happened two and a half thousand years ago in ancient Greece, it is said.

The Greeks were also the first people to strive for musical notation. Only with the notation on some sort of manuscript can we carry music on for future generations. For the simple melodies of the Greeks, it was sufficient to write down the letter names of the notes.

Later, the Greeks provided these letters with special characters showing the length of the tone.

Song of Seikilos

We have discovered up to twelve Greek melodies, which we can reliably translate into the new music notation. One of those few surviving songs, the Seikilos song, was a kind of awe-inspiring shawm with sharp and thin sound. Another instrument was the kithara, a string instrument in the form of a lyre, which was plucked. The inscription is covered with the characters of the Greek music notation with the text translated from the original Greek. 'While you live, shine have no grief at all life exists only for a short while and time demands his due'

The Greeks attributed their music to a high ethos. In their opinion, music shapes character. Good music inspires the joy of action, bad can diminish or even abolish people's free will. That's why music in education played a significant role. The Greek ethos of music, created by Plato and perfected by his pupil Aristotle, has survived the centuries. Beethoven was still filled with this ethos when centuries later he wrote his own music.

In addition to major sport events, the Greek state organized competitions in which the whole country participated. Those who carried the laurels at state events were celebrated and sung as national heroes where mighty wind choirs sounded. According to Plato's wish, all Greeks should be members of a choir.

So we know a lot about Greek music, but their sound will still be lost forever. As we ascend the steps of the Acropolis, if we use our imagination, we might restore some of the sounds of the life of yesteryear. The architecture and sculpture of the Greeks speak to us with the same force as it did two and a half thousand years ago. Many of the painting on vases and murals remains at least partially preserved today. Greek music, however, has died away despite this knowledge.

The Voice of the West, the extinction of Greek culture and being superseded by another, brought no advancement for the development of music. The Romans took over the heritage of the Greeks without decisively promoting their music. The high-minded connection with the ethos loosened in favor of sensual music. Now, above all, it should serve the enjoyment of life. Music was heard in the wrestling matches and as a stimulant at grandiose meals. In the late period, there were large musician ensembles. Otherwise, it would not have been possible to fill the 10,000 to 12,000-capacity theater with sound. Even then, music was considered indispensable for education. The emperors themselves were celebrated as singers. Nero went furthest in it. In his dying hour, he intended as a chronicler of all things of the court and gossip, not the crimes which he had done, but said only in vain self-congratulation: "What a singer knows, goes with me to the grave."

This brings us to those sections of history that connect more to the birth of Christ. Gradually, the countries around the Mediterranean lost their importance for the development of culture and thus for the development of music. Egypt, Persia, Arabia, Greece, Rome and everything they created there was subject to diminution and passing away.

Paths lead to the north in the forests of Central Europe, the art of sound flourished above all in Germans and the Celts. Then came the sounds that Christianity carried with it. The ancient gods were overthrown and condemned with them those sages who glorified them. That the hero singers lost their reputation through their displacement was by no means complete. Remains of the past were everywhere. Although the old gods and heroes songs were no longer sung in the castles and palaces, the songs of the vagrants, and the memory of Odin and Hagen remained awake on the highways and the taverns. The most faithful proved that the children have not forgotten the past to this day. In the side streets of the destroyed cities, they drew on the granite slabs with white chalk next to heaven and hell many ideas that go back to old pagan beliefs. To do so, they sing about Frau Holle, Goddess Holda, and others.

Christianity entered Europe through three primary paths for the north-wandering culture, which was repeated over the next two millennia. The one way over Spain, the Pyrenees and France became most prominent in advance of the Moorish culture. In the Middle Ages, the road through Italy has truly become a fateful way. The constant stream between north and south over the Alps was of the most lasting importance for the cultural history of the western world (occident). On the third way across Greece and the Balkans in the Middle Ages, the Turks invaded and caused a lot of suffering, but also brought some stimulation for the development of the music.

Invading Christians brought along all sorts of singing goods. The melodies of the Christians did not come from Hellas, but from the Orient, mainly from Syria. There the hymn had taken possession of Christianity. Of course, the wise men were modified many times, provided with new texts and sung to their unique circumstances. They consisted of free melodies without sharp rhythmic structure. These were melodies completely lacking in the motor accentuation needed for work and dance songs. Such a thing would not have been suitable for worship, in which the will of humankind does not humbly submit to divine power. The melodic power of these wise men and their suitability for the particular liturgical purpose was so high that they have remained alive to this day. Partly they owe that success the protective hand of the church.

Gregory the Great

The songs were always unanimous (unison), but were occasionally divided into speech and counter-speech between priest and church. This became immensely important for the development of music.

Bishop Ambrosius excelled in introducing these legends as songs. He worked around 380 AD in Milan and probably wrote some hymns himself. This is how the Ambrosian hymn of praise developed, which is still cultivated in Milan, Italy today. It consisted of simple sages, not only of the priest but occasionally sung by the whole congregation. This was the beginning of a liturgy. Because the singer of the Psalms stood in a raised place, leading to the steps (Gradus), one came to the word Graduale. From this, the common Mass Hymnal Book Graduale was developed.

The turmoil of those centuries, with the tremendous rearrangement of the migration of peoples, brought with it different hymns sung in different places. This created a serious threat to the hierarchy of the church where it was then necessary to arrange the hymnals of the church and to make it uniform. Pope Gregory the Great, who lived around 600 AD, was given credit for this work. This resulted in the Gregorian chant named after him, which is still considered valid today in the liturgy of the Catholic Church and has scarcely changed from the thirteen centuries since Gregory.

The first organ may be credited to Ktesibios, the son of an Alexandrian barber, around 200 years BC. Built in the 3rd century BC, it makes sense that he was also a good mathematician. Initially, the organ was used as a secular instrument. Starting from Rome, the first organs came to Gaul (present-day France, Belgium, northern Italy) and England. Pippin the Little and Charlemagne received such organs as gifts. These examples worked to show the powerful reach of Ludwig the Pious had in 826 for the cathedral in Aachen where the first German organ was built. To the people, it sounded like the roar of thunder and at other times so sweet and delicate, it was said that that women passed out. It not only replicated the lonely way of the Greek Aulos flute but the magic of a storm in nature.

In England, around the year 1000, there existed a giant organ with 400 metal pipes and 26 bellows that could play 20 notes. Later, the organs were built with keys to play them, were about ten centimeters wide and had to be pushed down thirty centimeters. One had to use fists and elbows as there existed the expression "to beat the organ."

Now the organ was an instrument of the church, of worship, and had become the worshiper. No other instrument has changed its purpose so often and so thoroughly. The organ belonged to the next millennium of the church where we see how it has recently, according to its old purpose, been made servile to secular purposes too. From the church loft, it wandered to the cinema where, as a Wurlitzer organ, it is intended to impress our souls compassionately.

The First Turn

To this point, the development of music occurred grudgingly if at all. Sometimes three to four hundred years went by without any decisive events. But around the year 1000 AD, the development of music became gradually more innovative. What had happened for millennia was overturned. What had never been anticipated became a reality.

Until then, there had been music in unison. The songs of the Germans and Celts were unanimously one voice, like those of the Greeks and Persians. Even if instruments accompanied the singing, it would not have been an independent part or melody. All voices sang the same notes or in octaves. Women and children of a choir would sing in the upper octave and the men in the lower. There had never been polyphony in our sense today.

Now the unanimous melody line began to split. The trunk of the tree forked into the branches. Of course, this process did not happen suddenly. Instead, it took decades, sometimes centuries, to move one step further.

The development of music was now concentrated in Central Europe. But it was not worked on everywhere with equal urgency and with the same success. Instead, the flame of progress lit up only once here, and then only once there. Somewhere the creative spirit was innovating. The fire often went out after a short time too. The monks innovation didn't stay in one place but was often passed on to another region. The spark almost always lit in a new home. Thus, the beginning, the flowering, and the extinction followed each other, and this was the gradual progress that took place in almost all the countries and all the big cities in Europe. They enjoyed their great moment but also spent time seeing the achievements of others. Paris, Florence, Vienna, England, Weimar, Munich, the Netherlands, Dresden, Naples, Venice, and many others were once given the stage in this genuinely European concert. The story of the emergence of the Occidental music is, therefore, a long journey across Europe.

To visit the locations of the first musical innovations, we must wander through the area around the shores of Lake Constance. Here lived the monks in the monastery of St. Gallen; Notker Balbulus, the Stammler, and Tuotilo. They expanded on the Gregorian chorales through the addition of strophic form and sequences. New verses and rhymes were added, giving a significant musical enrichment.

Even more momentous was what had happened since the year 1000 AD. The idea was to use a new interval, the fourth or fifth, sound like a shadow to a melody, or to leave the source sound as the melody progresses from note to note. Thus came two voices, one stationary and one moving. This was called Organum. It was significant as it was the beginning of polyphony.

In England something else came to the fore: the melody came in thirds and sixths. This was perceived as "wonderfully sweet harmony".

Such manners were called Gymel, which means dividing one voice into two but staying in the same range. Usually, the two voices would meet at the same note at its conclusion.

This Gymel was related to the fauxbourdon, or the wrong bass. They called it that because the lower voice was not the main voice either. At the time, that was considered something new and was hardly understood at first.

The upper voice was not always faithful in it's intervals. Instead, it gradually gained an independent life, melodically as well as rhythmically. Later, the discantus, as they were called, even ventured counter movements: when the notes of the cantus firmus rose, the notes of the discantus fell, and vice versa. This made the second voice completely independent. The main melody was called the Cantus firmus.

Just as this happened, St. Gallen and the island of Reichenau on Lake Constance sunk in historical slumber, and England's innovations went silent for a time after that. Now we have to go to France, where Gothic awoke. Architecturally, the Romanesque arch extended to the Gothic pointed arch. The areas were dissolved into upward striving branches. This is how the Gothic cathedrals of Notre Dame were built in Paris, in Reims, Amiens, and Rouen.

If we continue our march of progress, it leads us far into Europe and the monastery of Saint Martial in Limoges, and further to the Spanish pilgrimage site of Santiago de Compostela and many other places of Gothic piety.

In the following years, the individual voices soon gained more and more independence; a melody became a bundle of melodic lines set free; melodies played around with, connected with each other, and thus led an ever-greater life of their own. Over time, not only two and three such lines remained, but four, eight, ten or more.

The masters of the singing school Beatae Mariae Virginis of Notre Dame, under Leoninus and Perotinus, innovated as the construction of the cathedral took place. Their most important form was the motetus.

Mot, is that which motet originated from. A mot, a word, formed the foundation and was usually a tune, a phrase from the Gregorian chant. Around it, other lines could be strung, went their own way rhythmically, and were often sung in another language. It was like thesis and commentary, speech and rebuttal in one. Nevertheless, the two accompanying voices formed a unity with the mot. Incidentally, such a backing voice could again become a motto and thus receive new accompaniment voices. The style changed from Romanesque to Gothic

The motetus thus developed a transition from the rounded arch to the pointed arch. Independence of the voices characterized this advance. The syllables of the text are not sung simultaneously in the different voices, as with the case of the protestant chorale. Also, the richly flourishing choral art of our time liked to move in the style of the early motet. This whole epoch of music was called ars antiqua, or the old art. (1180 to 1320)

It was followed by the ars nova - the new art. The change did not happen to everyone's satisfaction, on the contrary: fierce fighting broke out. Music theorists came to the scene and defended their position in texts written in Latin. The church began to observe and combat the emerging polyphony, for it threatened the pure effect of the Word of God. There were already battles for "modern music" at that time, just as we still have to endure them today. The intensity of the conflicts was by no means mitigated by the vast and challenging effort to overcome distances.

The next development takes us to Italy where the austere Gothic was followed by the bright laughter of the Italian sun dispelling everything gloominess of the north: not to be bothered by the horrors of the plague year 1348 in Italy. Hellenic antique lucidity sounded stronger than elsewhere. The deadly plague eventually receded in all lands. To ward off the evil, people took boat trips and sang pious honeymoon songs, some of which have survived to this day. For here true joy overcame all the horrors of pestilence.

The music was now being developed in the courts of Italy and not in the dark-whispering naves of Gothic cathedrals. Music was no longer made to praise God, but to glorify earthly pleasures. Florence, Bologna, Padua, and other cities were filled with life. The whole existence was then bathed in music. Every day for the writer Giovanni Boccaccio's imaginative literature Decameron ended with music. Graceful dance moves were invented to divide peoples manners finely.

The poems of Petrarch, Boccaccio, and others were set to music in all sorts of new forms. Canzons and ballads were among them. The supplest form was the Madrigal, a song-style, in an original manner of a shepherd's song. Dante's friend Casella, whom he met while traveling, supplied the first verses around 1300. The most famous composer of ars nova was a blind organist named Francesco Landino in Florence.

Also, probably the most famous composer in Italy during the 14th century, know today as the Italian ars nova, he creating mostly secular works of music. Especially works of love and the magic of nature have been repeated themes. Unadulterated sensuousness and chaste behavior mingled with each other. The effort to portray reality, which became evident in the painting of this time with Giotto and others, also prevailed in the musical formations. The ars nova also reached out to France. There, the poet and musician Guillaume Machaut was their main master.

We would not have learned about the instruments of the time if it were not for the exacting customers of the painters of the time. They did not get tired of painting saints, angels, and martyrs, but they also painted the princes and patrons surrounded by many of the musical instruments of their time. It was natural that Francesco Landino, St. Cecilia, David and other figures, their gravestones depicting instruments they played from the time of the painter. The underlying contradiction was not felt. The wing parts of the Ghent altar, painted by the brothers' van Eyck, contain a whole chapter of music history and it's instruments.

The most important instruments were now the viola, the Rotta, an originally Celtic string instrument that was now bowed, the lute that had come to Europe via Spain, as well as the trumpet, drum, bagpipes, horn, flute, and many others.

These instruments were meant to accompany a vocal part polyphonically. Unaccompanied singing would not have happened often. Additionally, instruments weren't often assigned by the composer as in today's scores, as they just played along with the vocal parts. If a vocal part was not occupied, an instrument jumped in for it. If there were more singers or players available than voices, new voices would be added. Other times it would be ok if one voice were missing than the music intended. This kind of music making was very much in the vein of times and might even be seen today as improvisational. The work was not fixed, but was the only base for the starting point of making music. And in a wonderful sense, all those involved knew how to follow what the creator of the music wanted.

Fortunately, the fact that the old masters have captured instruments in their paintings have given us more understanding than had it only been manuscript. This brings us to an essential innovation of music: notation.

The complicated lettering of the Greeks left an unclear understanding of how it might really have sounded. What needed to be found was an unmistakable means to represent the ups and downs of the sounds as well as their duration.

The first remedy for this was neumes, where the text words were provided with small check marks and signs. This notation is similar to parts of the French language with its different accents.

The neumes were undoubtedly an essential improvement. However, they did not indicate to what level the voice should be raised, but only pointed to the direction, namely, whether to raise or lower the voice. The actual magnitude of the sound step was not necessary at first, because everyone knew the tunes. The music notation had the only task of a reminder or rather a kind of musical shorthand.

This early form of notation was not enough for music to advance as even the church in Rome was trying to unify its liturgy and stamp out any room for improvisation in its masses. It took a fixed system for the height and length of the notes to solve this. With the invention of the staff, this then became possible. Scale lines on top of each other were used to record the pitch. They were not always five lines, as seen in the staff we use them today. At first, one contented oneself with a line, because the melodies had only a small range. It expanded to two, three, and then five lines. The lines were drawn in different colors and the notes in such elaborate shapes that one deserved the highest esteem to interpret this high and long-lost art.

The notoriety of having improved this notation system is attributed to the monk Guido of Arezzo, who lived around the year 1000. It was he who shows his invention to Pope John, which allowed a singer to render an accurate performance of a melody without ever having heard the song before.

Note shapes were improved first as small black rectangles and squares. That's why they were called nota quadrata in the 15th century. The short note values were characterized as not only in pitch, but also it's duration. Today we use an almost unchanged system of mensural notation (scale = measure). Thus, our notation of today's music notation, which was completed around 1600, became increasingly standardized.

The Middle Ages designed the music almost exclusively around singing. The instruments were built and used the vocal ranges of soprano, alto, tenor, and bass. Each of these voices and their intermediate mezzo-soprano, baritone, etc. received their own key. An ornate point on the staff indicated the line on which c should lie.

Before 1000 AD, all reform attempts remained without result, the conclusion is not unjustified that in the Middle Ages, music was considered a science and, as such, stood alongside astronomy, rhetoric and mathematics. The fact that we still use the same keys that were developed centuries ago proves that it has been preserved without questioning its intrinsic value.

The ars nova also sank once again. The power of Italy was exhausted, at least in the field of music; the destiny of development determined another country, another people the creator of the new: the Netherlands. This is the beginning of one of the most productive chapters in the history of music.

Ministry and Mastersingers - Guilds and Folk Songs

The Minstrel musicians were not always the most respected group and were sometimes despised. Also known as Strolling Minstrel, Balladeer, and Bards, they went through the countryside from town to town to perform and make their 'keep.' They were mimes, actors, jugglers, comedians, roaming musicians, and runaway monks who populated the country roads. Among these vagabonds was poetry filled with themes of drinking, ridicule, quarrels, play, nature, and love songs. Within these themes a rough kind of thematic texture developed. These songs were also documented in the so-called Carmina Burana. This song collection of traveling students was found in the monastery Benedict Monks. The juicy liveliness of these folk tunes was celebrated during the last century when Carl Orff reworked, set to music, and released it as a stage work.

Also, there was a flourishing of secular music of its own kind: the art of troubadours. It was a secularization of ancient Mary. Until then, only Mary, the virgin mother of the Lord Jesus Christ, had been sung. This worship of the Madonna was transmitted to women in general. The worldly knights, the troubadours, paid homage to them. There were reports of noble deeds they had accomplished as Crusaders in the Promised Land with indications of chaste abstinence, occasionally mingled with dance songs. Ballads were sung, and its text gave an account of an exciting event from the time of our heroes. But this was just a later modification of this old dance form, the Ballata. Sometimes there were little dances played on the fiddle. These were the earliest forms of instrumental music. They were called Estampida. The word literally means "stamping".

From providence, the troubadours began to make their exit. The way leads us this time to southern France, Count William of Poitiers was one of the oldest troubadours. Bertrand de Born, Adam de la Hale, called "The Hunchback of Arras," and Richard the Lion Heart followed in the line of chivalric singers. Adam de la Hale lived in a time when honor and troubadour art sank, and the bourgeoisie awoke.

The troubadours moved from farm to farm, trying to outdo each other with the sincerity and artfulness of their songs. Diligent research in museums and archives has managed to find around 2500 songs with 250 melodies from about 400 troubadours. The troubadours were never allowed to accept compensation or rewards in any other form than in granted allowances. Otherwise, they would have been expelled from their community.

The Art of Polyphony

We last heard of art music when we talked about the sensual music of ars nova in Italy. Italy silenced again, if not for a long time, and gave the floor to a corner of Europe that had never before shown itself to be particularly creative in the field of music. Now it had his big hour. It was the landscapes of Burgundy and Hainaut. Slightly generalizing, we speak of Dutch music, which was above all an unprecedented harbor of polyphony. Like ship's flares, it's enterprising art shot out of the small tracts of land, not only in the music but also in painting. The heyday of Dutch painting ranged from the brothers' van Eyck to Rembrandt.

The Art of Imitation

The two centuries from about 1400 to 1600 with the dominance of the Dutch are filled with the high art of polyphony. We talked earlier about how within the year 1000 AD, the voices became more independent. The one melody split into two, three, four, eight, ten, and even more independent intoned voices, which run side by side and yet unite into a meaningful unity. The voices often come in succession. If there are voices with different melodic and rhythmic material, contrapuntal work or figurative music resulted. Counterpoint means nothing but point to point, punctus versus punctum. Each point of the upper melody corresponds to a point in the lower, still independent, but both points merge into a harmonic unity. Polyphonic music, that is, really polyphonic music, is always contrapuntal.

Of course, the voices do not have to be different. Sometimes the same motives and topics are interwoven. But they do not start at the same time, but may begin one after the other. They can start on the same note, but might also start on another.

The Canon

The meaning of the canon is that there is nothing in it but the theme itself. It accompanies itself. We know this from the common Canon-singing. After one, two or three bars, the next voice starts again and again as this game can repeat itself through four or more voices. The first canons were devised in England as early as the thirteenth century. Soon the new form wandered over the continent. It is evident that the masters of polyphony liked to use the alluring possibilities of this form. It was fun for them to increase the number of voices. After all, there were canons of up to 48, even into the hundreds of voices.

Canons Unraveled

In folk singing, we limit ourselves to the canons that use the same tones again and again. That does not have to be the case always. The canon melody can also begin on any other note on the tone scale. Thus, canons arise approximately in the third, in the fifth, as in any other interval. Occasionally, the canon theme starts as four voices. With every new melody beginning, four new votes are added. The canon was so enticing for the Middle Ages because it was not embracing gripping themes of the highest art, but more leisurely activities like Bosseln "The sport was connected to betting, drinking and disorderly conduct, often gaining a bad reputation and was banned a few times."

The Joke Canon by Joseph Haydn

Haydn's three-part canon can be sung forward, but also backward, as well with reverse notes and then back and forth again. One can also sing it in German and English. Haydn donated it to the University of Oxford.

Occasionally, all sorts of numerical mysticism got into the form of the canon. The canon became a mystery when many masters of these centuries attempted to surpass themselves in the construction of elaborate works. The theme of reversing, as in mirrored writing, popular in the Ottoman Empire, offered many opportunities for this. Up to Bach, the canon remained alive and well. Even Mozart and Beethoven found their fun in crafting new canons.

Here the contrapuntal arts were shown on completed works of later masters as a perennial structure of music. 200 years of polyphony going dutch developed only step by step. One school after another emerged at a gradual pace. In the baroque period, only Italian musicians were considered, now only Dutch musicians. All over Europe, the Netherland Dutch provided for their gifted musicians, as only a few remained in their homeland. Some moved to Germany, and many to Italy. The splendor of the Holy Sea lured them, and the popes sought to transfigure their realm more and more. The St. Peters Church in Rome was built. Michelangelo and other fine artists worked for the popes as Eternal Rome set out to become an ever more important and powerful center and refuge of the church.

Creating church music attracted the Dutch masters of music. Many wandered over the Alps to enrich themselves inwardly and outwardly in the south. But moreover, they were innovators. They founded Dutch schools and fertilized the flagging creativeness of the Italians, where their only significant contributions were in the art of musical reproduction.

Afterwards, a wave came from England, which in 1370 produced in John Dunstable an innovator of the new polyphony. Then followed, among others, Guillaume Dufay, Johannes Ockeghem, Jakob Obrecht and Heinrich Isaac from the Netherlands. With Josquin de Pres (1450-1521), a first high summit was reached. After him came Adrian Willaert, Jakob Arcadelt, then Orlando di Lasso and finally Jan Pieters Sweelinck (1562-1621) a noble predecessor of Bach and Handel.

After these Dutch masters, the hour for Italy came again. Pierluigi Palestrina was born in 1525, and culminated the art of polyphony. Following a meaningful stroke of fate, he died in 1594, the same year as Orlando di Lasso, who shortly before the turn of the seventeenth century brought another tremendous change in music.

Dutch art could be misunderstood if the technic of contrapuntal work were to be seen as the only content and meaning. Their polyphony was much more a reflection of a new world feeling. The new meaning of Dutch painting for its human depth had the same meaning in its music.

The Noted Master

There was Josquin des Prez, who is often called Josquin, who blended the cool-headed style of the Dutch with the hot breath of Italy, where he lived for a long time. Josquin was one of the first whose art was a personal statement. He became a master but also humanized the music. Martin Luther meant that when he said, "Josquin is the master of music, who must do as he wished; the other Sang masters have to do as the notes would have it." It was not for nothing that he was called a prince of music. Often Josquin has been compared to his contemporary the painter Raphael.

Josquin de Pres was a composer of worldly stature in the new era, when Europe had become so small, that it could no longer exist in all its separate pieces. As a master of the high renaissance style, he was no less at home than in the art of counterpoint. His version of a simple song has proven to be the most time defying, which he will undoubtedly have come to know on his repeated journeys: "Innsbruck, I must let you go". Josquin wrote both sacred and secular music, and in all of the great vocal styles of the time, including motets, masses, chansons, and frottole.

Adrian Willaert was born like Isaac in Bruges. Fate took him to Venice, which at that time was one of the most important commercial cities in Italy. In Venice, the untouchable city on the island, the Orient and the Occident touched each other. From here, the threads were spun to the near east and to all countries and cities of the Mediterranean. Venice was more prosperous than all the cities of Italy and therefore paid homage to a particularly sumptuous style, as it was also expressed in the Venetian painters of Titian and Palma Vecchio to Tintoretto.

For Willaert an externality should have become decisive. In St. Mark, where he worked as Kapellmeister, there were organs on two galleries. So it was obvious to use two choirs as well (antiphonal). This was nothing new to St. Marks Bassilica. But Willaert made this possibility more productive. The choir musicians in groups performed music on two galleries. Giovanni Gabrieli (1557-1612) wrote the music Sonata Pianeforte in Venice 1597. It is the earliest known music for brass instruments alone. Here the splendor, festivity, and colorfulness of his music had never been experienced before. His disciples, uncle and nephew Gabrieli, transplanted this to their own instrumental music. The aftermath of Gabrieli brought a broader range to the instrumental music which was to be followed by the great classical masters at the turn of the nineteenth century.

The Orlando di Lasso, who hails from Hainaut, also got to know Europe on youthful adventures. He found a permanent place of work in Munich where he led the court chapel, which still today consumes this glorious past. Out of the abundance of his works of which consist of more than 2000 motets that stand out as striking examples of this genius. Not without reason Lassus was called the "Belgian Orpheus" and at the same time praised as one of the most educated musicians of that century. He spoke five languages and was an outstanding connoisseur of literature of his time.

Prince of Music

In addition to the Dutch, several German champions also distinguished themselves in the style of polyphony: Jacob Gallus, Leonhard Lechner, and even more Hans Leo Hassler, half a century before them but above all the great Ludwig Senfl. He was considered the most famous German master of his time. All of them had the same inclination toward the simple German song. They liked to draw it into her contrapuntal style with their many interwoven structures. The primary music group consists of five singers (three men and two boys) and nine instrumentalists: Viola da gamba (leg violin), two zinke, lute, two trombones, flute, violin, harpsichord, and the music director.

The last link in this chain was Pierluigi Palestrina, with which the voice of Italy rose again. Palestrina belonged entirely to Rome, even though, despite all honors - he was called a prince of music - he did not remain undisputed there. Since he was married, he could not take a spiritual position. His music and his school were in perfect contrast to the glamor of the Venetians and to the gradually over-exploding artificialness of the Dutch. The church had to defend itself against both. Here threatened the danger of secularization, where the text was transmitted in a flood of sounds. The popes were therefore mindful of the whole, and to suppress the church music's power of the word, or at least to strangulate it.

Palestrina became a strong advocate of the church to this end. His tone was filled with fervent piety though it remained clear, calm, transparent, and did not fall prey to polyphonic intrigues. Before the attack of this secular music, the popes had to bow. Through Palestrina the church music has been preserved.

Hans Pftizner has described this in his musical legend about Palestrina: that it does not correspond to the historical facts. The Mass that was written for his patron Marcellus, who supposedly convinced him, was not written by Palestrina to fulfill a miracle in church music. He had already created it ten years before the Tridentine Council of 1563, on which these battles were fought. The glory of Palestrina as the savior of church music might just be a legend. This does not diminish the merit of Palestrina as his masses have always remained a sought after role model. If the church music wanted to renew itself in the centuries to follow, it turned their eyes to Palestrina. Of the many forms of that time, only three are prevalent as they frequently used again: The Mass, Motette, and the Madrigal.

The Mass has received its title in a 1554 woodcut from Rome, which names it peculiarly; Ite, missa est, which means: Go, the assembly is dismissed. These are the words of the priest in the Catholic worship. The word missa, meaning Mass, signified not only worship as a whole, but also the music for the evening meal in particular. Initially, the Mass consisted of only three parts: Kyrie, Sanctus and Agnus Dei. Later, Gloria, Credo and Benedictus joined. These six main parts remained throughout the year and could be supplemented when appropriate to the season. Time and again the Mass has been honored over the centuries with contemporary compositions. In the peak of polyphonic prowess, it was not the effect of instrumental ornamentation, but the subtler meaning of all the voices. Such extremes as four-and-twenty-part masses with up to up to three-and fifty voices were written.

The motet did not sit that big. It advanced out of the early motetus, as described earlier. Here phrases, passages, gospels, or epistles have been used to voice the melody in an imitative style. As soon as the text has a dramatic meaning, musical expression is allowed to switch. Depending on your needs, you can therefore, complete one part and start again. While the main movements of the Mass remain the same throughout the year, the motet is dependent on the annual and its festivals. Certainly, a motet can have a much freer form though with both humble devotion to God and praise to living a good life.

The New Madrigal

The madrigal, on the other hand, belonged to secular music. In the hay-day of polyphony, it flourished. There was hardly anything in common with the old madrigal of two hundred to three hundred years passed. The world had changed in many ways as folks have already sailed over to the New World. Reformation and Counter-Reformation began their struggle. The fair play of love sustained, renewed, and rejuvenated with poets, who coined the ever-young song of longing to another in lithe verses. There were also spiritual madrigals. The madrigalists took some of the folk song of that time, Frottola and Villanella. Jakob Arcadelt, Philippe Verdelot, Adrian Willaert and Cyprian deRore to name a few of the best masters of this art.

From the madrigal of the ars nova the new madrigal differed by a much more personal expression. The Renaissance was an 'i-am-strong' and 'self-confession' time. In the composition of imitative voices, a compelling art of the human spirit was achieved. What had begun with Josquin had now arrived at a plateau. Music was now an expression of the individual, but for the chosen few. They were called Musica Reservata, the music reserved for the connoisseurs.

This became fully apparent later on in the masters of the Madrigal, Orlando di Lasso, the Englishmen John Dowland and Thomas Morley, and in the great Claudio Monteverdi whose madrigals are still sung the most. Carlo Gesualdo - Prince of Venosa was one of that passionate uber-composer who only knew how to exult in the air or grieve to death. His resume was like a novel where he killed his first wife out of jealousy and spent his next few years as a tramp. Then he married Eleanor von Este of Ferrara, the bearer of a name known to us from Goethe's play 'Tasso' based on the life of the poet Bernardo Tasso. Gesualdo was friends with Tasso.

View Into the Future

The significant meaning of expression was the chromatic coloring of the sound. While the ancients moved only in the fundamental tones of a scale, Gesualdo and many other innovators in his direction took away all the secondary possibilities of semitones. Never before had the sheet music been covered with so many sharps # and flats b. (accidentals) In an unprecedented boldness at the time, he used semitone steps to juxtapose widely spaced keys with the expressive content of the words.

We call this music making with all non-scale semitones chromatic. Chroma is actually color. It was not the last time that a phenomenon of music was covered with a term derived from painting. The chromatic leadership really gave the music a new color: the color of the drawing's spirit. Emotions of the soul can affect the spirit such that one is no longer able to speak the words, but the meaning may still be revealed in music. Music had become confession, revelation, and confession again.

In the works of the last madrigalists, there was almost a pathological trend to limit the fatigue on all the musical refinements as if the fruit had become overripe and music had to seek ways of renewal.

The musicians of that time felt that themselves. One of them, Johann Hermann Schein, said:

> "The noble art of music has risen to the glory of God today, through the thoughtful and diligent, exalted, exquisite master of arts of the early and Teutonic nation, to such excellence of sovereignty, that it must be doubted whether it may or may not go higher."

Scheins contemporary, the Görlitzer shoemaker and philosopher Jakob Böhme, proved with his belief in the future of music as the wiser, when he wrote:

> "But now the tree has this kind of nature, the bigger and older the tree becomes, the sweeter it bears fruit."

Young Mozart – prodigy

For millions, his work was the epitome of musical harmony: Wolfgang Amadeus Mozart (1756-1791). The life of the world-famous composer, on the other hand, is subject to irreconcilable contradictions. Judged as a child prodigy at a young age, Mozart later fights in vain for artistic recognition. During his lifetime, the true meaning of his work was revealed only to a small circle of music lovers. It was only after Mozart's death that publishers and theater improvisers began to take an interest in his compositions, which were so gradually becoming popular and have since received innumerable interpretations.

Childhood in Salzburg

Mozart's parents did not always know that their smaller son was a prodigy. They needed four years to realize this. For the time being, they were concerned only about the life of their seventh child, born on January 27, 1756, and the following day baptized in the Salzburg Cathedral: John Chrysostom (that was the day saint of January 27), Wolfgangus (this name pointed to the mother, who came from St. Gilgen on Wolfgang Lake), Theophilus (that was the name of the godfather, in German: "Gottlieb", Latin: "Amadeus"). He should be called Wolfgang. The parents were justifiably afraid for the life of the newborn.

Already five of Mozart's siblings had died as infants, only the four-year-old Maria Anna (called Nannerl) had survived. Understandably the mother was very weak from his birth.

She had no milk for the child. At that time, it was a great misfortune for the more impoverished people, because only the richer ones could afford a wet nurse. So the parents decided to give water to little Wolfgang with barley or gruel, a diet many children died of. With this food, which Wolfgang got until the age of three, the boy remained small and weak and did not learn until very late.

He usually sat on the floor under the piano and listened quietly when the father was teaching his big sister Nannerl. Father Mozart had the position of "Prince-bishop of Salzburg court violinist and court composer", which entailed performing as a musician in the orchestra of the Archbishop of Salzburg. This was a valuable position to have as it had links with royalty and other connections.

The little Amadeus also sat under the piano when the father's friends came to practice. The court and field trumpeter Andreas Schachtner, as well as the court music director, court organist, the horn players, violinists, flutists, trombonists, and harpsichordists were all often to be heard making music at their home in Salzburg. All were members of the Prince-Archbishop of Salzburg Hof-musik-kapelle. They all frequented Mozart's apartment on the third floor of the Grain Alley 9 and practiced the new serenades, symphonies, trios, string quartets and wind quintets for the archbishop.

All Salzburg musicians composed (more or less pretty well) for everyday use - music for the "chamber" of the archbishop, for churches, festivals, and convent schools. At that time it was not customary to perform works by older masters. Leopold Mozart was considered a particularly fine composer, teacher, and his friends liked to listen to his advice.

The state of Salzburg was then one of the many German small states ruled by an archbishop. The state capital had about ten thousand inhabitants and thanked their wealth (and their name) for salt mining and salt shipping.

Salt was a precious commodity at the time as it was used not only to make food taste better but also to preserve its freshness for transport and storage. The then reigning Archbishop Count Schrattenbach was a friend of the theater and music. His small orchestra had the duty of providing him a live concert every day after dinner. Thirty musicians belonged to this orchestra. Wolfgang knew them all because Father Leopold Mozart taught them violin, piano, and composition.

Very carefully, Father Mozart examined the hearing of the child, whose nickname was "Wolferl." Was the boy musical as well as the big sister? He tugged on the violin and struck pure tones on the piano: yes, the child was happy about it. Soon the boy sang children's songs with his sister - he learned quickly. Wolferl's good ear was not taken or granted because the child had a peculiarity from birth, which initially filled the parents with concern: his ear canal was not fully developed, and his outer ear was a bit malformed. And then finally came the day when Wolfgang, was already over three years old and started taking his first musical steps.

It started by wiggling from mother to piano where he did not merely hammer on it with his hands, but eagerly sought out specific sequences of notes: the thirds of the cuckoo's call. "Koo-Kuck, Koo-Kuck," which he also sang. From now on, the piano was Wolfgang's favorite toy. "I want to play too!" He begged. "Please, dad, let me learn as well as the Nannerl!" The seven-year-old had regular piano lessons, learned diligently, and gave father Leopold a lot of joy. Leopold Mozart agreed and taught our child Mozart simple melodies on the piano. The four-year-old learned by leaps and bounds. The father proudly wrote down these successes in a notebook: "This minuet was learned by Wolfgangerl in his fourth year," it says, and another song was learned by the little one "at half past nine in the evening in half an hour."

The friends who came to visit looked attentively at the little boy. Extraordinarily, what this feeble kid could do! Wolfgang would surely become a good Salzburg musician like his father. One day the violinist Wenzl came to the Grain Alley to try out a new string trio with Leopold Mozart and "uncle" Andreas Schachtner. Four-year-old Wolfgang listened as usual, but then loudly and energetically demanded: "I want to play second fiddle!" The father shook his head angrily. "You still have not learned to play the violin properly. " "Playing the second violin is easy," said the little one. "I do not have to learn that first!" Uncle Schachtner, who loved the boy very much, asked his father, "Make him happy, Leopold." "Well, then with Mr. Schachtner. "The little boy happily picked up his child's violin, looked into the music book, and played the second violin part of the piece- without mistakes!

How was that possible? They continued to play their string trios, Papa Leopold and Wenzl played the first violin part and the four-year Wolfgang the second violin part. The adults could hardly concentrate because they always had to think: where did the boy learn to play the violin? The four-year-old had it only by watching and listening as well as learning to try it out in secret. Schachtner looked at the boy and discovered nothing else special though… This child, the little Wolfgang was not very pretty, not very tall, not very clever. He behaved childishly and defiantly like all children at this age. But with music, he was a prodigy. "The boy is not just a musician like us," Schachtner told father Leopold. "He's going to be an extraordinary person, better than any of us here in Salzburg."

Nannerl moved more and more into the background behind her little brother, no matter how diligently she practiced the piano and how wonderfully she played it. Was she jealous? Indeed, she did not show it. From all we know, both children loved the one another very much. Mr. Schachtner one day went home with Leopold Mozart and eagerly found four-year-old Wolfgang there writing music. "What are you doing?" The father asked. Wolfgang, concentrating "A concert for the piano. The first part is ready soon. "" Let me see, "the father asked the little one. "That must be something playable." Wolfgang defiantly:" No, it's not finished yet. " The father took the paper away. At first, he saw nothing but blotchy patches of ink: the child had held the pen way too deep into the inkwell and with each stroke made a big splash on the paper. This blob was then wiped it out by his hand. Such a smear! The two adults laughed about it. But then his father looked more closely and saw that notes were written between all the inkblots. Here was real music, albeit written down in a confused mess! "See, friend, how everything is correct and written according to the rules!"

Leopold exclaimed excitedly and showed Schachtner the paper. "Only you can not use it, because it's so hard that no human being would be able to read it." "It's a concerto," Wolfgang interrupted him proudly. "You just have to practice until you bring it out." And then he went to the piano to show how it should be played. "See, that's how it has to be." The boy tried to play, but could not quite master it. Nevertheless, his father and uncle Schachtner understood what he had intended to write. It was a solo "Concerto" for piano, too hard for a child, but all else was astonishingly correct for a musician to play. Now Wolfgang wanted to compose and learn the rules of how the notes can harmonize together.

The child begged him until the father finally gave in. The teacher, Leopold Mozart, described how he used this lesson with his son. First, he let Wolfgang memorize easy, foreign compositions by heart. Then he instructed the child to vary these tunes to make them his own. Since Wolfgang still had difficulty writing, he played his music on the piano to his father, who wrote the notes down on manuscript. From here it went step by step as a five-year-old, Wolfgang wrote pretty little dances for piano. As a six-year-old, he composed a minuet, which was later added as the opus number 1 in the famous Köchel Catalog of all of Mozart's future lifetime works of music.

The two Mozart children were never lonely in Salzburg. They had a dog, cats, and birds – as well as many friends. Guests came to the house often, because Mother Mozart was a very sociable, cheerful woman. Additionally, most of the parents had children of their own, so they always met in grand style as a group.

There was the Hagenauer family, who owned the residential building Grain Alley 9 where they all lived. Of the eleven Hagenauer children, Kajetan was Wolfgang's best friend. Wolfgang admired the ten-year-old for his organ playing, in which he was allowed to operate the bellows of the organ. Ursula Hagenauer was Nannerl's girlfriend. Then there was the Prince-Archbishop's personal physician. Barisani with eight children who were in Nannerl's and Wolferl's age, and the children of a servant and the surgeon" Gilowsky. On Sunday, the friendly parents often met at the popular target shooting of the Salzburg shooting guild, called the "Bölzischießen."

In the summer, people gathered in the gardens, in the winter in the larger apartments of its occupants. In the Salzburg circle of friends, the five-year-old Wolfgang (1761) appeared in public for the first time: He participated as a singer in a Singspiel (musical) on the archbishop's name day celebration.

All his life Wolfgang liked to sing: spiritual songs for worship, old folk songs and, as well as all together with friends, funny canons. Everything they learned, they learned from Leopold: playing the piano and the violin, composing, calculating, writing, French, English, and much more. They never went to school. Most of the children had to work, in the house, in the garden, shepherding, flower tying, or a thousand other jobs. For a musician, that meant learning an instrument to join in church music, writing music, singing in the church choir, playing the bellows of the organ, and various other musical endeavors. As the great gift of his two children became more and more evident, Father Leopold decided to change his life and to put himself entirely at the service of these "prodigies."

This turned out to be a big sacrifice for him because so far he had lived quite well as a pretty good musician and composer. Leopold had dreamed of becoming a Salzburg Kapellmeister (music director). He renounced this ambition in favor of the work as teacher and father of his children. We have much to thank Leopold Mozart for. Hardly ever has a composer as a child been so lovingly and at the same time expertly introduced into music by his father like Wolfgang Mozart.

Father Mozart did not force the children to play the hour-long scale, but made music a game, letting the children test their imagination with music and wrote beautiful melodies for them. Of course, Leopold Mozart was also often criticized: he had used the children, it was said he overwhelmed them with the belief that they all might be able to make money through the children. But one thing is just as sure: especially Wolfgang pulled it with all his heart to make music. As funny as the boy was otherwise – during this time, he was playing music seriously and very focused.

Mozart on Tour

When Wolfgang was six and Nannerl was ten, father Leopold had big plans for his children away from Salzburg. He thought to bring them abroad, and his children should be famous. He felt obliged "to proclaim a miracle to the world." The world for Leopold Mozart was then Vienna, the capital and royal capital of many countries ruled by Empress Maria Theresia, queen of Hungary and Bohemia. If Wolfgang was successful in Vienna, then he was famous. Leopold Mozart was a clever, cautious man as the children had not yet traveled and given a concert away from home. They took a small trial trip first in the form of a rehearsal and concert in Munich. Being the capital of Bavaria, it was only a three day coach ride away from Salzburg. Elector and then leader, Max III Joseph, who was nicknamed "the beloved" was a real music lover. Initially traveling was dangerous as there was a war in Europe lasting about six years. In the spring of 1762, Leopold Mozart dared it, and they left for Munich anyway. All four Mozart's, father, mother, and children, were very excited when they sat in the stagecoach leaving Salzburg.

At that time, traveling was with horses, and maybe a coach. It was tedious, expensive, and exhausting, especially with children. The stage-coaches rattled clumsily over the bad roads, got stuck in the mud in the rain. There were many accidents, sometimes the wheels or the drawbars broke, sometimes a horse shied, or it collapsed ill. When it was cold outside, the travelers wrapped themselves in coats and stuck their icy feet in lined sacks. They wrapped their heads in a woolen scarf - and they froze even as they were arriving at the coach station.

Six-year-old Wolfgang was a lively child, and the parents feared if the children could endure the hardships? Would they not practice seldom and forget too much of what they had learned? At each station, when the travelers were resting, the children took their "mute keyboard" out of their luggage and practiced to keep their fingers articulated. Wolfgang needed the music but hated finger exercises.

At the Munich court before Elector Maximilian III Joseph, Wolfgang had to get used to a lot of new things. The mirrored, marble-clad concert hall with unusual acoustics, the splendidly decorated piano, the many candles in the crystal chandeliers, but above all the many elegantly dressed people who listened to him. Finally, the little musician was praised. But Amadeus was not happy as he became very embarrassed and began to cry at all the new experiences. Leopold as Dad did not worry, as he knew Vienna would be in awe. The summer after returning home was spent more diligently than ever. The Salzburg friends were already in awe of the two Mozart children. Wolfgang and Nannerl were now almost famous, and it was known that they would soon perform in front of the great Empress in Vienna.

September 1762 the big journey that began with its many bags, suitcases, and a travel piano too. Arriving in Passau, after two days of travel with the stagecoach, they found the prince-bishop was in no hurry to listen to the Salzburg children. He had the Mozart family wait five days before he receiving only Wolfgang, but not Nannerl. As a fee for the performance, the little artist received a mere single ducat - a little more than four florins, which was about the sum for the Mozart's families' travel and overnight money needed for only one day. "At the same time we could have taken eighty guilders in Linz," said his father, annoyed, and pressed on to continue, downstream on a Danube river ship.

In Linz, in the inn "Zur Dreifaltigkeit," father Mozart organized a concert, to which he sold the tickets himself. It was the first public appearance of the prodigies. It brought success, a lot of money and a good advertisement. For some of the listeners immediately traveled to Vienna and spread the news about the two Salzburg prodigies there.

The Mozart family needed three days and two nights for the route from Linz to Vienna. On the way, when the ship had to stay docked, they got out and went not to an inn like the other travelers, but to the church. They could not always unpack the travel-piano to practice, but instead, Wolfgang now could learn to play the organ they had found in each church, an instrument for practicing.

On October 6, 1762, they finally arrived in Vienna at the landing stage at the "Red Tower Gate." What a noise here and confusion! Bumping and puffing! The Mozart family, surrounded by many boxes and suitcases and the travel-piano, became anxious about the many people there. At that time Vienna had about 200,000 inhabitants, twenty times as many as Salzburg, and the harbor was known to be particularly hectic.

In Vienna, although it was usually only cold at the beginning of October, now it was raining and storming too. The four trudged tired and anxious through the streets. Exhausted, they arrived only to be startled as it was very run down at their inn. Their room was dark. It had only two beds for the four of them, and Father Leopold complained bitterly that the children, sleeping with their parents in a bed, "at least allow us every night a few candles." In Vienna, even the cramped quarters were expensive.

While the children practiced diligently on the travel piano still standing in the narrow room, the mother was organizing the concert dresses and seeing that the wigs were freshly powdered. Father Leopold was always on the go to visit people and identifying possible concert venues. He couldn't lose any time, because every day in Vienna without a concert was a lost day without any money.

Leopold Mozart soon realized how scarce things had become in Vienna. It was said that the Austrian war coffers were empty and that the Empress had sold her silver things. There were no longer any beautiful festivals in the grand hall of mirrors in Schönbrunn Palace, and composers and musicians groaned because they received fewer orders to work than usual. 'What should they do if the imperial invitation doesn't arrive' thought Leopold Mozart?

His whole itinerary, indeed his plan of life for the two prodigies, was based on this imperial invitation. He gave letters of recommendation to all his musician acquaintances in return for advice and intercession. Of course, he also visited the imperial opera, where the latest work of the imperial court composer Christoph Willibald Gluck "Orpheus and Eurydice" had just come out.

Luckily on that evening, Father Mozart could hardly concentrate on the music, for he had heard that Archduke Leopold (a son of the Empress, later Emperor Leopold II) said "a boy is in Vienna playing the piano so well." Even the imperial family had all heard of these Salzburg prodigies!

Sure enough a few days later, the long-awaited imperial invitation arrived. On October 13, 1762, the event took place, to which the entire Mozart family was lifelong proud. Wolferl and Nannerl were allowed to show their arts to the imperial family in Schönbrunn Palace, in the Hall of Mirrors.

There they sat in the first row on golden armchairs: the portly Emperor Franz, although he was Emperor of the German Reich, but had little to say there, because the German princes governed their countries independently. Beside him his mother, the very plump, Maria Theresia, ruler of many countries for twenty-two years, next to the twenty-four-year-old Archduchess Maria Anna, twenty-one-year-old Crown Prince Joseph (later Emperor Joseph II) with his handsome Isabella, twenty-year-old Maria Christine, Maria Elisabeth, aged 16, Maria Leopold, fifteen, Leopold II, twelve-year-old Johanna, eleven-year-old Maria Josepha, ten-year-old Marie Caroline (later queen) of Naples-Sicily, the eight-year-old Ferdinand, the six-year-old Maria Antonia (later Queen Marie Antoinette of France) and the youngest, five-year-old Maximilian, later Prince-Archbishop of Cologne and Münster.

Mozart, of course, had to deal with almost all of these princes and princesses afterward. Nannerl and Wolferl played solo and four handed piano, and Wolfgang played the violin. Finally, he performed his own compositions and sang some songs to Nannerl's piano playing. The imperial family was very good at judging these two little musicians and knew they were doing extraordinary things.

Of course, all the imperial children played at least one instrument themselves, the boys violin or cello, the girls piano, and all had famous musicians as teachers. When the royal's children made music together, they formed a small private orchestra. Enthusiastically, the sovereigns applauded and shouted, "Bravo." The ladies-in-waiting and gentlemen, the princes and counts, did the same. Nannerl and Wolfgang bowed dutifully, as their father had taught them, beaming with pride.

Then Emperor Franz got up, he went to the piano and gave Wolfgang a task: he should not play with all ten fingers, but only with one - and a beautiful melody, of course. Wolfgang liked to show what he could and played a small minuet with one finger. Emperor Franz had another task: the keys were covered with black cloth. Wolfgang played through the fabric precisely and without mistakes. The audience clapped enthusiastically. The emperor praised Wolfgang and called him the "little warlock."

It was very honorable to play in front of the imperial family, but these tasks were too childish. The six-year-old became impatient and asked, "Is not Mr. Wagenseil here? He should come." Georg Christoph Wagenseil was a famous imperial court composer and piano teacher of the Empress.

Actually, Wolfgang's request was very bold. But Wagenseil, who was among the audience and had understood very well that something exceptional was going on, came willingly to the piano. "I'm playing your concerto, Monsieur Wagenseil," Wolfgang explained very confidently. "You have to perform with me." Wagenseil assisted little Mozart and stroked his cheek admiringly after the concerto. "You are a real musician." Wolfgang beamed.

Emperor Franz asked Leopold Mozart for a conversation in an adjoining room. The children were allowed to play together. Maria Antonia let her little dog run free. All apprehension to this important royalty had now vanished. The eleven-year-old Nannerl was still a little shy, but Wolfgang showed his joy and his affection as always very openly, about which Leopold Mozart wrote to friends in Salzburg: "The Wolferl jumped on the Empress's lap, got her around the neck and righteous kissed. In short, we've been with her from three to six o'clock." All his life, Wolfgang was proud of these three hours. After this event, there was no time to rest, as they had to go to a noble palace and perform a concert that same evening for a fee of six gold ducats.

Two days later, an elegant carriage drove up to the modest Mozart inn. The emperor's "Secret Paymaster" emerged from the car in his embroidered court uniform. He handed over a parcel to Father Mozart and announced that he would pick the children up for another concert. They will perform for the two youngest Archdukes, the eight-year-old Ferdinand, and the five-year-old Maximilian.

In the paymaster's package were two precious dresses, called "gala dresses," as a gift for the prodigies. The clothes were not new but used. At the imperial court, it was customary to give away children's clothes to subordinates. Nevertheless, the joy of this gift was enormous in the Mozart family. The children needed nice clothes for their concerts.

A few days later, the Mozart family received a leather purse with a hundred gold ducats as payment from the imperial paymaster. That was about 420 guilders and was more than Leopold Mozart earned in Salzburg during the whole year. Now everyone in Vienna wanted to see and hear the two Salzburg children.

Father Leopold stated in his diary: "The lords already order us four, five, six to eight days in advance so as not to be late." The two Salzburg prodigies became the biggest sensation of winter in Vienna. A listener wrote after the concert "The poor guy plays wonderfully. He is smart, lively, and a darling. His sister is a little master." continuing; "A lady gave the boy a kiss, after that he wiped his mouth." Father Mozart: "All ladies are in love with my children. I have never heard of anyone who did not say it was incomprehensible."

In return for their concerts, the children received many beautiful gifts; watches, rings, brooches, a children's violin for Wolfgang and even gilded shoe buckles. Of course, the Leopold preferred gold ducats.

The princes and counts let the prodigies be picked up for the concerts with elegant carriages and then bring them home again. They often wandered through Vienna four times a day, and they also performed two concerts a day. The father promised to buy his own coach as soon as possible.

Wolfgang was never again so successful with all the enthusiastic feedback from those weeks in Vienna. He had became acquainted with the most magnificent palaces and moved easily among the fine people. For the rest of his life, he longed for this luxury.

Sickness and new plans

Both prodigies were not used to such a busy life. Wolfgang felt increasingly dull and suffered from headaches. But his father was so enthusiastic about the successes that he did not take Wolfgang's complaints seriously. Before the second big concert in Schönbrunn, Wolfgang complained of pain in his hip. He played the concert with Nannerl, but he was, as the father remarked, "not quite as usual." At bedtime, he was feverish and showed painful patches on his skin. The big fear went around: was it smallpox? Leopold Mozart feared punishment from heaven for "being fortunate for fourteen consecutive days." It was not smallpox, but it was a serious disease, a kind of scarlet fever. For the next weeks, all concerts had to be canceled. An admirer of the prodigies sent a doctor who was a music lover.

For nearly fourteen days, Wolfgang was lying in bed with a high fever in a dark guest-room. Additionally, he also had a bad tooth that caused him pain and a swollen cheek. The boy was in a miserable condition. The frightened Leopold Mozart had Masses read in Salzburg for the son, and calculated precisely how much money he had lost by the canceled concerts: fifty ducats, over two hundred guldens.

The longer Wolfgang's illness lasted, the scarcer the money situation became. Another concern was his father's vacation was over, and he should have been in Salzburg some time ago. In long letters, he asked his Salzburg friends to beg for mercy and help with parts of his duties. Father Mozart became quite aware of how uncertain the future of his family was. Now everything depended on the health of this six-year-old boy. Wolfgang was always a fragile child. The fever sank, the sky cleared, and a very weak Wolfgang went to the piano and made music again.

The following day, the Mozart family gave their thanks to the doctor with a small house concert. They waited anew for another imperial invitation, but that did not happen. The great patrons were reserved, and the curiosity about the prodigies had subsided as the first sensation passed. The Mozart family was then invited to the public gala table at the Hofburg residence, along with many others. The invited guests had the honor of watching the imperial family celebrate the festivities, but there was nothing for them to eat there. Fortunately, the Empress recognized Father Leopold among hundreds of spectators and called to him, "Is the boy well again?"

While the parents waited for further invitations, the children had time to rest and to learn. The piano, violin, and singing, composing, writing, arithmetic, reading, Italian and French were the subjects of their study. The family finally found time to visit the famous imperial opera together.

Since the Mozart family urgently needed money for their return journey, they accepted an invitation to Bratislava in Hungary. They gave concerts there and were finally able to buy their own carriage. At the beginning of the New Year in 1763, they arrived back in Salzburg and told all their friends how they had felt at the imperial court.

Everyone was proud of the Salzburg Wunderkinder. Fortunately, the archbishop was not angry because of the long vacation, but rather congratulated Leopold Mozart on his successes in Vienna. Leopold received a promotion to become a vice-chapel master. As a thank you, the children performed at the name day festival for the archbishop and celebrated in their homeland.

Wolfgang was again, not feeling well. He was skinny for his age and became ill again shortly after returning home. This time he had so much pain in his fingers that he could not play the violin or the piano. This was accompanied by a heavy fever and significant fatigue. It was a rheumatoid arthritis, from which a child recovers only very slowly.

At the same time, his father was already preparing for the next trip to Paris and maybe even London. All of Europe should get to know the Salzburg Wunderkinds! The trip would undoubtedly be costly, but he was not sure if they would earn much money with the concerts.

The Salzburg friends helped and collected money for their trip. Mayor Haffner gave a hundred gulden and a member of the Gun Club three hundred. Those who knew personally powerful and wealthy friends and who lived along the itinerary wrote letters of recommendation. One should take the Salzburg children hospitably and encourage their talents.

The archbishop paid Father Leopold the annual salary of about 350 guldens and also granted him an extended vacation of one, two or possibly even three years. The mother improved the gala clothing. We do not know whether she was afraid of the big trip or not. Anna Maria Mozart was a healthy, humorous woman who, without complaining, took on all the inconvenience and cheered her family with her jokes.

Leopold Mozart spent months preparing to travel, wrote many letters, counted, and calculated. Every day they would go sixty or seventy miles, but Paris was more than a thousand miles away, not counting the many detours they had to make to give concerts in castles.

Each day of the trip cost at least four guldens and the stay in Paris even more. Paris was at the time the most expensive city in Europe. They would have to drive through many countries, pass through many customs stations, changing rules, different money, always dialects and languages, another food, almost every night another night's lodging. The children had to come to practice in spite of all the hardships because if they did not play well, the journey was pointless.

On this trip they took along a servant, Sebastian Winter, a twenty-year-old, whom the children loved very much. He was a trained Figaro, or barbers as they are now called. A Figaro was an important man in the 18th century, because not only were they trained for hairdressing and shaving, but above all to care for the precious wigs which no one was allowed to appear at royal courts without.

Sebastian would powder the wigs properly white as well as run errands, shop and sell concert tickets. Meanwhile, in Paris, the war had ended, which went down in history as the "Seven Years' War."

At the beginning of June 1763, the Mozart family embarked on a long journey abroad across Europe. On their way to their first stop, the Wasserburg Inn, they broke a rear wheel. There was a loud crash and the carriage overturned. The travelers crept out in shock: thank goodness, everyone was uninjured, but the horses could not continue. They stood by the side of the road and looked around the lonely unknown countryside.

Fortunately, helpers came from a nearby mill. They brought another wheel, but it was much too small. After felling a tree and fashioned the wood, the improper wheel was fastened to the carriage. Mother Mozart and the two children got in, but Leopold Mozart went with Sebastian on foot so as not to overburden the carriage. Exhausted, they finally arrived at Wasserburg Inn. It took three days to get the carriage ready to travel again.

Father taught Wolfgang how to use the pedals of the organ of the Wasserburg church. In Munich, the first major stop on their European trip, the Mozart family drove straight to Nymphenburg, the summer palace of the Bavarian Electors. Leopold knew a relative of the elector from the last concert and prelude concert was arranged in the castle for the same evening. After a long day's travel and a busy concert that night the children went to bed at eleven in the evening.

At the next concert, the seven-year-old showed something quite new. Wolfgang did not play from the music, but free from his own imagination on the piano and violin. From now on, this free fantasizing became the new highlight of their concert program. Further invitations filled out the ten days in Munich. Leopold Mozart was relieved to collect the revenue 175 guldens, just from the electoral family alone. From Munich, they traveled to Augsburg, Leopold Mozart's hometown where he had an advertisement posted in the newspaper. "These two extraordinary children had to be heard twice by His Majesty, the Emperor, and the Empress Queen. They were showered with gifts and then invited further to the highest nobility of the Viennese court. "

In Augsburg, Father Mozart was not thrifty and lived in the city's most distinguished hotel, the Three Moors. Leopold then bought a travel-piano from the famous Augsburg piano maker Andreas Stein. It cost over two hundred guilders but provided good service for many years.

The children met uncle Franz Alois Mozart, who had taken over the bookbinder's workshop from his grandfather. This uncle had a four-year-old daughter, Maria Anna Thekla, called by the Mozart children in Swabian "Bäsle." Later, "Bäsle" would become one of Wolfgang's best friends.

How Leopold Mozart had looked forward to success in Augsburg, and how was he disappointed! The Augsburg citizens were way too thrifty, and Leopold Mozart complained of their low ticket sales. "Augsburg has held me up for a long time and has done little to nothing good for me. What we made, we spent away again…, everything is costly. "

The next travel destination went through Swabia from one castle to another. On the way, the new travel-piano was carefully unwrapped at each post office and carried to the inn so that the children could practice. But even during the journey, they could not rest as Father Leopold gave lessons in composition theory, arithmetic, and writing. The children had a wooden tablet, a piece of paper on top of it and wrote while driving. Wolfgang maintained this custom as an adult as he kept music paper with him in his pocket using these hours in the stagecoach to good advantage.

The Mozart family got to know the city of Ulm with the famous Münster building and the great organ on which Wolfgang was allowed to play. They wanted to go to Stuttgart to the Duke of Württemberg, for which they had a letter of recommendation. Mozart was staying in his summer castle in Ludwigsburg instead, but the Duke said he was not interested in hearing prodigies. Leopold Mozart was angry, for they had traveled so far. He thought that the Duke's conductor from Italy might be to blame for this. This Duke in Italy wanted to "exterminate the Germans at this court" and let in only Italians, scolded Father Mozart. Moreover, this Italian man did not believe "that a child of German birth could have such a musical genius and so much spirit and fire." From an early age, Wolfgang heard his father scolding "the Italians." He, Wolfgang Mozart, would prove that he was better than all of them, he vowed.

Father Mozart, however, was wrong about this Italian musician's opinion. It was the Duke himself who had no use for music. He loved nothing more than his soldiers and spent most of his money on his army. Annoyed, they drove on to Bruchsal, and then to Schwetzingen, the summer palace of the Elector of the Palatinate. Here they liked it much better. The famous Mannheim orchestra, according to Mozart's father, "is without contradiction the best in Germany," played in the castle park, with all of Mozart's family together and happy again.

The Elector invited the prodigies to a concert in the castle. They played for four hours and thankfully received a purse of fifteen French Louisdor worth 165 guilders. In Heidelberg, they visited, according to Nannerl's travel diary; "the castle, the wallpaper factory, and a silk factory, the big barrel and the well where the rule lets the water fetch."

Once again, Leopold Mozart proved his business acumen and brought in the travel expenses by organizing a concert in an inn. Sebastian sold the tickets, and they made two hundred guldens in one evening.

Then in Frankfurt Leopold Mozart again put an ad in the newspaper in which he praised the musical arts of the children. At one of the four Frankfurt concerts, fourteen-year-old Johann Wolfgang Goethe was among the audience members.

Leopold Mozart told the Salzburg friend Hagenauer: "God grants us the grace that, thank God, we are healthy and are admired everywhere. Wolfgang is hilarious but also terrible. " Wolfgang was sometimes mean to his older sister as he annoyed her, made silly jokes, called her "Zizibe" because she was very sensitive and sometimes a little sad. She played the piano very well, but always the little brother was in everyone's focus. He was more versatile than she, able to fantasize and compose, to play the violin and the organ. However, in Frankfurt, she had greater success at the concerts. The father wrote proudly to Salzburg friends "The Nannerl suffers no more from the boy, by playing so that everything speaks of her and admired her skill." The same hustle and bustle occurred at each new location.

The father made contacts and gave wealthy patrons information from other musicians "What about concerts in France, in England, can you give me a letter of recommendation?" If there were not enough invitations coming in, concerts were organized in a hurry. Wolfgang practiced organ in the churches, which sometimes became their travel piano. If they did not have to give a concert, they used the free time for sightseeing learning something about history and art history. As it got gradually cooler, the children caught colds with coughs and could not sing. When a rest day was taken, Leopold's remedy was to apply "black powder," before traveling to their next commitment.

There is little written in the diaries and letters about Mother Mozart. She probably surrendered to her destiny without interfering with her husband's plans. Continuing on to Koblenz, Bonn, Brühl, Cologne where Leopold criticized the "dirty cathedral" in Aachen. On the journey to Liège once more, the carriage went on strike where an iron wheel on the front wheel broke. Sebastian went in search of a wagon master whilst the family found a small tavern for the wait.

Frozen, they sat down at the fireplace, where on a long chain hung a kettle in which meat and vegetables were sizzling. The Walloon-speaking landlord gave them food. Leopold wrote that "the door of the inn was always open, so we very often had the honor of having the pigs visit us and grunt around us."

They then traveled to Brussels, then the capital of the Netherlands belonging to Austria, where the affluent markets, and the good payment was an excellent reward. Leopold Mozart always calculated that he still needed two hundred guilders to travel to Paris. The precious presents given to the children from the noblemen in Brussels were not really helpful as they were two swords. Some of the other gifts were for Wolfgang, Brussels lace, a coat for Nanner, many cases, and tobacco cans.

With many letters of recommendation, they finally traveled in mid-November. Three days later, they arrived in Paris, where they stayed for five months. Finally in Paris the capital of France, it was unlike anything the Mozart's had ever seen. Paris seemed immensely rich when one saw the grand aristocratic palaces, the elegant carriages, and the luxury of clothes and hairstyles. According to Leopold Mozart, this vast wealth was shared by only a hundred people that lived in luxury amongst lots of waste. For most people, Paris was a city of terrible poverty such as the Mozart's did not know from Salzburg, Augsburg, or Vienna. Father Leopold wrote home full of horror, "that one sees the bad fruits of war without eyeglasses of all places." People suffer from hunger and disease. "They will not soon find a place filled with so many miserable and mutilated people." The streets are full of beggars.

It was challenging to go to the court of King Louis XV, as the people they met through referrals could not help here. So they had to wait for another opportunity. Wolfgang did not feel well in Paris either as he was homesick for Salzburg.

One morning his father heard him crying in bed. He wanted so much to see the Salzburg friends back, said the boy, making music in the Grain Alley with them and his father. The city of Paris scared him too much. The Mozart family did eventually find consolation with the wife of the Bavarian ambassador in Paris, a native of Salzburg. She took the countrymen into her beautiful house, spoke to them of Salzburg, and was a kind friend to them for the five months in Paris.

As a native of Bavaria and living in France, a very successful writer, Melchior Grimm, became a welcome helper. Grimm was a friend of the great philosophers Voltaire and Rousseau and knew all the great musicians of France as well as highly regarded by the nobility. Paris would listen to his judgment.

Grimm organized the children's first concert in Paris where he offered the money for the room rental, sold 320 entrance tickets, and even paid for the sixty large candles used to illuminate the hall. Most importantly, being a famous author, he presented the Salzburger Wunderkinder in a significant Paris newspaper, praising Nannerl's piano playing, and calling seven-year-old Wolfgang "such a rare phenomenon that one hardly dares to believe what one sees with one's own eyes see and hear with your own ears."

This first concert was soon followed by further invitations. The Mozart family quickly became acquainted with famous musicians who listened and critiqued how they performed music. Father Mozart agreed with his new friend Grimm that it was an outstanding level of music was performed here.

There was a great dispute between followers of French and Italian music, and Grimm took the side of the Italians, and his unjust disdain for French music. This was transferred to Mozart and deprived Wolfgang of Paris and what it had to offer even more.

The boy eagerly learned the rules of composition as his pieces became more sophisticated and inspired him compose more. Most of his time was fantasizing and improvising music on the piano and the organ. The father reminded him to write it down. In the meantime, he and Nannerl played mostly his compositions at the concerts.

It took six weeks before the longed-for invitation of King Louis XV to arrive. On Christmas Eve 1763 they took their carriage to Versailles, moved into a hotel, and attended in new black dresses and stiff French hats, the very solemn Christmas Mass in the royal chapel. Father Mozart was not dazzled by the splendor of this church. For him, the music was not decisive, and it did not satisfy him. The arias are "empty, frosty and miserable, hence French"; he only liked the part with the choirs. Still, to study the French motet style, father and son Mozart went daily to the Mass of the Royal Palace.

On New Year's Day 1764, they were invited to the public table. Wolfgang was allowed to talk to Queen Marie and kiss her hand. Luckily she spoke some German. At the organ of the castle chapel of Versailles, Wolfgang performed in front of the assembled court society. He played his own compositions and impovised on them freely.

The high royalty showed their delight and spoiled the children with praise and gifts. The prodigies also played before the king's lover, Madame Pompadour. To the curious Salzburg friends, Leopold Mozart described the forty-two-year-old as follows: "She must have been quite beautiful; because she is still clean. She is a big handsome person; she is fat, well in body, but very proportioned, blond, ... and has in the eyes a resemblance to the Empress. She gives herself a lot of honor and has an extraordinary spirit. Her rooms in Versailles are like a paradise." But she was haughty, and "still rules everything at the moment." Father Mozart was satisfied with the revenue of fifty Louisdor. Of course, half of this money was spent on the cost of staying in Versailles. There were no "Fiakers" or cheap accommodations there like in Vienna, and they had to pay for expensive chair carriers. This was practical, as in bad weather they could not walk in their elegant black shoes.

The success of Versailles meant the final breakthrough in France. One noble invitation now followed the next. They ate supper in the most distinguished houses in Paris, and a concert in the palace of Prince

Conti was recorded in an oil painting. The Mozart family was elegantly dressed. Father Mozart spoke French well. The children had their own language, and it was music. It was raining gifts: a gold watch, a gold-filled cardboard ring, gold toothpicks, sword straps, ribbons and flowers for bonnets, and scarves.

In Paris, for the first time, two Mozart compositions became engraved in copper and reproduced for others to hear and perform. They were piano sonatas with violin accompaniment, just as the two children liked to play them. Many Parisian musicians could also play them easily. The sale of these pieces brought a nice additional profit for the European family tour.

At the beginning of April, Father Mozart was able to send over two thousand guilders to Salzburg. The journey had been worthwhile so far, thanks to the excellent organization of Father Leopold Mozart. Wolfgang made rapid musical progress as the father raved in one of his letters to Salzburg "I can tell you, my dear Frau Hagenauerin, that every day God works miracles on this child. By the time we get home, he can serve the court." This desire to take up a permanent position as a musician at the court dominated Wolfgang's life again. The tender, sensitive child became ill again, this time suffering from angina and a catarrh.

Since the Mozart family had enough travel money, they decided to continue to the court of the King of England in London Some of the luggage, especially the heavy furs, they left behind in Paris, because they wanted to return before the winter. They had to part from the servant Sebastian, as he had gotten a good position with Prince Furstenberg in Donaueschingen. There were many tears at the farewell, especially with Wolfgang. Sebastian promised to tell a lot about the "miracle of Mozart" among his new masters, and to get a kind invitation to Prince Berger Castle.

Don Giovanni

The "Story of the woman seducer" Don Giovanni (Spanish: Don Juan), who as a punishment is sent to hell, plays out in Spain, and was worked on by many poets and composers. Also by Gluck in ballet music, which Mozart was most likely familiar with.

We do not know who first came up with the idea of choosing this material for the new opera, but it was either Mozart or da Ponte (his librettist). In any case, in the autumn of 1787 the work had progressed so far that the composer and librettist made their way to Prague to rehearse the new opera. Wolfgang and his wife Konstanze lived in the dark Old Town of Prague in the house "Zu den Drei Löwen", opposite of da Ponte in the house "Zum Platteis". The alley between them was so narrow that the two could talk comfortably out of the window.

One of the highlights of the opera was the "register" of the servant Leporello, in which he lists exactly how many women Don Giovanni has already seduced. These achievements are, of course, in the past. Now Don Giovanni finds it difficult to seduce: neither Donna Elvira nor Donna Anna let him catch them in the opera. Even the peasant Zerlina resists him. Don Giovanni has reached the end - and finally, in dark, wild music, he is dragged to hell during the splendid feast of the "Stone Guest". Konstanze said, "There are places in the ghost music of Don Giovanni that make your hair stand on end."

Mozart and da Ponte still worked very well together. But Salieri had meanwhile returned to Vienna after his Paris triumphs, had reconciled himself with da Ponte, and given him a libretto commission at the same time as "Don Giovanni." He called his librettist to come for a performance in Vienna. (That was his right). Da Ponte had to leave in the middle of work on "Don Giovanni" in Prague. Mozart's hatred of Salieri increased.

In the narrow center of Prague Mozart found it too dark and lonely. He needed people around him, especially friends who cheered him up. So he often went beyond the old Charles Bridge in the Prague suburb of Smichow, where the singer Josepha Duschek had a beautiful country house in the vineyards called the "Villa Bertramka." The Duschek was still a friend from his Salzburg days. She was now rich and famous as a coloratura singer and her nickname was the "Bohemian nightingale". She was a fervent admirer of Mozart, who had been in Prague for the performances of "Abduction", "Figaro", and for the Mozart Masses in the beautiful Niklas Church. Now she promoted the opera "Don Giovanni" and gave the composer what he needed to work: good food, fun company with games and evening dancing, a horse for the morning ride, dogs, birds, flowers in the park of Villa Bertramka.

Mozart often came back to the city late at night. There was little time to sleep because the next morning he went early to the theater to rehearse and had to toil very hard.

The Prague orchestra was "not as clever as Vienna." Mozart practiced relentlessly with the musicians. The singers should not only sing their arias beautifully but also think of the opera characters while remaining "natural." That was something new and very difficult for opera singers at the time: they were only used to singing one beautiful aria after another. Now they had to act, show emotions, react to other people in the opera, and to still perform the difficult music correctly. For love, anger, hate, lies, zeal seeking, everything had to be expressed as the composer wanted.

The first performance had to be postponed, because of the long rehearsals. At a festival opera for a traveling archduchess "Figaro" was performed instead of "Don Giovanni." The affluent Bohemian nobility appeared at the festival gala. Mozart, in his beautiful red tails with mother of pearl buttons and a white-powdered wig, sat at the harpsichord and conducted his opera. He was delighted with the enthusiasm from the audience. After, the work continued on "Don Giovanni," laboriously and exhaustingly.

He wrote Don Giovanni's famous seduction aria five times until the ambitious singer and composer were really satisfied. Would the Prague audience understand this dark opera, that it was "so completely different" from "Figaro", asked Mozart while walking a little anxiously with a Bohemian Kapellmeister. He reassured him that "everything that came from Mozart would be received enthusiastically by the Prague audience."

The premiere of "Don Giovanni" was to take place on October 29, 1787. Singers and musicians had studied the opera well. But two days before the premiere it was missing something important; the overture. The musicians were terrified. Mozart should finally sit down and compose it. It would all be a terrible failure without an overture! But he made no move, joked, spent his time with mischief and teasing, and enjoyed the desperation of his friends. He had already composed his overture, that is, finished in the head. He had not 'penned' it yet.

The night before the premiere he wrote down the "Don Giovanni" overture. The copyists had to work all day to copy the orchestral parts from the score, and at the beginning of the opera, they were not finished until seven in the evening. The musicians, singers, and composer had to wait fifteen minutes until the sheet music, still full of sand to dry the ink, finally lay on the music stands and the opera could begin.

The musicians had no opportunity to practice before the premiere. Was that good? Worried, Mozart conducted again. When the overture was rewarded with rejoicing and the curtain rose for the first act, very relieved, he praised the orchestra; "Although many notes have fallen under the desks, but on the whole the overture went quite well." The Prague "Don Giovanni" was a unique triumph for Mozart. "Connoisseurs and artists say that Prague has not yet heard music performed in the same way." The Prague newspaper raved about the new opera. The following performances became even better and even more successful.

The Pragueites tried to keep revered masters in their city for more operas. But Mozart wanted to return to Vienna. Konstanze was expecting the birth of their fourth child, and they had to move (again!). In addition, Christoph Willibald Gluck was severely ill in Vienna and would soon die. Would Mozart not finally get a good job at a royal court, as a successor to the big and famous Gluck?

As a farewell, Mozart promised his friend and hostess Josepha Duschek an Italian concert aria, but then again, he did not have time to write another down. Then she simply locked him in the garden shed of Villa Bertramka with music paper, pen and ink; he cannot get out until he has finished the aria! Mozart, on the other hand, threatened her with a laugh; he would destroy the aria if she could not sing it off the page and without flaws. Then he designed a very difficult aria and added a little mockery. The text was ambiguous in one place and could be translated as: "What shortness of breath, what terrible place for me to be in!" The "Bohemian Nightingale" passed the exam, and the aria "Bella Mia Fiamma" was preserved for posterity.

Years of hopes for an imperial position were fulfilled on December 7, 1787. Mozart became "Hof Composer "with a salary of eight hundred guldens annually. He was not happy about it though, as the new job was not connected with an important task. His was the small duty to write dances for the imperial masked balls for Carnival. On the other hand, the sum was quite high, and he earned as much as Salieri's position as director of the imperial opera. Then Salieri was promoted and with an additional salary of 1200 guilders to the court Kapellmeister and thus also appointed the head of imperial chamber music and court music of the Chapel.

The new salary did not release Mozart from the financial worries, which were more oppressive than ever after the birth (and imminent death) of little Theresia. Konstanze, who was severely weakened by four pregnancies in four years, became seriously ill. Mother Weber and Konstanz's youngest sister Sophie also took care of her for eight months. Mozart also watched Konstanze for many days and nights near her bed, always composing and writing. He made every effort to keep the troubled household quiet.

To spare her nerves, he did not play piano anymore. He received visitors and students in silence, with his finger on his lips and the whispered in French "Chut!" ("Still! Pst!")

It took half a year until "Don Giovanni" was finally performed in Vienna. The composer received an extra fee of 225 guilders. Two well-known Mozart singers stood on stage; Aloysia Lange sang Donna Anna, Catarina Cavalieri sang Donna Elvira. For some singers Mozart wrote new arias, and especially for the Viennese, a crude comic duet of the servants Zerlina and Leporello was added. Once again Mozart conducted the Vienna premiere. But the Viennese did not love "Don Giovanni." Nobody knew: Was that really an opera buffa? Surely there are fights, disguises, funny scenes, and a charming minuet. Yet at the same time there so much gloom, punishment, and death. The "hero" has no great aria to show his art. ("Give me my hand, my life" is more of a song than a 'showpiece'.)

If only, at the very least the Emperor had silenced the critics by his applause at the premiere. Joseph II, however, was in a new Turkish war with his army, only returned to Vienna ill in December 1788, and there he just had heard the last performance of "Don Giovanni." He too considered the music "too heavy for the singers," but boasted: "This work is heavenly. It is still more beautiful than The Marriage of Figaro. But it is not a piece for my Viennese city." Mozart's self-confident commentary: "Just give them time to chew on it!"

Mozart did not take the Viennese critics seriously because the most important of all living composers, "Papa Haydn," praised "Don Giovanni." Haydn: "The opera is not for the Viennese. But for Prague, rather than written for me and my friends." That meant that it was an opera for the real music experts, not for the "long-eared" people. Once again arguing about "Don Giovanni," Haydn ended the dispute with the sentence: "I can not make the dispute, but I know that Mozart is the greatest composer the world has now."

Haydn also knew about Mozart's financial worries and tried to help. But it was getting much worse for Mozart. The Turkish War devoured large sums of money and everyone had to save money. Mozart gave his own last concert in 1787. The others had to be canceled because too few tickets were sold. He had prepared such wonderful new compositions such as the late piano concertos, but above all the last major symphonies, including the famous forty-first, which later became known as the "Jupiter Symphony." This symphony was not performed during Mozart's lifetime. Even he never heard it.

The printed music was also hard to sell, and the publisher reminded the composer: "Write more popular pieces; otherwise I can not print and pay anything to you." The music was a holy thing to Mozart. The public compared his difficult, sophisticated art to the "popular" music they were used to and rejected Mozart. For example the "Jupiter Symphony", as house music, was useless. The listener must concentrate fully to even approximate the art and depth of this symphony. The majority of concertgoers were overstrained.

In contrast, Mozart's fame gradually spread abroad. New performances brought "The Kidnapping", "Figaro's Wedding" and "Don Giovanni" to other European cities. Mozart's students sang the music to the audience in concerts. Josepha Duschek and Nancy Storace sang Mozart aria at each of their concerts, piano and violin concertos, masses, and operas, quartets, and serenades were written down and performed by music connoisseurs. Mozart became an insider tip for music lovers all over the world.

Already music lovers from abroad came to Vienna to get to know Mozart. A young Dane, for example, described everyday life in Mozart's house in a Copenhagen paper: "There I spent the happiest hour of music I ever had. "I did not know where I was." Meanwhile, Ms. Mozart cut "keel-feathers for the music-writers-pen," a pupil composed, a little boy of four went around in the garden singing recitative, in short: everything about this beautiful man was musical! "

Mozart's music took several years to finally be recognized, though these years were too long for the composer. Now he needed help, for he had debts and money worries. He often felt sick and melancholy, and lost sleep due to his work. He now needed lots of time to write letters to rich patrons, such as the Masonic brother Michael Puchberg. He wrote about the significant sums of money; one to two thousand guilders he needed annually, "to get it right." Puchberg sent sums of twenty to two hundred guilders in response to petitions of Mozart's plight.

Dresden, Leipzig, and Berlin in April gave Mozart a new hope. His music students and Logenbruder Prince Karl Lichnowsky had to travel to Berlin and invited Mozart to come with him. King Friedrich Willhelm II, who ruled in Berlin, was an avid music lover who played cello quite well. Maybe he would give Mozart a good job at the Berliner Hof or some other assignment? Mozart composed four string quartets with particularly beautiful cello parts.

For the first time Mozart traveled without his Konstanze - and that was difficult for both of them. To cheer her up, he wrote her a farewell quartet, which gave us the piece similar to the bandle terzett (trio), in a lovingly cocky kind of tone, for the Mozart family household. Konstanze says goodbye to her husband: "Caro mio (my dear), ti lascio, o Dio! (I leave you, O God!), che affano! (devoted to you) "Mozart's answer:" Cara mia bagatellerl, io parto, tu resti, che pena! che tormento! "(Dear my little bagatellerl, I am leaving, you remain, such a pity! what a torment!")

They drove via Prague to Dresden. Mozart played his "Coronation Concert" to the Elector of Saxony and, in gratitude, received "a very nice box" with a hundred ducats; over four hundred guldens. In the Dresdner Hof Cathedral, he was invited to a competition on the organ. He triumphed over his rivals and scolded that he was "unable to properly execute a fugue." Mozart left Dresden as a winner, but without a composition commission.

Mozart was blessed with every letter from home: "I immediately went to my room in triumph, kissed the letter countless times before reading it, then devoured it more than I read it." At each stop, as in the old Wunderkind times, he sought out a piano or an organ and tried to impress his devoted listeners. Mozart played the music that was in his mind and which was never written down. He was invited to people's homes frequently for dinner. The soup was served and eaten, then the meat and vegetables. "So we had the choicest table music at our dinner and found him still sitting at the instrument after dinner", said the painter Dora Stock, who portrayed him.

Mozart went with Lichnowsky to Leipzig, where Johann Sebastian Bach had worked, and he heard a Bach motet for the first time, ("Sing to the Lord a new song"), sung by the St. Thomas Choir. "I can really learn from this " he exclaimed, asking for the score to study the music. The Bach Motets were not printed at that time. There was no score from the handwritten notes either, only the individual voices for the choir singers. He sat down with these many notes and composed the score from the many vocal parts in his head.

The highlight of his stay in Leipzig was when he played a one hour performance on the organ of the St. Thomas Church, on Bach's instrument. Mozart improvised, among other things on the Bach chorale "Jesus my confidence." Mozart immersed himself in musical dialogue with the admired "old" Bach, who had been dead for thirty-nine years and almost forgotten by Mozart's contemporaries.

Then he went to prepare for a concert in the Leipzig "Gewandhaus" (concert hall). In the orchestra rehearsal, the composer inflamed the musicians in such a way, "once stamped the time so robustly that he broke his shoe buckle to pieces." He repeated things so often and energetically that the musicians became foul. Eyewitnesses portrayed Mozart as a "small, deathly pale male" with considerable temperament when making music. He played exclusively his own compositions, all of which were not in print, so were still unknown in Leipzig. The concert was brilliant enough, on the part of the applause and the honor, but obtained a miserable review. "

The usual admission fee of one gulden in Vienna was too high for the people of Leipzig. This failure was even worse when Lichnowsky returned to Vienna and Mozart had to 'cough-up' his own travel expenses.

On his own, Mozart traveled to Berlin, where he was invited to perform his opera "Abduction.". At the end of May he performed in front of the Prussian court and received a well-paid commission from King Frederick William II for the string quartets and easy piano sonatas (which were never completed). After the bad experiences in Leipzig, Mozart did not give a Berlin Concert. He wanted to return to Vienna, and finally arrived safely on June 4th, where he hugged Konstanze around the neck.

In the summer of 1789, the revolution broke out in France. Mozart barely acknowledged the turmoil, for he was worried about Konstanze's health, she was expecting her fifth child and she was ill again. She urgently needed a cure in Baden, a small, yet quite medieval city thirty kilometers south of Vienna, which was known to have warm, healing springs.

Every other house in Baden rented rooms to spa guests. Week long spa treatment were very expensive. Again Mozart wrote letters to his friend Puchberg: "Unfortunately, but only in Vienna, my fate is so unfavorable that I can not earn anything when I want to." He wanted to give a concert for the list of interested parties, yet only one name had ever been found; that of the friend Gottfried van Swieten. Mozart conjured up Puchberg: "Bear in mind that without your support and honor, the peace and perhaps the life of your friend and brother will perish."

As often as possible, he drove to his wife in Baden and tried everything to cheer both of them up. In Baden, the Mozart family also visited the "Abduction" opera, performed by a traveling theater. The staging director was not obliged to perform the piece as the composer had directed. It was changed, simplified, funny inserts added, texts changed and all at will. Mozart mingled unrecognized among the audience. The opera troupe did not have a fine orchestra. The violist, for example, was an actor who had never learned to play the instrument properly. At the overture, "a little man" from the audience suddenly sat down with the violist, took the instrument from him, and played in his stead, wonderful and flawless. At the end of the overture he put down his instrument, shouting to the bewildered musician, "The gentleman is a krautesel!" and ran away. (Krautesel is a donkey that eats from the cabbage patch: out of a brother's Grimm story) After the performance, the director invited everyone to a feast in honor of the composer. How frightened the violist was when he saw who the "little man" was! But Mozart apologized: "I was a bit rude but had I not done this to you, the devil would have done it! "

During this time, the old friend Emanuel Schikaneder returned after a long journey back to Vienna, and was named director of the Freihaus Theater on the Wieden in the Black Forest. He was deeply shocked at Mozart's appearance; he found him sickly, burdened with debt, and far from his former success, moreover lonely, because his "dear wife" was back in Baden. Immediately Schikaneder took his friend in. Soon it became as wild and funny as before. Schikaneder loved beautiful women and wine and loved to gather "his children" around him, as he called his actors and singers. Mozart was feeling better than ever before.

The Freihaus Theater was a vast suburban theater with a thousand seats. In the middle stood a complex of buildings consisting of six large courtyards and many houses with thirty-two "staircases" and 225 apartments. These included it's own church, pharmacy, mill and workshops of all kinds. In the middle of the complex was a courtyard with a decorative garden, a fountain, benches and tables in front of an inn, where the theater people met. Mozart made friends with many of the people and recommended some singers and musicians to Schikaneder, such as his little protege, the now fifteen-year-old Anna Gottlieb. She got the lead role in a fairy tale opera, had great success, and was noted "as the first dramatic singer" in Schikaneder's troupe. Even Mozart's sister-in-law Josepha Hofer, a good coloratura singer, soon belonged to Schikaneder's opera company. Next her husband, an orchestral violinist, and then brother in law, the tenor Joseph Haibel (the husband of Konstance's youngest sister Sophie) joined.

This was Mozart's circle of friends in his last years; a jolly, not very distinguished, but fundamentally musical, society in which he found much human warmth. He loved the easy-going jokes and an unassuming tone. Here he forgot his worries for a short time. Some people in Vienna, of course, wrinkled their noses and said that Mozart was living in bad company. Schikaneder had just had his biggest successes in the role "Dumb Anton," a kind of baffoon, in the comic opera "The Stupid Gardener from the Mountains." This piece was so popular in Vienna that it received six sequels. Mozart also laughed at the jokes of "Dumb Anton." The friends asked him to write a funny folk opera, with Schikaneder as Kasperl. Soon came a fitting name: Papageno and to a Papagena.

The imperial opera company resumed performances of "Figaro." This did not bring the composer any money, but success and finally a commission: the opera buffa "Cosi fan Tutte", also based on a libretto by da Ponte.

Here the emperor made a joke, with the almost unbelievable plot, he alluded to an incident that was supposed to have actually happened in Vienna at that time; two young men of the society tearfully parted from their fiancée in order to go to the Turkish War. In reality, they stayed in Vienna, attended a big masquerade ball, disguised and masked, tested the fidelity of their fiancés', and tried to seduce each other's fiancée. The opera "Cosi fan Tutte" (All Women Do It!) is therefore a representation of Viennese society and its loose customs, although the plot's location is in Naples. Above all, it deals with the torments of the feelings of jealousy, under which Mozart and his Konstanz suffered immensely. Mozart set to work with great zeal.

He had less time for his students and other jobs - and again, no revenue coming in. Konstanze continued to be ill and needed a lot of money for doctors and pharmacists. In November 1789, a small daughter was born but died after an hour. Of the five children born so far, only five-year-old Carl was alive, a healthy, lively boy, who saw his dearest playmate in his father.

Again there must have been quarrels with Salieri. Konstanze later reported that Salieri's enmity had begun with "Cosi fan Tutte": he wanted to compose the opera himself, but then gave it up because he considered the theme "unworthy to be put into music." This annoyed him even more about Mozart, as he did not share Salieri's moral misgivings. There was also the issue with the principal singer. She had been cast in a Salieri opera as well as in 'Cosi fan Tutte' resulting in quarrels.

On New Year's Eve in 1789, Mozart invited Joseph Haydn and the financial backer Michael Puchberg to his apartment for a first "small opera rehearsal." The two were also in attendance on January 20,1790, at the first orchestral rehearsal in the Burgtheater in Vienna. On January 26, 1790, "Cosi fan Tutte" was performed for the first time. For the Viennese, the composer had hidden an extra joke in this opera; the maid Despina, disguised as a doctor, brings the allegedly poisoned lover back to life with a giant magnet. This was a reference to Mozart's old friend Mesmer. He had become famous throughout Europe for his new healing technique using magnetism.

But even this fun made the opera no great success, especially at the premiere, for the main character among the audience, Emperor Joseph II, was absent. He lay mortally ill in the Hof Castle and died four weeks later, forty-eight years old, deeply mourned by his court composer. Mozart had lost his most ardent patron. The new crowned Emperor was Joseph's younger brother Leopold, former ruler in Tuscany. Mozart still knew him from Florence, and hoped for his favor. Immediately he asked the new Emperor, in a humble letter, for the second post of Kapellmeister (behind Salieri), and also "for the grace of entrusting me to the royal family for musical instruction."

The new emperor had sixteen children. There was no answer. The new Emperor Leopold II entered a substantial legacy. In the east of the empire, the Turkish war still prevailed, which made the country poor. In the West, the French Revolution threatened to spread to the Austrian provinces. Queen Marie Antoinette of France, Leopold's sister, was in captivity with her family. Another sister, Archduchess Marie Christine, had to flee from Brussels as Regent of the Austrian Netherlands: the country was in open turmoil against Vienna, as was Hungary. The new emperor had his hands full. He had not been in Vienna for more than twenty years, and now had to work his way through things quickly and create order as quickly as possible to prevent the collapse of the great Reich (kingdom & realm).

There were really more pressing issues than court music. The two imperial brothers had not liked each other. Leopold dismissed many followers of Joseph II. Mozart kept his court office, but it was not an important place anyway. He was not promoted. The disappointment and dashed hopes attacked Mozart's health. He suffered from insomnia, headaches and rheumatic attacks, but above all a large measure of discouragement.

As a last resort for earning money, there remained the very thing he hated from the bottom of his heart. He had shown too clearly his distaste for "lessons" and was not a good teacher either. He had no patience if a student could not play the way he expected. He often arrived late, left early. He sometimes played bowling during composition lessons. He was one of the most expensive music teachers in Vienna and demanded ten times as much as his father in Salzburg. For no reason his many rich students kept coming.

Mozart's debts got bigger with the tailor, the cobbler, and the pharmacist. He had to raise money from loan sharks, and complained to Puchberg: "If you knew what it all means to me for sorrow and worry, it has prevented me all the time from finishing my quartet." He meant the commissioned work for the Prussian king.

The coronation in Frankfurt, occurred on September 1790, and was a magnificent tripartite time for the children of the new emperor. Salieri was the conductor of the festivities for that was his job as Court Kapellmeister. Mozart got no orders or work. But the most splendid celebration was Leopold's coronation as German Emperor in Frankfurt. For the festival music, the emperor engaged the court Kapellmeister Antonio Salieri and orchestra musicians.

In his distress Mozart decided to go to Frankfurt at his own expense. All the German princes were gathered there, and if one of them needed Mozart, perhaps they could pay him well? He exchanged his silver to buy a coach. Since Konstanze was too weak for a trip, he took the violinist Schwager Hofer along as a companion, servant and coachman. Mozart also had two new piano concertos, which he called "Coronation Concerts."

In September 1790, Mozart's last journey through Regensburg, Nuremberg, Würzburg, and Aschaffenburg to Frankfurt took five days. There he met influential people, asked for an audience with Emperor Leopold, and offered his services in vain. The city was swarming with people. The guests had brought their servants, their hairdressers, tailors, chambermaids, confessors, personal physicians, and musicians. Theatrical stages were set up in the market places where homages for the new emperor were performed.

The Hof-kapellmeisters of almost all German states were in Frankfurt, and of course were the best musicians. How Mozart would have enjoyed this festival hustle and bustle in better times! But now he remained uninvited and mocked: "Tschiri chichi - the best is to flee." He wrote to Konstanze with longing, "I rejoice to you like a child. When people could see in my heart, I should be ashamed. It's so cold for me, freezing cold. Yes, if you were with me I would perhaps find more pleasure in the kindly behavior of the people against me. But it is empty. "

Ironically at the destination of this expensive and exhausting journey, in the glittering coronation city of Frankfurt, he stayed away from all the festivities and worked with great reluctance on an old

Viennese order to play some ducats in his wife's hands. It was a piece for Orgelwalze (music box), a mechanical instrument, for a Viennese wax figure cabinet. On Coronation Day, Salieri conducted the Coronation Mass in the cathedral; he was the most famous musician in Frankfurt. Mozart got permission to give a concert only after a waiting period of three weeks. From the rehearsals we have an eyewitness account of an orchestral musician: the "small, very lively and agile" conductor had often jumped down from the piano on the stage over the prompter's box into the orchestra trench, giving instructions to the musicians and then taken the same way back. This was certainly not a good way for a composer to get his respect: this Mozart was really a weird guy!

The guests were very exhausted from many celebrations, and many had already left. Mozart played his two "Coronation Concerts" in front of an almost empty hall, and also performed with his brother-in-law Hofer a duo for piano and violin. The trip to Frankfurt brought nothing but debts of about five hundred guilders. On the return journey, Mozart gave a concert in the castle of Mainz to the Elector and received 165 gulden for it. Then he carriaged to a German speaking "Figaro" performance in his beloved Mannheim and was greeted enthusiastically.

He briefly stopped in the city of his ancestors, Augsburg. He did not visit his cousin Bäsle as she had meanwhile become the lover of an Augsburg canon (church official) and had no contact with her relatives.

In Munich Mozart was allowed to play for the royal couple of Naples. Stop in his hometown of Salzburg? ...he avoided it. Should he show himself to the sister and the old Salzburg friends, so unsuccessful, so tired, so sick? On November 10, 1790, he arrived exhausted in Vienna and found the apartment into which his family had moved in the meanwhile. The twelfth move in nine Viennese years! It was on the first floor of a beautiful house on Rauhenstein Alley in the middle of the city. It was very large and quite expensive with an annual rent of 330 guilders. It had a billiard room, and Mozart's horse was in an annex barn in the yard. The furniture, including the pool table and piano, were on loan and pledged to a lender.

On his arrival, Mozart found a letter from London in which the director of the London Opera offered him "the place of a composer in England." He should come to London at the end of December, stay for half a year and "compose at least two serious or comic operas at the direction of the directorate", for a fee of 2400 guilders. In addition, he could give concerts and accept other assignments. Why didn't Mozart accept this offer? What held him in Vienna, where he had no chance of success? We can only assume that the appointment was really too soon for such a long journey, and Konstanze was ill. Without his "wife" Mozart really did not want to travel.

At the same time, another composer boldly accepted the English offer: the fifty-eight-year-old Joseph Haydn. The English concert agent who organized Haydn's journey also made a brilliant offer to Mozart for the following year: 1791 - Mozart's year of death.

In December 1790, "Papa Haydn" said good-bye to Mozart. Mozart asked Haydn whether he was not afraid to make such a long journey in the middle of winter. Mozart asked anxiously, "and that even in his old age?" "I am healthy and have my full strength," answered Haydn cheerfully. Then Mozart; "Papa! They are not raised for the big world and they speak too few languages! " Haydn replied curtly and confidently, "But my language we understand it all over the world." When he left, Mozart burst into tears. "I'm afraid we'll say goodbye for the last time," he explained. But Papa Haydn expectantly embarked on his journey, where the two years brought him much honor, 24,000 guldens of income, and famous compositions.

Mozart remained in Vienna in great solitude. He started The Magic Flute and his worries grew larger, but the Mozart family made every effort to forget them often. Once a servant met the couple eagerly dancing and asked if his wife would like dance lessons? "But no!" Mozart laughed. "We will just freeze, and we have no money for firewood."

The Mozart family still had a heart for friends. They loved a full, loud house and feasted generously. Konstanz's youngest sister, Sophie, vainly scolded "false friends, bloodsuckers, worthless people who served Mozart as fools and whose treatment damaged his reputation." Above all, she was annoyed Anton Stadler, a talented clarinetist. He exploited Mozart's good nature, lured him with money, stole a promissory note in exchange for silver. Stadler owed Mozart 500 guilders, which he never paid. He was the best of all clarinetists, and that's why Mozart put up with all of it.

Mozart composed one of his last concertos, the famous clarinet concerto KV 622 for Anton Stadler. His most faithful friend Annerl Gottlieb, who had long since grown into a mature singer, stayed close by her beloved teacher. He promised her to write big operatic roles for her, though he had received commissions for only one.

He wrote once again for the wax-figure music box and two string quintets for an unknown source. Then a bookseller and lodge-brother needed some nursery rhymes for an illustrated song album. Mozart wrote the songs that have long since become folk songs; "We children, we really enjoy the pleasure" and above all "Come on May and turn the trees green again." As a court composer, Mozart also composed dances for the imperial royal masked balls; minuets, German dances and Ländler.

A friend gave Mozart the opportunity to premiere a piano concerto. That was on March 4, 1791, the last time Mozart performed in concert. The hope for an imperial opera commission was not fulfilled. But there was still his friend Schikaneder with his suburban theater! Schikaneder knew better than anyone else what his audience wanted: a buffoon with a pretty girl in bird gowns, princes, princesses, a wicked queen, a wise priest, an ugly moor as a villain, three pretty boys as lifesavers, and splendid scenery with machines, sinkings, thunder and lightning, fire and water magic and so on.

Pieces with magic were still in fashion in Vienna. The sensation was to write a piece for "Kaspar the bassoonist or the magic zither", played by Schikaneder's competition. He, Emanuel Schikaneder, urgently needed such a magic piece for his theater. From the magic zither you just had to make it another instrument: a magic flute, because the intended tenor Schack was also an excellent flutist.

Mozart hesitated. He wanted so much to revive the old Thamos theme of Salzburg, the story of the noble Egyptian king and his priests, Isis and Osiris, a play that praised the idea of Freemasonry. Schikaneder was also a Mason. He took the Thames story with him into the "Magic Flute." From Thamos became Tamino, who with the help of the flute, passed all the exams and is accepted by the "initiated priests" and gets his Pamina. At the same time, the piece was a magic opera, a comedy of a buffoon, a hymn to the Free Masons and much more.

The main roles were written to match the singers on hand. Schikaneder got Papageno again, his talent role as a comical bass buffo and folksy, funny songs that brought him certain success. Mozart dedicated to his sister Josepha Hofer as "Queen of the Night" with her high voice with two breakneck arias. Schikaneder brought in new scenes up until the last minute, whether they fitted the whole or not.

The main thing was the success. This is how the "Magic Flute" became an adventurous collection of pieces on the surface. Anyone who takes the trouble to understand the plot might be confused though; first, Sarastro is a villain, then suddenly a nobleman. The Queen of the Night character is a poor mother robbed of her daughter. Then she is wicked. Actually, the text is very directed against women, but Pamina is still included in the circle of "initiates." Many books have been written about the many mistakes of the "Magic Flute." But Mozart's music makes all these considerations less important.

The modest use of a suburban theater becomes a musical marvel that everyone experiences and understands differently, which always challenges new interpretations, yet remains mysterious and ambiguous.

Mozart's health was very bad that summer, his very last. He was lonely and sad. Konstanze went back to Baden. His letters were as tender as ever and traveled there as often as possible. At five o'clock in the morning he set off to be in Konstanze's arms five hours later. On one of these short visits, as if casually composed without much thought, the forty-eight bars of the choral work "Ave verum corpus" were written for the feast of Corpus Christi in Baden. It shows Mozart's introspective and serious mood at this time.

Composing was difficult for him then, because he needed a cheerful mind and balance, and Konstanze next to him. He wrote in early July: "When I think how funny and childish we were together in Baden and what sad boring hours I spend here. I am also not happy about my work, because, as usual, as time suspends and to talk a few words to you, this pleasure is unfortunately an impossibility. If I go to the piano and sing something from the opera, I have to stop right away. It gives me too much sensation."

Schikaneder did what he could to advance the opera: he invited the singers, led by Annerl Gottlieb, into a wooden house near the theater, ordered wine and good food. Mozart was brought back into humor with all sorts of jokes. He had to finish the "Magic Flute"! Konstanze, who was again expecting a baby, learned about these fun evenings in Baden, and became jealous.

Mozart, on the other hand, could not suppress his jealousy of a young man whom he himself had sent to Baden, his pupil and assistant Franz Xaver Süßmayer, ten years his junior. The artist scolded in his letters on the "sour-mayer", was irritated and injured by him, whether rightly or wrongly, we do not know. In this mood he wrote Papageno's amusing arias, the coloratura of the Queen of the Night, the love arias of Tamino, and the splendid, desperate music of the Pamina.

His friend and librettist da Ponte had to say goodbye. The new emperor had dismissed him and even expelled him from the country. The lyricist went to England and asked Mozart to come with him. In England so many friends and admirers lived there. He said Mozart would be better off there. They would write together many great operas. But Mozart refused as he was in the middle of the work for the Magic Flute. Now he could not leave Vienna. Maybe in half a year

Requiem

Then came the commission that deeply shocked Mozart and indeed darkened his life: an unknown, "long, leaner man in gray clothes" delivered an anonymous commission for a funeral mass in Mozart's apartment; a requiem. Mozart, oppressed by money worries, had to accept a hundred ducats! He thought a piece of church music fits well with his plans as he had applied for the post of cathedral conductor of St. Stephen. He would need church music for it. The dark look of the mysterious messenger, the anonymous commission, haunted him in his dreams. Sickness, melancholy, work overload, and the loneliness away from his wife all caused mortal fear in him.

What Mozart never learned was that the client was a certain Count Walsegg, who, more than enough, tried composing himself. After the death of his wife, the count wanted to perform a funeral mass and sought a composer who wrote them for him. He wanted to pretend to be a composer, that's why he was secretive. That he was thinking of Mozart is a sign of how run-down the thirty-five-year-old was.

In the middle of July Mozart picked up Konstanze from Baden. On July 26, 1791, the sixth and last child, Franz Xaver Wolfgang, was born in Rauhenstein Alley. It had a malformed ear like the father's, a lucky sign; a new Mozart?

Shortly thereafter, Mozart had to interrupt his work on the Magic Flute and the Requiem. Leopold II was to be crowned as King of Bohemia in Prague, and the loyal Prague composers would perform their favorite Mozart opera with the composer of the coronation mass. The opera had to be finished in four weeks. The score was in no hurry to write itself. It was "La Clemenza di Tito" by Metastasio. A hymn of praise to the kindness and gentleness of the Roman ruler Titus, and thus to the newly crowned Bohemian King Leopold II, and all other rulers whose tribute this text has been repeated. Even Gluck wrote music on this theme. Again, an opera seria like the Munich "Idomeno". By now this form of opera had become old-fashioned, and Mozart had long since evolved from it. But could he turn down two hundred ducats, after all, almost nine hundred guilders? So he went to work.

Konstanze: "He often composed until two o'clock and got up at four in the morning, an effort that contributed to his death." There was no hour of recovery. One morning his hairdresser, astonished, observed Mozart while on horseback, talking out a chalkboard, and writing notes. His constant exertion is to be noted for "La Clemenza di Tito." There are wonderful arias in this opera and wonderful orchestral passages. But a real musical drama like the "Don Giovanni" or the "Figaro" it wasn't.

The work was wrestled from a sick body and a sad-tempered spirit. Mozart also asked for help for the first time from Süßmayer, who wrote the recitatives. In mid-August Mozart left for Prague with Konstanze and Süssmayer. As they were about to get into the coach, the "gray messenger" appeared suddenly, (now for the third time), and warned Mozart to finish the requiem. Konstanze comforted him on the speedy return. Mozart remained speechless. Again this fear of death!

He composed tirelessly during the journey and at the inn at night, always in the fear of not being able to cope, of dying over worked. Salieri was also in Prague. He conducted the solemn procession of the new royal couple in St. Vitus Cathedral and other splendid concerts. Mozart was allowed to conduct a performance of his "Don Giovanni" in the presence of the royal couple and, a few days later, the first performance of "La Clemenza di Tito."

The new opera was unsuccessful. First of all, the listeners were already tired of all the festivities of the Coronation Day. They also weren't voluntarily in the opera audience as only official participants in the celebrations had received tickets, i.e. the imperial royal court, the domestic and foreign diplomats and important representatives of Bohemia. Among them there were only a few music connoisseurs and supporters of Mozart. Only later performances in front of an educated audience brought success.

Mozart took his two hundred ducats fee – and continued to work on the "Magic Flute" in Villa Bertramka in Prague with his friend Josepha Duschek. He was able to relax, go bowling and play pool. The Prague friends saw with dismay how forced Mozart's cheerfulness was. He was sad and nervous, timid and "disturbed by thoughts of death." He sought consolation from his Masonic brothers. Several times he went to the Prague lodge and conducted his cantata "The Mason Friends" for the brothers. When leaving Prague in mid-September, there were tears. The big hurry was fitting, because the premiere of the "Magic Flute" was due to take place in Vienna on September 30, and the composition was far from finished.

On September 28, Mozart still wrote the priest's choir and the overture. Süßmayer helped to write the parts. The orchestra rehearsals did not help the seriously ill composer. Yet he still conducted the first performance from the piano, with Süßmayer sitting next to him to assist if Mozart perhaps fainted. The "Magic Flute mesmerized Vienna's suburban audiences" with it's music as well as the fairytale like action, lavish scenery, and all the theatrical thunder that Schikaneder masterfully used.

Schikaneder as Papageno, the sister-in-law Josepha as Queen of the Night, Sarastro and Tamino were all celebrated. The happiest was Annerl Gottlieb as Pamina for in the last few months she had trembled more than anyone else about the sick master, had comforted him, amused him, and was now happy for him. A very sad love story.

Konstanze traveled back to Baden right after the premiere. Mozart was alone with his work on the Requiem and his fear of death in Vienna. As often as possible he visited his performances of the "Magic Flute." He took with him the joyful seven-year-old Carl, his mother-in-law Weber, and the horn player Leitgeb. Even the court Kapellmeister Salieri and his favorite singer went to the new success in the suburbs. Mozart proudly told Baden, "how much they liked not only my music but the story and everything together." So Salieri's and his hostility to Mozart could not have been that bad.

After the performances, Mozart sometimes sat alone in the nearby beer house "To the Silver-Snake". Here the servant of the house watched him with his head resting on his right hand, brooding, "Mozart looked unusually pale, his powdered blond hair was in disarray, and his little braid was carelessly bound." The waiter spoke to him, told him a story "of Turkish music" that Mozart always laughed at. But Mozart resisted; "No, I feel that it will be too exhausting. I am affected by a cold that I can not explain."

In mid-October he traveled home with the little Konstanze. He was very ill and fantasized and (according to Konstanze) "that he was poisoned." "I know that I have to die!" He exclaimed. "Someone gave me 'aqua toffana' and accurately predicted the day of my death, and they ordered a requiem for that. I am writing it for myself." At that time people in Vienna were talking a lot about the poison aqua toffana, a mixture of arsenic and hydrocyanic acid, which, taken in small portions for a long time, slowly leads to death.

Mozart could only explain his increasing weakness from this poison. In fact, he had severe kidney disease, and the damaged organs gradually poisoned his already weak body. Konstanze, who had returned home, urged her desperate husband to set aside the funeral mass. Again he found solace in the idea of the Free masonic cult and composed the "Small Masonic Cantata" for the inauguration of a new temple in Vienna. It was the last composition he wrote in his catalog raisonné. (a comprehensive, annotated listing). He conducted the premiere on November 18, and sang with his brothers and the final chorus to a text by Schikaneder. This music is another text, the national anthem of the Republic of Austria. This was his last evening in the circle of his friends, and the last time playing music together to cheer the sick. He returned "very proudly" and said (according to Konstanze); "If I did not know that I had written better things, then I would consider this my best work ... Yes, I see that I must have been ill to think so wrongly, I would have taken poison. Give me the requiem again, and I want to keep working on it."

Three days later he had to go to bed. His hands and feet were swollen. He had terrible pain at the slightest movement. He had had these rheumatic inflammations since childhood, and now they were unbearable. His friends did their best to help the patient. Longing, the patient waited for news of the "Magic Flute" and heard with pleasure that the theater was sold out every evening. The nights were bad and Konstanze woke up to him.

On the 4th of December in the morning he looked fresher. Konstanze's youngest sister Sophie came to visit. She was greeted warmly by Mozart with the words; "Alright, dear Sophie, that you are here. You have to stay here tonight. You have to see me die." Sophie tried to calm him down. But he replied, "I have already the taste of the dead on my tongue, and who will stand by my dearest Konstanze, if you do not stay here?"

Süßmayer appeared every day to work on the requiem. Mozart had come to the "Lacrimosa" ("tearful"). The main voices for the other parts were sketched, and Mozart showed Süßmayer where and how to insert the remaining parts. In the evening they sent for the doctor. It was Schikaneder's theater doctor who could not come until after the evening performance had ended. He made a cold vinegar wrap on the fever hot forehead. The sudden cold made the patient tremble. Sophie; "His last thing was still how he wanted to express the timpani in his Requiem with his mouth, I still hear that." Then he fainted and died shortly thereafter.

It was December 5, 1791, one o'clock in the morning. Together, his friends and family dressed the dead body and moved him to his study next to the piano. Gradually, they gathered around Mozart, loudly moaning and crying. Later, the owner of the waxworks department took off the death mask. Konstanze, the twenty-eight-year-old widow, was so broken with pain that she needed to be taken care of by the doctor and was unable to give instructions. Gottfried van Swieten organized the funeral. With only sixty guldens of cash in the house, he advised a third-grade burial, the simplest kind. It cost eight guldens fifty-six cruisers for the church and three guldens for the wagon.

The next day, December 3, at three o'clock in the afternoon, the corpse was blessed on the outside of St. Stephen's Cathedral, in the open air, in front of the cross chapel. Friends, pupils and relatives took part in this short ceremony without music. Konstanze remained ill at home. The coffin was placed in the death chamber and was brought informally, without solemn escort, in the evening to the cemetery in the suburb of St. Marx. This lay five kilometers from the city, over a very bad road in a lonely area.

Nevertheless, two Mozart pupils wanted to follow the wagon, but soon had to give up their idea, "because the driver drove the horse in a greater hurry and they could no longer follow." Even at the funeral the next morning there were no witnesses. Mozart was buried in a deep grave together with five other dead. A tombstone was forbidden on such graves, as well as flower arrangements and mourning ribbons. This is why we do not exactly know where Mozart's grave lay, just about the place where the dead were buried in the time in question.

There exist many a horrible story about this funeral. It was not at all extraordinary, but as Emperor Joseph had stated; "to make the exaggeratedly sumptuous and expensive Vienna funeral ceremonies simpler and cheaper, and to relieve the population, he had issued a funeral ordinance." After the consecration, the coffin was to be driven out of the narrow inner city at night to the distant new suburban cemeteries, and buried there in shaft graves consisting of four adults and two children each. All downtown cemeteries were leveled because of health hazards.

Only those families who bought their own tombs were allowed to hold ceremonious burials. Of course, a rich patron could have bought his own grave for Mozart. But Mozart's friends would had probably been so surprised by the quick death of the thirty-five-year-old that they were compelled to organize the funeral within a few hours.

The grief in Prague was incomparably greater than in Vienna. On December 14, 1791, the orchestra of the Bohemian National Theater held a memorial service in St. Niklas Church. For half an hour the bells rang and the church was overflowing with over four thousand mourners. One hundred twenty of the best Bohemian musicians, led by singer Josepha Duschek, performed in honor of Mozart.

As usual, the deceased's assets were accurately calculated. Household goods, clothes and books had a value of about five hundred guilders. Three thousand gulden of debt stood in front of it, with the tailor, and cobbler. The pharmacist at Puchberg alone was 1415 guilders, a very high sum. Puchberg assisted the widow in this difficult time and reassured her that he did not need the money for the time being. Many years later Konstanze was really wealthy and paid the money back to Puchberg.

After the shock of the news of Mozart's death, the family got help from everywhere; charity concerts, money gathering, and donations. Konstanze later sold her husband's works. She received almost four thousand guilders from the Prussian king alone for eight compositions. The requiem was completed by Süßmayer, and Konstanze got the agreed upon fee. It was first performed in Wiener Neustadt in 1793, as the work of the composer "Count Walsegg".

The seventeen-year-old Anna Gottlieb was so inconsolable about Mozart's death that she never sang the Pamina role of the "Magic Flute" again. She lived as a poorly paid actress and singer, never married and died in 1856 after a long life of remembrance and grief. She was buried in the cemetery of St. Marx, not far from Mozart's tomb. A memorial plaque is there.

Joseph Haydn also grieved deeply. "Posterity will not have such a talent again in a hundred years!" He complained, repeatedly emphasizing that Mozart was better than he, Joseph Haydn. Still years later he could not speak calmly about his death, and apologized; "Forgive me, I always cry in the name of my Mozart."

Konstanze experienced Mozart's fame following the period after 1800 his major works appeared in print. She became famous as "Widow Mozart" herself. In 1809 she married the Danish Legation Counselor

Nissen. He was a fiery Mozart worshiper who wrote the first biography of Mozart. After his death in 1826, Konstanze lived in Salzburg, very close to the widowed and blind Maria Anna Freiin von Berchtold zu Sonneburg, the former Nannerl. The two women still did not like each other very much. Nannerl died in 1829, Konstanze in 1842. She thus survived her first husband for more than half a century.

Mozart's sons remained unmarried, so there are no surviving offspring of grandchildren and great-grandchildren. Carl Mozart was educated by Prague friends, became a civil servant, and died in 1858 in Milan. The father had secured him a good income, and thanks to a new copyright law, from the proceeds of three Parisian "Figaro" performances, Carl was able to buy a country estate in Italy for ten thousand francs. The younger son Wolfgang, only five months old at the time of his father's death, received a good musical education from Mozart's friends, but did not fulfill the exaggerated expectations and died in 1844 as a pianist, music teacher and composer in Carlsbad. Mozart's death mask was exhibited in the wax museum on Kohl market in Vienna, as well as a wax figure who had been dressed in his original clothes. A music box played those pieces that Mozart had once so reluctantly composed for money. The wax museum was unfortunately not preserved, any more than the copy of the death mask that Konstanze possessed. At some point it fell to pieces. Konstanze looked satisfied that "the ugly thing was finally broken," and threw away the pieces. Posterity does not know what Mozart really looked like. The few bad pictures contradict each other. On each Mozart looks different. Even the story of his life cannot explain the "miracle Mozart." To know what it is, one has to listen to his music.

Folk Music and Folklore

Folklore is the knowledge of the people since the English explorer Williams J. Thoms used the word "folklore." For the first time in 1846, it has become a widely used term in all languages. It is composed of two old Anglo-Saxon roots. "Folk" corresponds to our same-sounding word people, and "lore" means knowledge. Folklore is, therefore, what the people know without having been taught it. It is knowledge of instinct, intuition, tradition, and indigenous culture. Folklore includes fairy tales, legends, customs, ceremonies, habits, poetry, songs, and dances.

Folkloristic music is born within the people, made by the people for the people and also has a particular tradition. It is also music without artistic ambitions and is a pure expressive feeling of their folk soul. On one hand, these conditions are not as easy to fulfill, as they seem at first sight. On the other hand, folklore has become a branch of research. It has many complicated rules that distinguish it from sociology and ethnography.

For a long time, people simply spoke of folk music terms that are less scientific but easier to handle. Folk music was songs made by the people that live in the vernacular and dances that came from the tradition. By "folk music," we understood that music was first written and made for the people. Afterwards, they were perhaps recognized, adopted, and assimilated. We touch upon the field of folk music when we speak of the composer Franz Schubert's 'Linden-tree,' which, as it is called, is a little 'shattered' into the vernacular. It has become a folk song according to our concept, although folklore does not consider it so, mainly because the author is known.

Real folk music should be anonymous. But is there the creation of melodies in the people themselves? Has not all of our authentic folk songs maybe centuries ago been composed by someone? Invented and sung for the first time with such success that they took possession of it or it passed on orally? There are European tunes that have been alive for four, five, even six centuries. The majority has characteristics and expressions, which immediately lead us to their origins when we hear them. Without being able to explain it, for the most part, we can perceive certain songs and dances as Spanish, Italian, or Russian.

But what is "real" folklore and what is "only" folk music? Especially in the last hundred years, in which we have broadened our knowledge in the field of folk music, it is increasingly tempting composers to incorporate national styles into their music. Not only those from their own country, but those borrowed from any country. Imitations of folk music that lead to folk music, but also to art music, are example like Bizet's 'Carmen', Rimski-Korsakov's 'Spanish Capriccio' and 'Indian Song.' Often certain regions have cared for them for centuries without realizing it; only out of need, in certain moods, at certain seasons, at war or peace, harvest or plague, in love, at the cradle and at death, or in the mind to relieve the soul. Folk music is as old as humans, and when the first cultures arose the division between folk music and "cultivated" music, i.e., art music, started imperceptibly at first, but then deeper as time progressed.

There have been epochs in all cultures, as popular and art music ran parallel, were close and fertilized each other. At other times, they moved away from each other as they were consciously segregating upper class from the lower class, for example. The minstrels and troubadours of the European Middle Ages were deeply rooted in the folk song and even enlivened many works of polyphonic art in the 14th to 16th centuries when highly trained composers used it as the subject of polyphonic works.

The great composer Joseph Haydn processed several Slavic and Hungarian melodies from his native country in his symphonies. Beethoven treated Scottish and Welsh sages, solely for the pleasure of real folk music. The romantic epoch "discovered" the folksong and used it with enthusiasm. Chopin would be inconceivable without Polish accents, Liszt hard without the Hungarian element of his music and Gustav Mahler incomplete without his native Austrian Empire.

Connections between folk and art music "Folk song is either a song that has been written where the composer or its origin is no longer known and has passed into the vernacular, or one that is known or " popular," and is simple and melody and harmony are easy to grasp is composed in... ," Hugo Riemann defines the term in his lexicon. Riemann tacitly denies that folk music can arise "in the people," though he expressly mentions it, but with the explanation that "the poet and composer are no longer known." He annuls the possibility of a pluralistic creation, of the emergence of music "from the masses." Finally, and "simply and easily understood ... composed," mixed Riemann folk melody and folk harmony.

It is by no means said that his definition must be thrown overboard as obsolete and inaccurate. In fact, such close connections exist between folk music, art music, that a separation is not easy. Are not the North American songs by Stephen Collins Foster related to the "real" folk songs? For several generations, they "live" in the people and are perceived by other peoples as "typically American." We mentioned cases in which folk music found its way into art music. We could offer Chopin and Liszt a wealth of other composers. Particularly interesting are instances such as Manuel de Falla and Béla Bartok; they have not used a single, genuine folk melody, but they have met the folksy tone with such precision that the image of Spain or Hungary arises before the listener's eyes.

Perhaps one could speak of a big circle: music is born in the people, rises to art music, and after a certain period, its decline fertilizes folk music again. A cycle that never ends and to prove it a test case is Latin

America. Latin America's folk music is relatively young, and similar to the old Native American Indian melodies that would have been preserved, are difficult to find. Where Native American music still exists, it has mingled with later influences. The European immigrants certainly brought along their folk tunes to the new country. However, these were for the most part condemned to fade away. As in countries with a strong lineage, the customs, costumes, dances, and songs brought with them were rapidly shared and mixed.

One might imagine it at the playground, the children of innumerable peoples meet, and so the songs that each one brings with them from his parents' home are quickly mixed up or left aside to be forgotten. It turns out that Carlos Vega has credibly demonstrated the majority of today's folklore consists not of folk songs brought along, but of imported art music. As the upper social stratum of the 18th and 19th century introduced fashion dances and songs from the cultural centers of Europe, the same court dances were danced in Madrid, Lisbon, and Paris. Also in Vienna, London and Rome, we see later on the same ballroom dances; the Gavotte and Minuet; later the Waltz, Polka, Quadrille, etc. The South American lower classes watched the upper classes in the palaces or on the estates and imitated them. The gaucho dances were created in apparent imitation of European social dances. These ballroom dances have long since disappeared in their countries of origin, but they still live in South American folklore. Here are still the "open" dances where only the fingertips are touched as in the European tradition of centuries past. And the forms of music have clearly "fallen socially." What was a monopoly of the upper classes two to one hundred years ago, is now folk music and has become folklore.

One more thing can be clearly demonstrated in the living example of South America; that folklore and folk music arise from what would be rejected as popular in Europe. In Latin America, folklore still occurs today, every day, every hour. Many songs penetrate the vernacular, which have just been written by a librettist, a composer, printed by a publisher, recorded on records, registered with a society to collect royalties.

Songs are what Riemann said in the last words of his definition: Society today denies them the status of folklore; but how will the same songs and dances be in a hundred years?

Meaning, value, and unity of folk music

Folk music is alive and should be considered in constant flux and constant renewal. As new songs emerge then accepted by the people, others are slowly forgotten or unconsciously reshaped. Most go by like "popular hits" and as fashionable creations useful for the times. What distinguishes a folk song above all else is its duration, its permanence, which may only be measured after centuries have passed. Anyone who truly understands how to read and hear old folk songs often learns profound things from history and the past. Yet more rarely, the names of rulers of whom the history books are about, but the joys and sorrows of the people of which history scarcely records. Diseases, invasions, oppression, and hunger are included in it, as are the joys of existence accessible to humanity; wandering, love, and the changing of the seasons.

In folk music, instruments, songs, dances are inseparably merged into a great unity. Every nation on earth has it's own. Perhaps we can do nothing more than show how global music is, how all countries are expressive in song and dance. When they sing and dance, what they know, they are one people. Not because their dances and songs resemble each other. No, because the emotional impulses always drive them and are the same everywhere.

Ludwig van Beethoven

A modern time calls on the artist to live consciously in the present. The past artist's life and deeds were regarded as being independent of the general social existence of their environment, and were based on the idea that art was for its own sake. Even in earlier centuries, the artists were servants. In Bach's time, music in the royal cities was the expression of courtly representation. In the citizen cities, the musician was a town musician, an organist or cantor, the representative of the citizenry. Music was composed because the delivery of new utility music was required as a matter of course. All of the works that today are regarded and praised by music history as an expression of their time in style and content owe their existence to such an attachment to the artist's order.

The strict division of the eighteenth century brought with it an equally strict separation within the various artistic genres. The opera, the most sophisticated form of the Baroque expression of life, served almost exclusively to represent the royal court with some exceptions in politically independent or commercially wealthy and independent cities, such as Venice, Hamburg, Nuremberg or Leipzig. The bourgeois representation was served by festival cantatas, the musical needs of urban patricians and students, suites and concerts for the collegia musica, church cantatas and organ chorals, as well as the tower music of the instrumental trumpeters, dances of the art violinists, and "beer fiddlers" playing at the festivities. The music of the journeyman and maid in the city, yet no one took notice of the peasant music practice as it was unworthy of notice. It was from here that springs forth a new life to art and music.

Even that period, which we today call classical music, would be inconceivable without the ever-renewing contact with the simple music of craftsmen and peasants. Haydn took on the imperial reproach of being a "joker" when he summed up the forces of empowerment, using folk elements in his music, which he welded into the form of the classical sonata and symphony.

Italian serenades and Salzburg dances combined in Mozart with the features of court opera to form a classical unit. Moreover, Beethoven's life's work would never have retained its vitality for ages and generations if not the inexperienced and untrained listener in it immediately felt that healthy core of folklore. However, Beethoven did not grow out of the people as Haydn did.

It had been generations since his ancestors had lived as Flemish peasants and craftsmen in the Liège, Mechelen, and Brussels districts, with a cruel campaign of the Spanish oppressor where one was burned at the stake as a "witch" in 1595. This was against the Dutch who pressed for bourgeois freedom. Then the Beethoven family had moved to the Rhine River as candlestick makers and his brother Ludwig, a musician. Ludwig had been first chorister and singer of Mechelen, then in the church choirs of Leuven and Liège. He founded the Bonner Hof-kapelle in 1733 for his bread as a singer. He held the title of Kapellmeister for four decades.

Bonn, the city where the court Kapellmeister Ludwig van Beethoven worked, was for several centuries' residence of the archbishop of Cologne. The court Kapellmeister served various jobs in this ministry, which was connected to the secular sovereignty over an extensive Rhine area. The lavish Klemens August, a Bavarian prince had made Bonn into a resplendent residence full of festivals, masked balls, and theatrical performances. Unfortunately, the prince Maximilian Friedrich had followed and led a politics of sparseness to the point of avarice. It was a time of consolation, which curtailed costly court balls, wild boar hunts, and reduced the salaries of his court officials, but at least the court musicians were treated relatively lightly.

Within the palaces a dainty chatter of ladies and gentlemen filled the court halls, where a sober hand was dealt of enlightened absolutism, their rulers worldview, which became ever louder among their society. The intent was a call for freedom of the "nonpolitical" paths of scientific academies and German national theaters. The Bonn court also wanted this outlook, which made concessions to be firmly in control. It was also in the spirit of the Enlightenment that in 1781 the Catholic Elector awarded the Theater Music Director Christian Gottlob Neefe, without claiming his "Protestant religion," the title of Court Organist.

Court organist Neefe soon had a capable young assistant: the grandson, still in his boyhood, of the former Court Kapellmeister Ludwig van Beethoven and son of the court tenor Johann van Beethoven. The young Ludwig van Beethoven was born in mid-December 1770 in the small rear building of Bonn Alley 515. The entry in the church records indicates the 17th of December as the day of the baptism. Since it was the custom to baptize the children as soon as possible, the 17th or 16th of December 1770 may be accepted as a birthday. A few years later, the family of the court tenor van Beethoven moved out of the Bonn Alley house. Johann van Beethoven did not have the balanced, robust character of his father, the Kapellmeister. As long as his wife lived, there seemed to be order and modest petty bourgeois wealth in his home.

A playmate of his son Ludwig, Gottfried Fischer, whose father's house he visited several times, described the family as follows; "Johann van, Beethoven, court tenor, claimed his position punctually. He taught the sons and daughters of the family English, French, and imperial envoys, gentlemen, and daughters of the nobility, and also to the public; lessons in piano and singing. He often had more to do than he could handle. He also often received additional gifts. This kept his household well."

The Beethoven family's way of life began to collapse with the progressive illness of the housewife Maria Magdalena. After her death, in 1787, the court singer sought solace in drink, so that in a list of residents from the year 1790 already the twenty-year-old "organist Beethoven junior" is recorded as a housekeeper: Johann van. Beethoven had been 'dispensed' from duty, and saved from the ban of exile from Bonn only through the efforts of his son and because of the merits of the old court Kapellmeister.

Johann van Beethoven soon recognized the musical abilities of his eldest son. At that time, a musician was far from being as specialized until later on. Grandfather Ludwig had been a church singer, performed on stage, and conducted the court orchestra. Likewise, Johann van Beethoven was not just a singer. We may assume that he also allowed the son to play the piano. He might have learned 'figured bass', improvisation on a keyboard and instrumental accompaniment, and perhaps compositional arranging. The young Beethoven was also well versed in organ playing at an early age. At times, other Bonn musicians took over the lessons of the thoughtful, stubborn boy.

The court organist Heinrich van der Eeden might have taught him occasional acting, singing and flute lessons, and also from an elegant but lewd musician Tobias Friedrich Pfeiffer. He also served the Beethoven's food at their home. The member of the court band, cellist Bernhard Mäurer, reported on the musical education of little Ludwig; "Often, when Pfeiffer had been drinking with Beethoven's father in the tavern until eleven or twelve, he went home with him, where Louis was in bed and fell asleep. The father shook him impetuously; crying, the boy, gathered himself and went to the piano, where Pfeiffer stayed with him until the early morning when he recognized his unusual talent."

Under these circumstances, little emphasis was placed on the general education of the child. "Beethoven's education was neither noticeably neglected nor particularly good. He learned reading, writing, arithmetic and a little bit of Latin in a public school, music to which his father kept him uninterrupted and strict," says Franz Gerhard Wegeler, who was five years older than Beethoven and was friends with him at an early age. Playmate Gottfried Fischer even claimed; "He did not learn much at school after his father's statement, that's why his father put him so early on the piano and stopped him so severely." Beethoven felt these shortcomings, which are revealed in all of his letters with uncertain spellings, and in his household books as calculation errors.

When the University of Bonn was opened in 1786, he probably also belonged to its listeners and with his own zealous and critical reading of poetic and philosophical writings, he achieved energy that allowed him to express in 1809: "There is no essay that will be published I have not read. Without even the slightest claim to actual education, I have endeavored, from childhood to grasp the meaning of the better and wise of every age. Shame on an artist who does not consider it his duty to bring it at least so far." The court tenor Johann van Beethoven had tried at an early age to make money with the talent of his son.

In March 1778 he announced a concert of two of his "Scholares", indicating the age of his son as the age of six. (Ludwig van Beethoven also considered his year of birth to be 1772 until his fourth decade in life.) In the year after this first public concert of the boy who had been forcibly prodigal, Christian Gottlob Neefe came to Bonn. As music director of the theater and court organist, he developed an active musical life in the Rhenish royal capital. There, the young Ludwig van Beethoven, whose genius Neefe recognized immediately, received the first methodological teacher.

The following year in 1781, he made a trip to Holland, and was allowed to represent the court organist Neefe at the organ. This year also saw the first printed composition of the barely twelve-year-old, published in Mannheim: Piano Variations on a March by the Kassel composer Dreßler. They were followed in 1783 by three piano sonatas, which the young composer, certainly on Neefe's and his father's advice, dedicated to the Elector Maximilian Friedrich. These works, which are almost unknown today, called "Electoral Sonatas," were the result of strenuous study. Neefe did not tease the young Beethoven with petty rules but influenced him with examples.

The "Well-Tempered Clavier" by Johann Sebastian Bach, which was at that time rather unknown to musicians, was studied so thoroughly that Beethoven memorized many of these preludes and fugues throughout his life. In addition, Neefe made him versed especially with the piano sonatas and the leading textbook "Trying to play the piano over the true nature of" by Philipp Emanuel Bach, who had far outshined his father's fame in the second half of the 18th century. This book wasn't for piano playing alone but was necessary for the performance practice of his time. Beethoven later based his own teaching on this.

In a music journal, Neefe reported on his pupil, that which he foretold a bright future. If he could travel and educate himself "He would certainly become a second Wolfgang Amadeus Mozart if he progressed the way he did." In 1787 he succeeded in obtaining a study trip to Vienna with Mozart for the new Elector and Max Franz for Beethoven's pupil. In 1784, Beethoven's organ playing aroused the court orchestra's admiration. Neefe had the young Beethoven receive the title of second court organist in1785. The payrolls also listed him as a viola player.

What kind of services did the young Bonner Hof musician have to perform? In the first place, according to the spiritual condition of the Elector, first and foremost church music was played. In the theater, where Neefe was himself a vital singer, songwriter, and acted as a "singer-song director and clavic harpsichordist," Beethoven sat on the viola and pianoforte.

French and Italian comic operas were predominantly performed. The new Elector from Vienna brought with him the taste for German singing plays (Singspiel) and operas. Beethoven introduced the orchestral musicians to Dittersdorf, Mozart's, 'Abduction', "Marriage of Figaro" and "Don Giovanni." The ideas of human liberation and fraternity spilling over from France took root, and above all in the hearts of youth. The university professor Eucutius Schneider, a fervent admirer of French revolutionary ideas, who was later executed by the Counter Revolution in Strasbourg, gathered the progressive students around him. From the cathedral, a self-proclaimed hymn proclaiming the battle of the Paris citizens on the royal fortress, the Bastille, was resounding.

Can one even doubt that the boy Beethoven was passionately seized by these new ideas? Konrad Pfeffels words from his song "Who is a free man? The one to whom only his own will can give laws! " Is it the daily song of his friends? Schiller's revolutionary dramas, his "Robbers," his "Fiascos", were read and discussed in the circles of progressive Bonn citizens.

These ideas of republican virtue, as designed by Schiller, never left Beethoven, and a statuette of the Roman hero of the freedom Brutus was still a constant ornament of his home in Vienna. Bourgeois Bonn was also in a musical relationship with Ludwig.

In a report from Bonn published in Hamburg in 1787, "Cramersche Magazin": "Music lovers growing rapidly among the locals. The piano is excellently loved; we have here several Augsburg pianos and other similar instruments." (The pianoforte replaced the old harpsichord at the time.) It is also reported that they liked to sing Rhineland folk songs in these circles. This is a critical reference to the connecting threads between Beethoven's work and folk music. His folksy, serene songs, such as "Urian's Journey," may have been sung in such social circles as in the case of Frau von Breuning, to whom Beethoven revered as his second mother.

However, the somewhat awkward, but gladly cheerful and often uncomfortable atmosphere of his father's house, found Beethoven seeking to forget. He soon became friends with the four children of Helene von Breunings, and above all with Eleanor and Lorenz, whom he taught piano, and with Stefan, who later worked as a lawyer in Vienna. Wegeler later married Eleonore von Breuning and through his "Biographical Notes on Ludwig van Beethoven" reported many facts about the composer's early years in Bonn. He published these Reminiscences in 1834 together with Beethoven's pupil Ferdinand Ries, whose father was "formerly the Cologne music director of Bonn, Beethoven's first protector," The Reminiscences are dedicated to him.

Franz Ries was a violinist in the court chapel and later music director, whose violin lessons were enjoyed by Beethoven. He remembered those lessons with gratitude when he then promoted Ferdinand Ries selflessly in Vienna.

In the series of figures that influenced Beethoven's first two decades of life in Bonn, he was also allowed to dabble as a composer from Dux in Bohemia. Count Ferdinand von Waldstein, whose prophetic entry in Beethoven's genealogical book on his final move to Vienna "Through Uninterrupted Diligence you will receive Mozart's Spirit from Haydn's Hands," was a brilliant observation.

Later, Beethoven broke with the rather adventurous Count, to whom he dedicated one of his most potent piano sonatas in 1805: the opus 53: Waldsteinstein. Today it is called the Waldstein Sonate, after Waldsteine who died in 1823 in Vienna, completely impoverished by bank speculation.

In the first days of November 1792, Beethoven embarked on his journey to Vienna, which was to kidnap him forever from his native Rhineland. The voyage went through the war zone at the beginning, because at the end of 1792 the frontier posts of the French Republic, as recorded in the picture of Goethe at the "Campagne in France" in the same year, had even advanced over the Rhine into Rhenish Hessian territory service.

Perhaps the inmates of the traveling coach heard from afar the revolutionary songs of the French people's armies, the Marseille Laise or the "Chant du depart," still echoing in the marching variations of the "Eroica" Symphony.

The twenty-two-year-old Beethoven arrived in Vienna at the end of November 1792 with a considerable number of finished or semi-finished compositions, above all chamber music, glowing with enthusiasm and hopes. Vienna was not unknown to the young musician; he had been there five years earlier when he was seventeen. But the stay had not lasted for a long time. He had played for Mozart, who at first mistrusted the young Rhinelander, but then became more and more enthusiastic about the young genius.

Soon, however, his native Bonn had recalled him, where his mother was dying. In the meantime, Mozart had also died, misunderstood by the court and without economic support from the bourgeoisie, which was only slowly becoming culturally independent. But Haydn, in spite of retaining the title of Princely Esterhazy Kapellmeister, the cultural dissolution of the bourgeoisie from the courtly-aristocratic society was just as evident in his work.

On the return from a concert tour to London, Haydn made a stop in Bonn and gave a benevolent examination of compositions by the court organist Beethoven. Thus the young musician of the Rhine, who had been on leave to Vienna, could indeed hope to receive "Mozart's Spirit from Haydn's Hands." He quickly found a home in Vienna and its surroundings. Perhaps the streamlined Austrian low mountain range even reminded him a little of his home on the Rhine River.

Opposite of the modest, small-town Bonn, Vienna had an active life in a metropolitan and stimulating sense. Here the intellectual life of the Habsburg state was concentrated. The feudal lords from Hungary, Bohemia, Croatia, and Galicia had a rendezvous in Vienna during the winter months. They also brought their musicians with them, so that there were plenty of folk music suggestions of all kinds. Added to this was the natural musicality of the indigenous bourgeois population, which manifested itself in ballrooms, public garden concerts, and in the singers' theaters of the suburbs.

The young Beethoven had to feel as though he were being transposed into another world. However, there were also things that would probably make him less satisfied compared to home. In Bonn, despite the spiritual rule, a freer political air had flowed on the whole. From forward-looking France, the ideas of the Enlightenment and the ideals of freedom, equality, and brotherhood had been brought to the people.

The cataclysmic events of the Great French Revolution of 1789 did not find any foothold. After all, Elector Max Franz had to flee from the

March of the French Revolutionary armies and seek refuge with his imperial brother, where he died in 1801. It only took a few years until the French troops abused by Napoleon for his anti-revolutionary and imperialist policies, pushed the rest into slumbering. "Holy Roman Empire of the German Nation" on the battlefield of Austerlitz and they marched into Vienna.

For the time being, the magnates of the Habsburg monarchy still had politically and culturally influence, although the replacement of the feudal lordship was already clearly emerging. Many of these aristocrats intervened at an early stage in the capitalist economic system, which is now coming to power in Germany. For example, the princes of Lobkowitz maintained industrial factories on their estates in Bohemia. Others, such as Count Waldstein, made money transactions, and Beethoven also belonged at times to the customers of the banking house of Count Friess.

With the decline of feudalism, which had suffered a fatal blow throughout Europe as a result of the events of the French Revolution of 1789 and its aftermath, the maintenance of art, which up to then had been reserved almost exclusively for the ruling class, was abandoned. First, when he came to Vienna, Beethoven had quickly found his way into the aristocratic Viennese nobility through the recommendation of the Bonn Elector and Count Waldstein.

The splendid Baroque building of Prince Ferdinand Kinsky was as familiar to him as was the palace of the artistic Prince Karl Lichnowsky, who had at times been Mozart's pupil. In these families, Beethoven taught, much to the displeasure of the Viennese artists, who were not very well accustomed to the "newcomers," new sound effects of his new compositions. The lessons of Joseph Haydn bore fruit, although Beethoven later unfairly claimed that he had never learned anything from him. Of course, the great master of the classical symphony did not abandon himself with trifles, such as ticking off false vocal progressions.

Lessons were more fun and stimulating than school had been. Beethoven, who always worked on his perfection and filled in gaps in his knowledge, sought precisely this lack of severity. Therefore, he was happy that Johann Schenk, not only known as a composer of the successful musical play "The Village Barbeque," but also as an able theoretician, took care of him. Although it may have happened behind the aged master Haydn's back, whose artistic Beethoven recognized without envy, whose nature was in many ways opposed to his.

Beethoven had other Viennese musicians advice and teaching, during Haydn's stay in London. The famous counter pointer Johann Georg Albrechtsberger and the Italian court master Antonio Salieri, are responsible for the answers to Beethoven's questions of vocal writing. Taking into account his numerous works written in Bonn, Beethoven began to re-count his compositions in Vienna from Opus numbers. As early as 1795, three piano trios, possibly dating back to Bonn, appeared and were published as a work of a not yet well-known foreign young master. In a thoughtful consideration, he dedicated them to Prince Lichnowsky who alone ordered 27 copies with his relatives.

Significantly, after hearing this trio for the first time, Joseph Haydn had advised the composer not to publish the third work of the group, whose time he had apparently not thought had come. The old master will have been astonished that the younger fellow had made the breakthrough so quickly using the unusual and new.

The same year 1795 saw Beethoven's first appearance in a public concert after he had already established himself as a wonderful pianist and imaginative improviser. In aristocratic and bourgeois salons and at competitions of the virtuosos the most outstanding Viennese pianist had been left far behind. Beethoven's pupil Carl Czerny, who later became a well-known pianist reported about one of these competitions in his autobiography, "I still remember one day when Gelinek told my father that he had been invited to a party for the evening, where he was about to hear a foreign pianist. We want to joke about him," added Gelinek. The following day, my dad asked Gelinek how yesterday's fight had failed. "Oh," said Gelinek quite downcast, "I'll think about yesterday. Satan is in the young man. Never heard anyone play like this! He fantasized on a subject I had given, as I had never heard Mozart fantasize. Then he played his own compositions, which are in the highest degree beautiful and magnificent, and he produces difficulties and effects on the piano that we have never dreamed of. "

In a short time, Beethoven had a firm foothold in Vienna. Soon he was surrounded by a large and loyal circle of acquaintances and was often in love affairs, to which he was envied by noble and wealthy cavaliers. He could now afford servants and riding horses, and in 1801 he reported in a letter: "Since last year Lichnowsky, who, as unbelievable as it is to you, has told me, always my warmest friend was and remains (there were also small disagreements among us), a safe sum of 600 florins, which I can draw as long as I find no suitable employment for myself; my compositions carry me along, and I can say that I have more orders than is almost possible that I can satisfy. And I have a publisher for everything, and even more, if I want to be on my own guard: I demand, and you pay!"

The more that old Haydn was out of the public eye, and the others withdrew from the work, the more the eyes of the musicians and music lovers turned to Beethoven. For some thirty years Beethoven had become Vienna's leading musician. But dark shadows hung over these apparently happy circumstances.

Already in 1798, Beethoven began to complain about his ears. The suffering worsened. Despite some improvement periods, the composer's hearing decreased more and more over the last three decades of his life. At first, the high notes failed; his pupil Ries tells how he takes the master on a walk in front of the gates of the city. He drew attention to a flute-shepherd, but although Beethoven heard the words, he no longer heard these sounds and became exceedingly silent and gloomy. He consulted the most prominent doctors, but the progressive destruction of the auditory nerves was unstoppable by medical science. Beethoven's prognosis of deafness was the most tragic fate that can strike a musician. With relentless cruelty it struck, just as later the characterful German songwriter Robert Franz and the Czech master Friedrich Smetana met.

It came to shattering scenes. In 1818, visitors observed him said "The master was leaning over the piano. With his clenched fist, he hit the keys and cried out in despair: "I hear nothing, nothing at all!" Discourse with the outside world has become increasingly difficult over time. Beethoven was noted in conversation books in which his visitors wrote their questions about his mood. Under the pressure of this fate, Beethoven's happy Rhineland temperament understandably declined to melancholia.

In 1802 he wrote a will in the beautiful surroundings of Vienna, which he had loved and which had made him twice as aware of the gap between the cheerful nature and his own misfortune. In the lovely Heiligenstadt, where he liked to visit frequently in the summer, he wrote this "Heiligenstädter Testament."

In the harrowing document, the internal struggles caused by Beethoven's illness speak out: "O people, whom you consider hostile, stubborn, or misanthropic, or explain how wrong you are to me. You do not know the secret cause of what seems to you ... Born with a fiery, lively temperament, even susceptible to the distractions of society, I had to separate myself early, to spend my life alone... For me, rest in human society, finer discussions, reciprocal exercises may not take place. Alone, only as much as the highest need requires, I am allowed to get involved in society ... There was little lacking, and I ended my own life - only her, art, holding me back. Oh, it seemed impossible for me to leave the world until I produced all that I feel like ... " To inherit his small fortune, if you can even speak of his meager fortune, Beethoven used his two brothers who had followed him to Vienna. Karl came first as a musician, then as a bailiff, and later Johann, who was a pharmacist. Karl, who died in 1815, left behind a son, also named Karl, who later casually denounced his uncle's life.

Although Beethoven's works are an expression of his life, confessions of his great soul, and his noble humanity, they never reflect the petty momentary moods of the composer. Only in this way can it be understood that in the same summer of 1802, which brought the composer the cruel knowledge of his presumably incurable bodily suffering, a work like the second symphony.

Beethoven had waited a long time before he emerged in the symphonic field, wonderfully conceived by Haydn and Mozart. It was only on the 2nd of April, 1800 that he had introduced his first creation of this genre to the public. It has long been content to regard the first two symphonies as "precursors" of Haydn's and Mozart's "Beethoven" as the "true" symphonist, without paying any attention to how much new, frighteningly and unusually influential this work was at that time.

These new features are first and foremost stylistic elements that Beethoven had brought with him from the Rhine. These are the features of the vigorous, marching rhythm-preferred music of the French Revolutionary period, in which numerous important French composers had reflected the heroic spirit of the time. Within Beethoven's works, such as the Third Piano Concerto, the Third, Fifth, and Seventh Symphonies, and in the opera "Fidelio," his spirit reflects the history of Europe as a whole.

The verdict, then spoken against the Second Symphony, that it was "too heavy" and a "blatant monstrosity" is unjust. General Bernadotte, the first representative of the young French republic in Vienna who was vehemently opposed by the Austrian aristocracy and the misled masses, became acquainted with Beethoven and referred him to the personality of the Consul Bonaparte.

In his Symphony No. 3, Beethoven expressed more clearly than ever the concept of freedom and moral dignity that moved him. At first, in General Bonaparte, Beethoven saw completion of the humanitarian liberation that begun in 1789, the annihilator of the old feudalistic structures of states, which held all peoples in bondage. He therefore proudly wrote the words "Buonaparte" and "Ludwig van Beethoven" on the title page of his Third Symphony.

It, therefore, had a deeper meaning that in the concluding sentence he reused a theme from his ballet The 'Creatures of the Prometheus' cited in 1801: the parallel between the light-bringer Prometheus and

Napoleon is intended. There was a horrible awakening for Beethoven when he learned that Napoleon, the republican consul, had set the imperial crown on his head.

Angry, Beethoven tore up the title page of the symphony, which henceforth was called "Sinfonia Eroica, composed to celebrate the memory of a great man." The entry of Napoleon and his troops into Vienna in spite of all the respect and friendliness he personally showed, affected his work to the extent that the premiere of his opera "Fidelio," which took place eight days after the invasion, had little success. It is understandable that the frightened Viennese had other worries these days, and that the French soldiers visiting the theater were not the general audience.

The text was almost literally a translation of an opera narration that had just been put into music by the French composer Gaveaux and by the Italian Paer. Fidelio belonged to the so-called rescue operas of the French revolutionary musicians. The heroic act of the woman liberating her husband from the dungeon and the present-day fate of the oppressed humanity against political tyranny is expressed in the shattering chorus of the prisoners.

These were thoughts that were first pronounced by the artists of the French Revolution of 1789. They set fire to the freedom-thirsting personality of Beethoven. Fidelio still strongly influenced the artistic development of the young Richard Wagner style of Beethoven's only opera. On stage, it had reached the place where it belonged.

The first decade of the new century was the most fruitful of his life. He wrote numerous piano sonatas, among them in the new form, "Fantasie" sonatas op. 27, the three sonatas op. 30, the "Waldstein" Sonata and the "Appassionata". In addition to the oratorio "Christ on the Mount of Olives", the overture to the drama "Coriolan", the music was commissioned by the Russian Ambassador Count Rasumowski and used Russian folk-song themes. Goethe's "Egmont", the Choir Fantasia, the 3rd and 4th Piano Concerts and the Violin Concerto were the works of the symphonic kind, and the 5th and 6th Symphonies were a symbol of rebellion against all storms and afflictions of the life and the finite victory of man over them. This, the so-called "Pastoral Symphony" by Beethoven himself was a confession of the master to nature, but not in a petty imitation of natural sounds and natural sounds, frozen to an end in itself, but "more expression of sensation than painting."

Around 1810, Beethoven was generally recognized as one of the leading men of German intellectual and cultural life alongside Goethe. Bettina Brentano, the later wife of the poet Achim von Arnim, described it in romantic exuberance to her idol Goethe as the ideal of a human being, and Beethoven himself assured the Weimar poet of his esteem. When both the poet and the composer met in Teplitz and in Carlsbad in person, a predestined disappointment was inevitable.

The Weimar Minister of State Goethe's excellence and Beethoven's embodying republican virtues were all too different in nature. Goethe called the musician an "untamed personality." Among the friends who understood him, he sometimes sat down to the piano without being asked to donate from the fullness of his imagination. If you wanted to force him against it, then he became rude, took his hat, and went or even threatened to become violent. This happened, for example, to Prince Lichnowsky, who urged him to play in front of his French billeting officers, and he insulted him: "Prince! What you are, you are by accident and birth what I am, I am through me! There are princes, and there will still be thousands, Beethoven there is only one!"

Therese Malfatti and a large number of ladies from Beethoven's acquaintance, especially his pupil Countess Therese Brunsvik and her relatives, Countess Giulietta Guicciardi, were brought in connection with one of the master's most original and characteristic writings, the letter to the "Immortal Beloved." To this day, nobody knows who was the recipient of this ardent confession of love, when the letter was written, and whether it was ever sent or later returned to the writer. No doubt several times in his life, Beethoven had the desire to see a beloved woman by his side. But the fear of being ignored because of his suffering or, in the matter of noble ladies, being rejected because of his civil status made him silent any time he thought he had found the right one. His song circle "to the distant beloved "sounds like a salute to the unattainable goal. Therefore, he continued with his ill health, quarreled with the women in waiting, and moved without having canceled his rental contract, continuing to pay rent in several places.

He was glad if his acquaintance, such as the famous piano maker Nanette Streicher occasionally worried about his wellbeing. Even though his communication was increasingly affected by his hearing discomfort, Beethoven remained a public figure. He learned that in the great political events of 1813-1815, it had ended with the defeat of Napoleon. This collapse of a man, who had made himself a tyrant by betraying the revolutionary idea of freedom, equality, and brotherhood of all men, filled Beethoven with satisfaction. Not out of a chauvinist sense of revenge, but conscious of his national dignity, he had regretted that he would not be able to beat the Corsican with his weapons: "If, as a general, I understood as much of strategy as I, as a composer, understood counterpoint, I would give him something to do!"

Although we know of no direct sources in which Beethoven would have commented on the attempt to free the Tyrolean under Andreas Hofer or about the defeat of Napoleon in Russia, we know from the pen of his Adatus and later biographer Anton Schindler to what extent artist was familiar with the history of nations. Also to Schindler's astonishment, Beethoven had a clear awareness of the connections between art and politics: "But we must gradually become accustomed to our poet on this, his own - to visit completely unknown areas, because one side of his nature has irresistibly pushed for this direction and carried political character."

The wars of liberation had sparked a wave of German national consciousness and were also considered by Beethoven as a step towards the liberation of the people. He planned, therefore, a mass song on the battle of Leipzig. Since, as Schindler reports, he "possessed intelligence and knew how to preserve his secret thoughts right before his death," it is not known what he held in common with the orderly dignitaries of the "dancing congress."

Europe from Vienna did not lead to freedom at all, but into a new era of reaction. High-minded Beethoven would not have thought much of these people. The term "princely rag," which he occasionally uses, does not imply sincere devotion, and his saying, "Something smaller than our 'great ones' does not exist," also leaves nothing to be desired in terms of clarity.

Through his art, Beethoven intervened directly in current affairs in those years. The mechanic Johann Nepomuk Mälzel, who is still known today for the invention or at least improvement of the metronome measuring time, persuaded the master to compose a work for one of his music boxes, as Haydn and Mozart had occasionally created pieces of music for this machine. He suggested writing the composition as a tribute to the victory over the French by the English troops at the Spanish city of Victoria, as musical battle paintings have always been trendy. (Already after the battle of Marignano in 1515, the French composer Clement Jannequin created a naturalistic imitation of the war-like event in the form of a choral Trojan horse).

Beethoven, then at the height of his fame, agreed and composed his noisy sound-image "Wellingtons Victory at Vittoria", This made Beethoven's name more famous in the version for orchestra with two mighty percussion batteries than the eight symphonies, the other orchestral works, the many piano and chamber compositions and the opera "Fidelio".

Beethoven performed this completely forgotten composition with both the leading musician of Vienna, and others willing participated. Even Court Kapellmeister Salieri did not think it a pity to lead the considerable drum arsenal as a conductor. The composer conducted himself, though not being his best work, and did not hear, and as the soloist singer Wild reported, "at the crucial moment Kapellmeister Umlauf took over the command staff, while the orchestra was meant to follow him, Beethoven did not notice this arrangement for a long time ... " Certainly not without thought, the composer always coupled his battle-painting at these national celebrations with the seventh symphony, which, since Richard Wagner's bold interpretation, is still often one-sided "Apotheosis of the dance." "Wellington's victory in the battle at Vittoria" also cemented Beethoven's fame, and especially in the case of amusing people, so that the composer, as one of his visitors reported, declared the work to be stupidity.

The Viennese could not hear this "stupidity" often enough. Therefore it was performed again for about six thousand listeners at the end of the "Great Musical Academy" including the guests of the Vienna Congress, on November 29, 1814. One may safely assume that Beethoven kept his head high in the waves of national enthusiasm of those months. Perhaps even the Austro-Prussian-Russian reaction that started as a result of the Vienna Congress did not surprise him anymore. For a politically clear-sighted person like Beethoven, it had to become clear that the crushed Napoleonic despotism would not yet be replaced by the rule of the peoples.

But Beethoven's combative nature did not hesitate even when he fell back. It is precisely from the first decade of Metternich's reaction that Beethoven's willing Secretary Schindler reports on the revolutionary progressive attitude of the composer. Schindler even summed up the motives which could have "determined Beethoven to be a consistent opponent of Austrian state policy, the government, as well as the imperial court," and as such he names among others: "the arbitrary and corrupt administration of justice attacks by the police, the bureaucracy of the state apparatus, the debauchery and demoralization of aristocracy, the interestedness of the court in artistic things."

Beethoven stood in sharp contrast to all these obstacles to the freedom of the human race, such as in the Ninth Symphony and the "Missa Solemnis" which defied all obstacles and annoyances in their own existence of which he was not lacking. In his sixth decade of life, Beethoven's creative soul flowed more slowly. However, this was not due to a lack of ideas, nor to the difficulty of directing what was heard only internally, but rather to the ever-stricter standard Beethoven applied to his work. He had the musical laws of form, and the expressions of his great role models were adopted by Haydn and Mozart and created his formations, which belonged to only him.

Now a new generation has grown up with new art and language content. Goethe despised them and called them the new "the sick," The old, however, were called "the healthy." Beethoven hesitantly found access to the unique creations of Weber and Schubert. Of course, he would have recognized the progressive newness in the opera Freischütz, but he would probably have had no inclination for such romantic material. He apparently planned to compose his successor to his "Fidelio," who in 1822 had finally been included in the program in Vienna. A romantic fairy-tale opera "Melusine" was offered to him by the revered poet Franz Grillparzer. It was not for a man who had written "Fidelio" and who was involved in immense subjects such as "Faust," "Romulus," "Brutus," "Macbeth" or 'Odysseus.'

The breadth of his experience becomes astonishing when, as his conversation notebook betray, sometimes his deepest thoughts alternate with childish, jokes, or genuine gratitude for his friends. This breadth is reflected in his work, which above all is the relationship between artistic creation and folk music, and is far from being fully understood. Already in the Rhine of Bonn he had enjoyed the songs of the boatmen and farmers. Its tunes and songs had entered into his work with artistic design. Even in his seemingly subjective creations, the sounds of folk music, are not unlike the great classics of Joseph Haydn.

The sonata and the symphony from the demarcated districts of court aesthetic were given back as a gift to the people of his homeland. Anton Schindler and Beethoven biographer tells us vividly of Beethoven who loved the art of the Viennese street musicians. What Beethoven had to say to the great public, he expressed in such mighty works as the Ninth Symphony and the Missa Solemnis. Music lovers were not disappointed when the artist, who was only forced to write a solitary name, in truth the connection with life and with people anxiously seeking, presented to them the demand he made at the conclusion of his Missa solemnis: "From the heart - may it be so to heart again!" The invitation to his "Academy," the fashion of the time of the extraordinarily long and luxurious concert on the 7th of May, 1824, which brought the Ninth Symphony and parts of the Missa Solemnis, pulled all Viennese interested in Beethoven's art into the theater.

Despite his deafness, Beethoven appeared to himself at the conductor's podium. He did not even hear the applause of the crowd so that a participating singer turned the master around so all could see him at least. It was severely noted that the court balcony had been left empty, although Beethoven personally invited the imperial family - a remnant of the aristocratic courtly art sponsors. Beethoven's music became the bearer of cultural life of the bourgeoisie. Now there was a paying public as the bourgeois friends of art. Monarchs and aristocrats, who used to be the commissioners of the artist, now belonged to the talistic basis for developing musical life.

Beethoven spoke to them with his great joyful hymn to the Ninth Symphony, which like his purely instrumental works, but now exaggerated by the word, established Schiller's demand for humanity and brotherhood. The same will of the artist sounds from the Missa Solemnis, which breaks the frame of liturgical church music and leads to the sublime demand for peace for the people.

> Joy, beautiful spark of Divinity
> Daughter from Elysium,
> We enter, drunk with fire,
> Heavenly One, thy sanctuary!
> Your magic binds again
> What convention strictly divided;
> All people become brothers,
> Where your gentle wing abides.
> Courage firm in great suffering,
> Help there, where innocence weeps,

Eternally sworn oaths,
Truth towards friend and foe,
Mens' pride before kings' thrones --
Brothers, even if it costs property and blood, --
The crowns to those who earn them,
Defeat to the lying brood!

(poem, 'An die Freude" - Friedrich Schiller)

The aging Beethoven, who was still driving restlessly from apartment to apartment, opened his last home in the autumn of 1825 in the "Schwarz Spanier Haus", which had once been named after the black robed Spanish Benedictine monks. There he produced his late compositions as he studied with growing astonishment the works of Franz Schubert. Schubert sincerely esteemed him, but hardly ventured to approach him, and devoted a work of variations to him in 1822.

Ludwig van Beethoven took his last breath on the afternoon of the March 26, 1827, while a spring storm raged outside. He had suffered much in the final months of his life, so that the friends visiting him and his self-sacrificing biographer Anton Schindler, who had been immersed in the changing light of the story, also lived through difficult days and weeks.

The last rays of light in the patients suffering from liver shrinkage, which only occasionally relieved pain through puncture of the abdomen, had been a correspondence from the Mainz Music Publisher Schott and a letter from the Philharmonic Society in London, which sent him a pound of 100 pounds sterling to commission 10th symphony.

Beethoven dealt with his last days of life with the sketches of this unfulfilled work. Beethoven's funeral turned out to be a memorial service for the whole community. Schools were closed, and the military was mobilized to keep traffic off the streets. Eight bandmasters walked with candles beside the coffin, friends, and defenders, among them Franz Schubert, Carl Czerny, and the violinist Ignaz Schuppanzigh, followed his casket.

After a spoken eulogy written by Franz Grillparzer (Austrian writer), Beethoven was buried in the Währing Cemetery. A little more than a year later Franz Schubert was buried close to him. Since 1888 his remains, like the numerous other artists and scientists, have been buried in honorary graves at Vienna's Central Cemetery.

Beethoven's work has remained alive for generations, proclaiming human and moral strength in every measure. Also the features of his face, as painters and draftsmen portrayed him with different temperaments and rendered by nature in 1812. In1827, the deceased man supported this knowledge, that the humanity in Ludwig van Beethoven was a role model to live by.

Frederic Chopin

A man who used to surround himself with luxury and beautiful things was understandably demanding in the choice of his friends and acquaintances. In the process, it is peculiar of him that he was less interested in the poets with whom he often frequented than by their art as one might suspect.

The most important French romantic and realists of that time, Victor Hugo and Honore de Balzac, were among a few of the great number of poets and literary figures that were his Parisian friends. It did not seem as if Chopin had the same interest in their novel way of life and art even though music aspires to some of the same heights as literary art. Something happened to Heinrich Heine, whom he knew and who left us a nice little description of his playing. He said Chopin's piano rivals Kalkbrenner, and Thalberg did not fare very well against Chopin in Heine's opinion. He seemed uncomfortable that he was the egocentric in the musical field. His attitude toward the great composer Hector Berlioz, whose music was undoubtedly repugnant to him because of its crude coloristic and decorative effects, seemed out of place. Perhaps for Chopin as a being the 'new one', it was difficult in the beginning to understand the contradictory intellectual currents of the French capital.

The bourgeois aesthetic has compartmentalized almost all creative artists between the restoration of the French monarchy after Napoleon's final defeat and the revolution of 1848 with the collective term "Romantic." This conclusion is made without their ideological and creative content differences sufficiently clear. Between the subjectivist, Catholicizing Chateaubriand and the initially loyalty to the king, such as that in the ministerial chair Lamartine on the one hand and the poetically and politically revolutionary Victor Hugo on the other hand, later under Napoleon III to emigrate, to name but a few - there were hardly any connecting bridges.

Chopin's sympathies were probably with romanticism, which, as Victor Hugo had demanded in the famous preface to his drama Cromwell, declared reality and truth to be the subjects and design principles of art. It is no coincidence that the realistic Italian opera master Verdi was deeply touched by these features of French literature. Nevertheless, Chopin probably sensed something divisive between him and this progressive romanticism, which in a new storm-and-surge (Sturm and Drang) attitude, took hold of individual expressive elements and destroyed the classical forms. All the more so did the poet confess to Bach and the German classics, of which Beethoven, however, did not address him in equal measure with all his compositions.

The illustration of Chopin's personality and piano playing from the pen of Heinrich Heine excerpted in the following wording: "It would be unfair to speak on this occasion of a pianist who is most celebrated alongside Liszt. With Chopin, it can be proved right that it is not enough for an extraordinary person to be able to compete with the most skillful of his art through technical perfection.

Chopin is by no means satisfied by the fact that other hands applaud him because of their mobile ease. He strives for a more grand success: his fingers are only the servants of his soul, and his soul commends those people who listen not only with their ears but with the soul ... Poland has given him chivalrous sentiment and historical toleration; France light elegance, and grace, Germany dreamy depth, but nature gave him a slender, delicate, a sickly little figure, the noblest heart, and genius. One must grant Chopin in every sense of the word genius. He is not only a virtuoso but also a poet. He can reveal to us the poetry living in his soul. He is a poet-musician, and nothing compares to the enjoyment he gives us when improvising on the piano. At this moment he is neither a Pole, nor a Frenchman or a German, but he betrays a higher birth: he comes from the land of Mozart, Raphael, and Goethe. His true fatherland is the land of poetry. "

Of course, Chopin deeply loved and revered the Polish poets living in Paris, although they did not express themselves as enthusiastically about Chopin as Heinrich Heine. Adam Mickiewiez was particularly close to his heart, describing Poland's suffering and the oppression of peasants by the nobility in his great epic "Pan Tadeusz," written in Paris. According to Chopin's own remark, several of Mickiewicz's poems are said to have inspired the composer to his ballads. Even the older generation poet and political writer Ursyn Niemcewiez, who went to Chopin's first concert in Warsaw in 1818 had also sought shelter in France after the events of 1831 (November uprising in Poland), was one of Chopin's familiar acquaintances. Of the painters of his time, the romanticist and revolutionary Eugene Delacroix, inspired one of Chopin's most expressive music with genuine sympathy and betrayal in the music?

It can be assumed that the inclination and understanding in the encounter Delacroix-Chopin not on full of reciprocity. This can also be observed in Chopin's relations with many other artists, such as Giacomo Meyerbeer, Mendelssohn, who valued him more than he appreciated them. But to some extent, Franz Liszt, whose playing inspired him, and liked his compositional formlessness as "realistic simplicity." For clarity of form and inner simplicity, he considered the most crucial foundation of all creation. But he met the composer Robert Schumann, to whom he had much to thank.

Chopin visited Dresden and Leipzig to help his artistic reputation in Germany. The visits in Leipzig were of particular importance in 1831. Robert Schumann had just published an essay in the New Journal of Music, repeatedly pointing to the Polish composer. His first meeting with the Leipzig musician and the music lovers promised to be particularly profitable, especially as Friedrich Wieck was eager to show the guest his daughter Clara's skill as a pianist. Schumann was hoping for an opinion of the German pianist, rumor had it, to help Clara's reputation.

Surely it was Schumann's own conviction when he reported; "Chopin was here, but only a few hours spent in closer circles. He plays exactly as he composes." After Chopin's visit the following year, Schumann's enthusiasm for the honored guest was repeatedly expressed in the magazine and letters. Mendelssohn, too, was delighted with Chopin's visit to Leipzig. They knew each other from Mendelssohn's trip to Paris and had also spent some pleasant hours in Aachen and then in the Düsseldorf at a colony of painters at the Lower Rhine Music Festival of 1834, in which Chopin had participated. Felix Mendelssohn told his sister Fanny about his impressions, which he had of the foreign friends, but just because he was so positive, in order to dispel their skepticism towards Chopin; "There is something inherently peculiar in his piano playing and at the same time so masterly, that he can be called a quite perfect virtuoso ... It was nice to be together again with a decent musician, not with such half classics, but with one who has his own strong direction and if however different it may be from my own, I can get along splendidly with it; just not with those half people."

The artistic personality

The musicians and music lovers who surrounded Chopin during his lifetime presumably had not enough time to appreciate his special and unique character. All listeners were mostly delighted with Chopin's piano playing, but even the young concert player Chopin had sometimes been accused of lacking energy and volume in his playing.

Chopin realized that he was playing in a different, transparent, and almost trivial way, and for that very reason he preferred the more intimate salon. Here, there would be only a few dozen listeners compared to the great concert halls or the theater.

As an inimitable peculiarity of his performance practice, his "tempo rubato," that is, the art of deliberately making small variations in the measure of time, was used to bring a piece of music to life. This type of performance, which was mainly cultivated in the supporting melody, maintained the master using metrical precision in the left hand accompaniment, was misunderstood by many of his followers. They bristled at such relaxations of the tempo into sentimental feelings of revelation. On the other hand, Chopin is often said to have amused his friends by chopping down his polonaises and mazurkas into the strictest march tempos, as most dilettantes did in ignorance of its nature and style.

From none other than his French contemporary and Parisian fellow-citizen Hector Berlioz, who, like Schumann, Wagner, Liszt, Weber, Hoffmann and other artists of the Romantic epoch, handled the writer's pen with equal ease as the pen, comes one of Chopin's most unambiguous portrayals of art. It appeared in 1833. It reads: "To be able to estimate him [Chopin] fully, I think he must be heard at close range, more in the salon than in the theater, and free himself from any biased opinion. You could not apply it to him or her to use his music. Chopin is as a performer as well as a composer a unique artist. He has not the slightest resemblance to any other musician known to me. His melodies, which are always soaked in Polish forms, have a certain wild carelessness that irritates and captivates precisely because of their strangeness. In his etudes, one finds astonishingly deep combinations of harmony; he has come up with some sort of chromatic decoration that he applies in several of his compositions, the effect of which can only be described as unusual and piquant."

"Unfortunately, there is hardly anyone but Chopin himself who could play his music and give it that peculiar attitude, the unexpected, which is one of his main charms. His presentation is permeated with a thousand intricacies of movement, the secret of which he alone knows and which one cannot determine. There are incredible details in his mazurka. Moreover, he has found the means to make them doubly interesting by reproducing them with the last degree of delicacy, in extreme piano (softness), with the hammers only lightly stripping the strings, so that one prefers to approach the instrument and point the ear would like to listen to a concert of air spirits or goblins. "

Chopin has passed on his performance style to many of his students. Among them were gifted ones, who showed themselves worthy of their teacher. The untalented students paid a small fortune hoping to be regarded as pupils of, or maybe become one of Chopin's favorite pupils.

The master's peculiar sense of unique timbres in the pianos of his time, especially the piano makers of Pleyel and Erard, were also expressed in his teaching. In contrast to the teaching of the time, were the finger acrobatics of Czerny's lessons, which were technically diffi-cult and contained less tonality. Chopin's music started in keys with E major or H major (B), thus keys with many omens, as he also used them for the most poetic of his compositions with fondness.

Apart from his own creations, the piano works of Bach, Beethoven, Mozart, Clementi, and Hummel served as compositional inspiration. Beethoven's works, such as the so-called Moonlight Sonata and the Sonata op. 26 are useful templates for Chopin's musical direction. Conversely, the works of Mendelssohn, whose neoclassical coolness one thinks would have impressed him, and especially Robert Schumann, to whom he owed his reputation in Germany, but to whose works he found no relation that he did not play or study them.

To a Parisian publisher, he is said to have commented on Schumann's original piano work Carnaval, "This is not music!" We will hear another almost identical judgment of Schumann on a work by Chopin, but there these words have no pejorative meaning, as in the case of the 'Carnaval', on the contrary, an expression of extreme emotion. Such one sidedness of the verdict was probably the result of his inner thoughts of his great-ness, which hardly any other could tolerate being near him. Chopin, with his own compositional technique of sound lines, represent distinct style with almost no role models. At least the works of those composers, against whose background Chopin's style, are hard to be found today.

Louis Spohr's somewhat thin-blooded creations, for example, which he greatly appreciated, and whose chromatically softness and harmony deeply impressed him, comes to mind. The popular compositions of Mozart's pupil Johann Nepomuk Hummel, with its many pianistic ornamental styles, and the piano poetry of the Irishman John Field, whose Nocturnes, which seems rather weak today, led directly to Chopin's works of the same genre.

The brilliant virtuoso pieces by Kalkbrenner and Moscheles, and above all the compositions by numerous smaller masters of Chopin's native country, whose national mood influenced and enriched the beginning of his creative journey. The value of admiration and with such speed he has found himself processing the foreign impressions that inspire upon him into his own compositions.

When he left his Polish homeland at the age of eighteen or nineteen to make his way into the world, his compositions already exhibited a master craftsman. Even among the works of this ingenious artist, a development and maturation process can be observed. It is difficult to recognize this, not least because of the exclusive use of the piano and its limited minor musical forms, but primarily in his dances, mazurkas, polonaises, waltzes, with their repetition and sequential principle constructed lyrical-epic structures.

While Chopin engaged in a combative dispute with the form of the symphony and sonata, as before with Beethoven, Schumann, and Liszt, a change in style manifests itself to a great extent with the idea in music drama stage work, such as in Weber or Wagner. What appeals to us, especially in his art today, is the musical bond that resonates within every bar of music. For us, Chopin embodies the awakening of the native sense of art, which can only be understood as a result of its social political insights, and the lessons that life had given it. It is therefore in line with those artists of other European nations who have undergone a similar development and who already verified Friedrich Wolf's words in their day; that art is also a political weapon. This was recognized by the Czechs; Smetana, Dvorak and Janacek, by the Russians; Glinka, the "Novators" (Mussorgsky, Rimsky-Korsakov, Borodin, Balakirev, Kjui) and finally Tchaikovsky, by the Hungarians; Erkel. Then, crossing the century are the Hungarians Bartok and Kodaly, in Denmark; Gade, and in Norway; Grieg, at sometimes reminiscent of Chopin in the harshness of his harmony. Chopin's harmonic innovations, which put him in line with Liszt and Wagner, are a reminder of the composer as a 19th century musician. While his "Polish spirit" is how he spoke is transient and anchored in time.

It's not a coincidence that Berlioz, in his characteristic as mentioned earlier of Chopin, pointed out the harmonious innovations of the Polish artist. As an example, besides the études, Berlioz could have referred to Chopin's mazurkas, where he supplemented short motifs with repetitive techniques based on Slavic folk music typology, with their highly bold harmonic reversals and shifts. The mazurkas, with their characteristic rhythms, are very peculiar, in their varied moods oscillating between melancholy and popular bluntness.

Today, we are especially fond of Chopin's works. The polonaise, on the other hand, reflects more of the pronounced knightly attitude of the Polish aristocratic class. Chopin had a modest predilection for these chivalrous images, which sometimes seem to see candlelit banqueting halls and sumptuously dressed dancing couples, while the mazurkas are said to have an unmistakable peasant look.

Chopin's waltzes are once again revealed by another spawning ground. They are the "Valses" from the atmosphere of the European salon. Chopin's waltzes are much more stylized and above all, leaving behind all utilitarian art, largely poetized. In their attitude, they sometimes touch on the piano style of Weber, which Chopin highly appreciated.

All of these dances, plus the naturally softer, more delicate like, Night Songs of the Nocturnes, and such famous pieces as the D flat major, Berceuse (Lullaby) op. 57, or the Barcarolle F sharp major op. 60 were, for a long time, depending on the varying degrees of its technical requirements, became the play-thing of the lay musician who enriched himself with pleasure and ability.

Chopin's sonatas, études, preludes, scherzi and ballads were destined for the concert hall from the beginning. It must be admitted, however, that Chopin did not pile up his sonatas after a long considered plan like Beethoven, but that he put them together in one attempt. For example, the funeral march of the B minor Sonata, which had become famous around the world, was initially finished as an independent piece, and then the other members of the group revived it.

The determination of Chopin as an outspoken piano composer meant that his small number of chamber music works and his songs were hardly noticed at the time. Although Robert Schumann did write about his Piano Trio op. 8, in which he said; "Is it not as noble as possible, as enthusiastic as any poet has ever sung, singularly in the smallest as well as in the whole, every note of music and life?" Forgotten is also a late chamber music work by Chopin Trio, op.65 in G minor, Sonata for violin, cello and piano, premiered at his last Paris concert. At that time the composition aroused more amazement than enthusiasm, so that the pianist Moscheles, stated; "For me it is a wildly overgrown forest into which only a ray of sunlight sometimes penetrates." Through the frequently used mazurka rhythm, through up beats and in the melody through the excessive "Lydian" fourth, the composer emphasizes in his songs the folk-national element.

The last song of this series was "Poland's Mourning Song," which the English Chopin biographer Niecks perspective of 1888 wrote, "deeply felt, but in his terrible monotony also oppressive." It also proves that Chopin would have been capable of outstanding achievements in the field of song writing if he had not confined his circle of life to the elegant Warsaw and Parisian salons. Of course, the somewhat detailed presentation of the genre and personal style of Chopin's music must not give the impression that it limits the essence of this unique art. All this is understandably a consequence of his human and artistic attitude, not its cause.

Chopin's works were the natural results of an artist's work in which his senses made him a romantic. At the same time, it was limited to the essentials, and to the classicistic rejection of formlessness and exuberance, it carried features of realism. Chopin's music, 170 years after the death of the master and over 210 after his birth, has shed the last fetters that had been determined at that time by time and society.

The "Polish spirit" of this music is understood everywhere today. Chopin's art is alive throughout the musical world. It is now transmitted and received as a message of the early musicality of the Polish people, who were finally free after centuries of oppression.

The Romantics

Even though the Germans were especially susceptible to the pervading fashion of romanticism, the new spiritual life captured the whole continent. France, for example, after the war of liberation, was repelled from the influence of Germany. Madame de Staël acquired fame as a mediator between France and Germany. In general, women did not play such a significant role in any given century as in this one for she enabled her incipient emancipation. But in the fine touch of romance, an individual female element came along too. How often were the prophets in their own country the least so?

Hector Berlioz was a master composer who kindled the wildfire. This again was a truly romantic trait, although his phantasy of imagination was creative for his century, his work remained behind the proclaimed ideal. Berlioz was already heavily criticized during his lifetime. Nevertheless, Claude Debussy was probably a fan and once thought that Berlioz was the favorite composer of those who did not understand music much. But the significance of Berlioz in music history is indeed more important than its position in concert halls. Excess was his personality when it came to the romantic Berlioz that Berlioz wrote memoirs.

Bach would never have waited to observe his life from the outside to account for him self and others. But the romantics loved to look in the mirror. They liked to make nature the favorite subject of their detailed observations. They bored into themselves, and their works were basically nothing but answers to this mental dissection. Incidentally, Berlioz was also active as a music writer, something that many of the romantic composers did. Also, many were literally at the crossroads between literature and music. The biography of Berlioz is a novel where he would not expose himself to the charge of exaggeration. His love experiences were all one rage. The adolescents, whose red cheeks had brought him out of his mind, he worshiped again as a gray-haired man, standing on the threshold of old age, with glowing cherubic cheers.

On the other hand, there were situations in his life that one couldn't explain away. Hector Berlioz was always close to the edge of madness. This too, characterizes him as a high romantic, within a healthy mix of instability. The case of the mentally ill patient is even then more captivating for the romanticist's examination. It was no coincidence that many romantics really went mad, and paralysis was not always to blame. The romantic excess leads to confusion, fantasy, and incredible-ness. For Hector Berlioz that excessive grew from his life and work. He needed a new way for his art and it was clear to him as anyone ushering in a new epoch.

Since Berlioz wanted to create sound paintings, he was particularly interested in the orchestra. There was only the classical orchestra of the time. Until then, a specific size with no desire to enlarge it. If Beethoven demanded special instruments such as the contrabassoon, it was only an exception, not the rule. Hector Berlioz found Beethoven's orches-tral size pitifully lacking. He dreamed of a large orchestra. At that time, Handel's oratorios were often performed in mass occupations of double and triple choirs. It was believed that an orchestra with 200 strings would have to make ten times more impact than an orchestra of twenty strings. Such huge groups were the right idea for Berlioz, only that he went far beyond.

For his ideal orchestra, he wished for 120 violins, 40 violas, 45 cellos, and 33 double basses, or around 240 strings. For the woodwinds, he thought of an average score of 12 to 15 musicians for each instrument, plus 16 French horns. The influence of 30 harps and 30 pianos was particularly useful. His imagination was perhaps even busier for the drummers. On the whole, he wished for an instrumental body of 465 players. Of course, several conductors were needed, especially since he also asked 360 choristers to sing along with them.

On the whole, the orchestra of the thousand was in the lead. This fantasy was so enticing that later Gustav Mahler chased after it, and with greater success. It was really a romantic fate again that these bold dreams faced a harsh reality. As the bawling sounds of his large orchestra rushed past Berlioz's inner ear, life almost denied him anything that could have led to the fulfillment of that dream. He created in memory of a French general, four orchestras in four different places. Of course, they had to be led by four different conductors. Thus Berlioz took up the old Venetian technique of the double choir, only now he doubled the orchestra of old Gabrieli again.

Berlioz also implemented the introduction of the third woodwinds, which became standard operating procedure for Richard Wagner. Now there were no longer two flutes in the orchestra, two oboes, two clarinets, two bassoons, but three of each. A piccolo, oboes, the cor anglais (English horn), which has neither anything to do with England nor a horn, but a deep and sonorous grand oboe usually accompanied by a flute. The bass clarinet and the bassoons supplemented the two clarinets by the contrabassoon.

Of course, the strings had to be strengthened too. Even Wagner had to endure many feuds with his directors and be financially powerful. For Beethoven, an orchestra of 30 to 40 men was considered good. Half a century later, 70 to 80 players were needed. This growth of orchestral occupation continued for quite some time.

New colors

Berlioz enriched the color palette of the orchestra through the multiplication of the instruments as well as introducing new effects. The strings were divided into subgroups, which gave the sound a larger range. The instruments could follow higher and lower when the music asked for division.

With flageolets special effects were achieved. Flageo tones are produced when the strings are lightly pressed in places and the vibration passes from the wave crest into the wave valley. Flageolets sound hollow and ghostly. Since the romantics liked to imagine spirits of the underworld, dwarfs, mandrakes, mermaids and other goblins, the romantic music sought out such effects.

The concertgoers were well versed and aware of the new direction of music. The meaning of those changes is similar to the classical organ, which had new 'stops' added to increase the color range. The orchestra pieces in the sense of Berlioz on the 'future music' were paintings in heavily applied colors.

The same thing happened in art paintings at the time. The counterpart to the romantic color scale in the orchestra was the open air colors that the romantic masters of the nineteenth century fought for. The distant horizon, and the wind roaring in the pictures of Caspar David Friedrich wanted to conjure up the passionate tone creators in their own way.

Berlioz was not only a revolutionary in the means, but he also sought a renewal in content and substance. It seemed certain to him that one could no longer create a symphony in the spirit of Beethoven. He considered 'absolute' music to be exhausted. Absolute music is works we call life confesses in tones, where there is no extra musical content that represents and describes anything. It is nothing but music.

The allure to sacrifice the absoluteness of music had always been tempting. Music that describes itself did exist. Many things that point in this direction must not be taken too seriously. Haydn by no means contradicted the absoluteness of the music when he gave his symphonies names. Beethoven went a step further in this, both in his piano sonatas and in his symphonies. But Beethoven had the deciding word in his symphony. "More expression of sensation than painting," he wrote. So he was not interested in a naturalistic description of something extra musical.

Berlioz, on the other hand, chose an entirely new way. The starting point, the basis of his composition, became a precisely fixed program. It could, for example, be a poetic work of world literature like Romeo and Juliet, or Harold in Italy. Later personalities, poets, philosophers, and nature were described, as well as the mountains or maybe the sea. This new direction initiated by Berlioz was called program music.

The most successful and most lasting work of Hector Berlioz was his 'Fantastic Symphony'. In it, the experiences of a hero were described in a musical story. We accompany him to the countryside, where the path leads him to the place of execution. Each musical scene is full of exciting experiences. The hero of this symphony was, of course, no other than Berlioz himself. This work was a music biography. Berlioz described in his ways of Damascus unequal naturalism, as Beethoven had done when he walked along the stream and listened to the song of the birds.

After the high heat of this vaulting romantic, the fire of German romantics like the violin master Louis Spohr or Felix Mendelssohn-Bartholdy seems tame. Mendelssohn, too, was traveling across Europe for compositions. His Scottish Symphony, the Italian, and the Hebrides Overture, which are among his most successful works, also show a programmatic impact. Between song and passion, even if he allowed them to echo the folk melodies of those countries, Mendelssohn remained much more connected to the classical form of the symphony and was far from being as dependent on programmatic music as Berlioz. The mild temperature of his personality did not seek the new in such an exciting way. Mendelssohn was an authentic bourgeoisie, evolved in his politically quiet decades. In the house of his parents near Potsdam Platz in Berlin he reversed everything that had rank and name. This bourgeoisie tended to softness to sentimentality. The tears of overly intense emotion that often flow in the verses of Heinrich Heine, meet us again at Mendelssohn.

To develop opposing forces, he tried to renew the contrapuntal art of Bach and Handel. But not everything is possible after the cat is out of the bag. The inspiration of Mendelssohn is from ancient times long ago and far away. An essential event for Mendelssohn was the performance of Bach's St. Matthew Passion. The fiery spirit of the twenty-year-old defied the times. With this performance, Bach's work only really came to life. Until the Bach's music had been forgotten or thought of as being old and uninteresting.

Mendelssohn's songs and words have understandably played a significant role in nineteenth-century chamber music. Romantic elf magic represented in fantasy old fairy tales and legends was best represented by young Mendelssohn's compositions. At the age of seventeen, he succeeded in writing the composition of the 'Midsummer Night's Dream.' The loving description of elves magic was truly romantic language.

The violin concerto written later was in many ways related to this overture and belongs to the standard solo repertoire of soloists today. Merchants and businesses appointed Mendelssohn music director in Leipzig of an orchestra that was funded by average business people. This was a significant turn of events as music was, till then, the realm of the palace and castles.

Mendelssohn also started the grand concerts that led to today's tradition where tickets are sold to any interested public audience member. The orchestras went public everywhere in a concerted handover. It is unthinkable that a princely patron of the arts should still have an orchestra for evening entertainment, as was the case in Haydn's time. The cities, the provinces or the crown ran the orchestras. Only there were fewer princes as patrons of music. Following the example of the people of Leipzig, public symphonic concerts were set up everywhere. Mendelssohn was one of the first traveling directors.

No less important was Felix Mendelssohn-Bartholdy support for education in Leipzig, Germany. It was here that the most important music college was built, even though it was still a conservatory. For decades it was considered to be the best training center for professional musicians, both at home and abroad. All musically gifted from the countries on the edge of Europe sent their best to Leipzig. This gave rise to a stream of musical influence that one cannot underestimate.

Two master musicians and composers of the keyboard in the nineteenth century became trailblazers. Frederic Chopin and Robert Schumann were both born in 1810. Chopin was the child of a Frenchman and a Pole. Born in Warsaw, he moved to Paris after his education, during the July Revolution. The spirit of Paris was also a musical center. Here were the movers and shakers who created the significant decisions of art. Franz Liszt, the German from the Hungarian state, arrived after Chopin and Richard Wagner.

Chopin brought from Poland the Slavic passion, the primal and revolutionary of his proud people, but above all his musical rhythms. In Paris, he acquired the smoothness, the perfection of form, the supple, the glittering and the French scent. Chopin quickly became a hero of the Paris salons. Here his music found its real home. When he sat at the piano, the spirited and charming listeners who sat at his feet sank into ecstasy. His breathy play on the black keys spread an atmospheric glow that hinted at nirvana.

It did not remain hidden, though, and this passionate glow stuck in this sensitive artist. As cascades plunged over the keys, listeners sensed a fate hiding behind the music. Chopin never saw his homeland again. He never forgot the suffering of his people, always threatened by world politics. It resonated in all his work. Chopin's life was a pretty romantic life. In Paris he met a clever and creative woman in George Sand. Like many of those women of France in these literary decades, she felt compelled to expose her inner life in novels to the world. The coolness of her mind was masculine. While Chopin, always ailing and coughing, collected the last of the power to write his piano fantasies, she smoked black cigars to stimulate her "mind." Their commonality was determined by love and hatred at the same time. Finally, they had to part as she died in the arms of another.

He, too, was one of those who had gone out early when he had not even reached the age of forty. We admire Chopin's piano art mainly because of the almost unimaginative originality of his creations. In general, he wrote only in small forms. But each of these etudes, ballads, waltzes, preludes, mazurkas, and polonaises wears it's own mask. A kingdom begun by Schubert, Mozart, and Bach blessed his ingenuity. Chopin developed brilliance, a firework with sparkling string of tones, with a full-hand of keys, as neither Schubert nor Beethoven had known.

One of the prerequisites was the new technique of the piano, which was much faster and allowed quicker repetition of each sound struck. The virtuoso was becoming a sociological phenomenon. So far the music has always been written so that lay people could perform it. All the music had been more or less house music. Bach drew students to perform his passions, and even Beethoven performed his music with orchestras filled with music lovers. Of course, as early as the eighteenth century, some professional artists shone with a technique that was not available to everyone.

Franz Schubert wrote compositions for the piano like the Wanderer Fantasy, which he could not play. Only what no one could or at least could not accomplish, the overcoming of the impossible, had the prospect of being valued and wooed. The favored performers, who were able to conjure up this magical game, were showered with rejoicing and money for it.

The rage around Niccolo Paganini knew no bounds. He became a legendary violinist and composer. It characterizes this period of bourgeois music culture, for better or worse, that at that time a violinist could arouse the people to an enthusiasm such as today's world championship fight or rock concert. That something so earthly as the virtuoso could begin and complete its rule, its tyranny in yearning, and with drunken romanticism, a feature of this tense time. Piano art has gained a lot through this. But the music culture as a whole had to pay dearly for this splendor of virtuosity.

Robert Schumann was born in Zwickau. Saxony and Thuringia, which had already produced so many great composers, once again proved to be fertile musical countries. Schumann had to fight long before he could devote himself to music. At first, Robert Schumann wanted to surrender to the virtuoso career. He fell for the foolish idea to strengthen the problem child of the pianists, the fourth finger, by mechanically pulling it up in a noose. Tendinitis was the result, and the virtuoso path quickly ended. Schumann's clear, cool, and infallible view of classical approach always proved its worth. Schumann has become one of the most important music writers among the masters of the art of music and has remained one of the most celebrated. His musical style we still appreciate today as a catechism of music.

The desire for musical writing led Schumann to found his own music magazine. The "Neue Zeitschrift für Musik" (the New Magazine for Music) has a written chapter on music history. His first article was on Frederic Chopin and his last, Johannes Brahms. Schumann thus became the link between two generations, which made up two focal points of this century. Schumann's journalistic sense also brings some sensational discoveries. He found the score of the 'Great' Schubert's C-major Symphony somewhere under dusty notes, which Schubert himself had never heard.

Like Chopin, Schumann began with piano compositions, though he did not follow purely musical forms. He was one of those for whom composing was a story in tones. His compositions took on a rhapsodic freedom of form and movement. Schumann at first limited himself exclusively to writing works for the piano.

Clara, the daughter of his master Friedrich Wieck, became the beloved of Schumann's heart. The intimacy of their mutual affection left us a gripping romance novel. It stands worthy beside the togetherness of Dante and Beatrice. The only reason why he cannot be compared to the love of Romeo and Juliet, is after a long struggle, he brought fulfillment to their wishes. The father of Clara rejected the appreciation of Robert Schumann. He was an economically unsecured musician.

Schumann had to win over his wife. In the years of the separation from her, he had suffered, and all his piano works became glowing love letters in tones. When Clara and Robert Schumann finally found each other, much changed in Schumann's life. The youthful fire disappears. From the Storminess became a masterful poet, as on E. T. Hoffmann an Adalbert Stifter and Caspar David Friedrich followed a Schwind and Spitzweg.

Schumann wrote piano and violin sonatas, including the exceptional Piano Concerto in A minor, one of the pearls of this genre, four symphonies, several oratorios, among them the Faust Scenes and Paradies and Peri. With all admiration, especially for the 1st and 4th Symphony's, the Manfred Overture, and other creations, it is rightly maintained the claim that the small form of composition was actual Schumann's strength.

The poetry of his songs proved worthy of Franz Schubert. Nobody has praised the beauty of the country, the dew of the moon and the poetry of the flowers and blossoms better than Schumann. The 'Scenes from Childhood' for the piano show in each bar a master of the highest rank. He wrote these gems in the hope of later marriage and children. Schumann dreamed up these little family creations in which goodness and the happiness of safety within musical poetry combined to form an incomparable wreath. This is the dreamy and admirable image of a family idyll from the middle of the last century. Only when we sing the blissful melody of reverie, we know the complete Schumann.

His work was a romantic tragedy in that his path did not lead to these heights, but on the contrary, unstoppable to a never-ending decrescendo. This mainly caused his severe mental illness, which eventually led to his becoming a victim. Where his cheering talk of bold conquests ended in the night of madness. That night when Schumann jumped off a bridge into the Rhine River, then languished for two more years in the lunatic asylum, was a screaming counterpoint to the fantastically sweeping singing and poetry of his young years.

Clara Schumann survived him by forty years. Worrying about the many children, few of whom were healthy, demanded the hardest strain from her. Her career as a pianist continued. While she repeatedly struggled for the works of her husband, she met the young Johannes Brahms, who became more than just a musical companion. She, who had been admired by Goethe, led her life in a different way than her husband's two masters of the high romanticism, reaching almost to the end of this century.

With the romantics in the limelight, it is time to revisit the development of the opera. The Italians, inventing opera, were now finding German champions after several years. Since Mozart there was German opera or rather a German Singspiel. Even the story of the opera no longer resembles the trunk of a tree that shoots powerfully in one, but how branches and leaves spread out on all sides, there were now several types of operas. There was the mighty branch that the German reformer Gluck had created. The renewed operatic spirit quickly dissipated with Gluck's death, and the opera once again got on the way it had previously had.

For example, to the so-called Grand Opera there were huge choirs, elevators and mass scenes in it. Great examples of this genre can be found in Luigi Cherubini, who originated from Italy, and created German musician's spirit and lives in France. Daniel Francois Auber gave an admirable example in the 'The Mute Girl of Portici' with elephants on the stage, But Gasparo Spontini, who served as General Music Director in Berlin for two decades, made it almost legendary. With him, it was no longer possible without huge trumpeter choirs on the stage, and when that did not pull crowds in anymore, elephants appeared. Spontini still had to realize that this was too much for the audiences. The spirited Berliners used a theatrical scandal in 1841 to chase him away like a troublesome intruder. He survived after all, he had been a real highlight of the grand opera.

For in Giacomo Meyerbeer's works, this genre was often embarrassing. There was no question that his operas were clever, especially in the river scenes were thrilling theater to watch. But the lack of real invention and innovation could not be ignored even with the best intentions. That's why Schumann, Wagner, and other grandmasters could not do enough in their conviction for musical content. That is why we today leave the operas of Meyerbeer to the archives.

At the turn of the nineteenth century, the French loved operas with tragedy. In dark ravines there had to be as many gunshots as often as possible. Without prison and death it seldom went off successfully. The reason for this is possibly the senses had become dull in the horrors of the French Revolution, so that powerful sounds had to be struck in the senses. Guillotine and opera stages were closely associated in those years. In the evenings, the imagination was stimulated by a number of sensations, sought satisfaction in one of the sixty theaters in Paris, which were always sold out.

The opera style that developed in this time is called the horror, rescue or show opera. This genus soon became established in Germany with Beethoven's Fidelio. This opera greatly influenced the genus, and once again showed what a spirit like Beethoven can do with the thematic content. The wonderful power of his musical language has refined the black and white horror story of Florestan and Leonore to grandeur. If anything it is here that proves what is said of the ethos of Ludwig van Beethoven. Here the story has a French actress, whose action takes place in Spain, reinforced by a German who lived in Austria, did no harm the unity of the work. Once again, Beethoven's music in the opera triumphed over all other elements.

In addition to the Grand Opera, the French developed a cheerful style with the opera comique. The sense of tingling rhythms, charm, and the enjoyment of witty phrases, especially when playing the game of inexhaustible love, have benefited them. That is why the cheerful operas of the French have kept fresher than their Grand Operas, especially Fra Diavolo by Daniel Frangois Auber, King for a Day, Lonjumeau's Postillon by Adolphe Adam, and The White Lady by Frangois A. Boieldieu. In the French opera lyrique, their sense of the melodic facade could almost be self-sustaining. They also proved to be masters of delicate yet luminous instrumentation. Regular works of this genre were created by Charles Gounod with Margarethe and Ambroise Thomas with Mignon. They could have tried to compose an opera based on the profound writings of Wolfgang v. Goethe, though the audiences preferred to stick to the cheerful operas of the French.

An exceptional work that unites all genres and at the same time rises above them is Georges Bizet's Carmen. From the first to the last act, we experience choirs and staging in the style of the grand opera. In between, one delights in the sense of opera lyrique, and others in the scenes corresponding to opera comique. The concern where this genus belongs only clouds our enjoyment of this masterpiece. From the refinement of the instrumentation and the polished form, as expressed in the four preludes of the opera, to the dramatic drawing the masterpiece Carmen of scenes and characters is magnificent to the end. It is characteristic that in a round robin question of the most esteemed musical work, most of the votes went for Bizet's Carmen.

Carmen, like many others, did not have any success at the premiere. Bizet died soon afterward. A friend replaced the spoken dialogues with recitatives. Only after its world success set in did one resort to the original version. It is a characteristic of the opera comique that the plot is entrusted to some spoken dialogue. The opera comique thus approaches the Singspiel in its form. This is the difference and contrasts to the grand opera. We would understand Friedrich Nietzsche's enthusiasm for Carmen better if he had not used it to insult Wagner, and the fact that the philosopher of time became the passionate advocate of an opera who shows that there must be something special about this work.

Everything in the Italian opera has always been born from and centered on the singing voice. The primo tenore and the lamenting street boy sing from the same spirit. Woe if a composer did not satisfy the wishes of the audience and gallery with emotional solo arias. The Italian opera creations particularly delight when they brought a piece of their bright, sparkling life, full of sunshine and carefree, to the northern climates. Gaetano Donizetti composed and premiered Don Pasquale in 1843. The story is of the young ward with his old uncle, which is presented here for the umpteenth time.

The same is true of Gioacchino Rossini. There is an endless delight when the tunes of the Barber of Seville begin to giggle. In this delicately spun and cheerfully dancing Tone-spiel lives the real brio of the south. Heart and sensation gladly remain silent when so much tingling grace compensates. The most beautiful is the crescendo in the first finale with the big drum, where finally everything goes down in a thunderous vortex. At the premiere of this work, everything went completely wrong. All imaginable theater glitches rendezvous on this evening. When at the end, a stray cat from the street appeared on the stage and was chased away by Count Almaviva with his sword drawn, everyone burst out into laughter. It was not until the next evening that the Romans realized that they had been given a grand new opera.

The Viennese were noisier than most audiences as they did not know anything about Franz Schubert. Three decades before, Mozart had received a cold reception, as did Anton Bruckner six decades later. But Rossini cheered them and let them forgot about their magnificent monument Beethoven for the moment.

The joy of 'Barber of Seville' is understandable. There was a wonderfully naive anachronism in it for the composer, as it was just a piece of theatrical material and had to be fabricated every year at the opening of the season. The theater is a world of its own.

The fairytale of the German forest

At the time when Napoleon was going to St. Helena and Goethe was writing the West–Eastern Diwan, Rossini scribbled the score in thirteen days for this ancient love game full of delicious improbabilities. There developed a division in Germany between the cheerful and serious opera. Here the romantic opera was created and maintained. In this context, the name E.T.A. Hoffmann must be mentioned. It is true that his most successful opera Undine does not appear in any German opera house repertoire. But the fact that this poet and painter wrote it in the first place proves the intimate connection between romantic music and other arts.

Everything that the romantic opera desired and what possibilities it contained were fulfilled in the free will of Carl Maria von Weber. It has often been said, most recently and most emphatically by Hans Pfitzner, that the German forest plays the leading role in it. Never before or later have forest scents and forest poetry been translated into opera. The shimmering of the sun in the forest, as the horns in the overture recount, and the ghastly F-sharp minor ghosts of the Wolf's Gulch have never before been heard. The premiere of the Freischütz on June 18, 1821, meant more than a regular theater event. In the history of the opera, written by Eduard Mörike, the enthusiasm it brought was a breakthrough for the national opera.

While Weber's Freischütz was performed in the theater on the Gendarmen Market in Berlin, defying all resistance, Spontini haunted the Linden Opera as a tyrant. Only the Italian opera reigned. In Dresden, the control of the Italians was still so strong that the premiere of the Freischütz was not enforced at all, although Weber worked as Kapellmeister in Dresden and founded and promoted German opera.

It was about much more than German or Italian opera. From the wars of liberation, a national uprising developed. The students joined together to form fraternities and demonstrated about their homeland.

Like all great wars, the war of liberation had brought new leadership to power. Now the moment of the bourgeoisie had come. In the years shortly after the war of liberation, it developed its best forces, while unfortunately only too soon, for the citizens became philistine and less understanding about art, music, & literature.

This young bourgeoisie citizenry hoped and waited for an opportunity to find itself manifested in something symbolic they might all get behind. Then came Freischütz, which fulfilled and exceeded all their hopes. The people of the unrest had finally been found, as in the opera character Max, who got lost and found his way back to the right lane. Or about the female character Agathe, who had something mysterious within her. So the audience loved the dark forest with its adventurousness, rain showers and ghosts that invite to all sorts of superstitions. So they believed in the good in man. The songs Weber had written were now the bourgeoisie's own.

The morning after the premiere, all the street boys whistled the 'maiden's wreath' (Jungfernkranz Lied) with other songs and arias. The most famous was the hunting chorus from the Freischütz. The effect of the Freischütz was also an extraordinary around Europe and other continents. Soon after the Berlin premiere, this opera was performed mostly in an appalling cacophony; first in the northern countries, England, south, and the southeast. Freischütz played an essential role in the endeavor to reach a final agreement between Germany and France. German immigrants performed it with meager means in the haciendas of South America. For them, this was the German homeland at it's best. With Freischütz we easily forget that Weber has given us other operas: Euryanthe and Oberon. Nothing else can change this, much as we enjoy his virtuoso piano works and folk songs.

The premiere of Oberon was the last artistic event in Weber's life. He had taken his leave of absence in Dresden and had traveled to London to rehearse the work, which had already been completed with this last effort. On leaving, he knew he would never return. Really his life light in London was extinguishing like a flickering candle. It was his successor in Dresden, Richard Wagner, who succeeded in restoring his spirit to his homeland.

Richard Wagner – the monster of genius

His name was Richard Wagner, a composer of great music though his internal struggling plagued his humanity. Sometimes regarded as insightful, seeing only the outer image placed in a way far more vibrant and more devouring than any other creator of art. It is difficult to extract the essentials from the variety notoriety of Wagner's public persona.

Wagner was born in 1813, in the year of the Battle of Leipzig. In the early and defining years of his life, Heinrich Laube, David Strauss, and Ludwig Feuerbach influenced him. After a stay in Paris, he held a post for a year as music conductor in Dresden. This was the only time in his life he had nothing else to do but to compose operas. The Royal Court Kapellmeister was overcome by the waves of the onrushing politics and revolution.

The role of Wagner as a political revolutionary, however, is usually exaggerated. He was nothing more than a confused bully. His plan for government reform had to remain a utopian dream of the artist. After all, he met Michael Alexander Bakunin, the Russian anarchist, who led the uprising in Poland and Bohemia and then in Dresden. Maybe Wagner would have become a real revolutionary had he not emigrated. In the middle of the century, he did not succumb to the pessimistic philosophy of Schopenhauer. His fate brought him to the royal friendship of King Ludwig. It was tragic that his patron of the arts was a mad man, and the philosopher of Wagner's music was Friedrich Nietzsche. In the years of the monarchs, Wagner became an advocate of the federalism of Constantin Frantzscher. When all hopes waned in Munich, and the alienation between him and Bismarck remained insurmountable, he allowed himself to be carried away by the emerging Central German centralism, he built the long-planned temple of his art in Bayreuth.

The years of his creation of music and his theater in Bayreuth brought so many technological advances that one called his century that of science and industry. While he created his "The Ring of the Nibelung" opera, the capital of Karl Marx arose. Bernard Shaw interpreted the "The Ring of the Nibelung" in the sense of the socialist theory. As Wagner saw Carl Maria von Weber still limping to the opera rehearsal, he could even have traveled to Goethe. At the end of his journey, Ibsen was at the zenith of his work, and the time of naturalism came. During the years of his childhood, and the court painter of the Bayreuth master, was Franz von Lenbach, Vincent van Gogh was already painting.

At the beginning of Wagner's career, the opera had a history of almost two and a half centuries. What had been initially sought out had never been fulfilled in terms of form. Besides, great music had been scored. Wagner greatly valued the Freischütz, Fidelio and Don Giovanni operas. But the opera as a whole had never found the position that Wagner held according to his views. Of course, the weaknesses of the operas, written in the generation before Wagner, particularly excited him. He thought that poetry played a miserable role in opera. There are opera stories from those decades that nobody has understood until today. Not a dramatist but rather text cutters were at work. Wagner knew the plight of Weber and Beethoven with their librettists only too well.

Wagner's unique talent enabled for the first time that one and the same artist created both word and sound. We owe this ideal case to the emergence of his music dramas. The term music drama means nothing more than the convergence of poetry and music in equal partnership. Neither in poetry nor in music did Wagner continue on the paths of tradition, but he sought and soon found his own way. Above all, he enlivened poetry through the development of new and evolving material worlds. Greeks and Romans had long since exhausted themselves as the stories poorly reconciled with the unreality of music. The present is not realistically performed in the opera, because the singing man in the modern costume is an unbearable contradiction.

Wagner acted as a true romantic when he opened the German saga for the music drama. It called for interpretation, clarification, and amplification through music, whereby there was still the opportunity to incorporate streams of experience of one's own humanity and the contemplation of contemporary issues.

One thing is common to all of Wagner's works: the idea of salvation. This, too, was due to Wagner's own humanity as well as his life phases. Only the actions of his first creative half part of his life are fundamentally different from those of his second. In the Holländer, Lohengrin and Tannhäuser, the heroes seek redemption in human and earthly love. In the Ring of the Nibelung and Tristan and Isolde, the Mastersingers and the Parsifal, salvation is found in renunciation and denial. This change of direction was brought about by Wagner's acquaintance with Arthur Schopenhauer's Theory of Wisdom, although this triggered only more vehemently what would otherwise have developed in Wagner.

Wagner's strong affirmation forces often broke through this pessimism, which caused contradictions especially in the Nibelungen Ring. Decisive for the present and the future was the idea that dramatic works were no longer parallels to an unconscious world view, but that they were underpinned by the doctrine of a philosopher of the time for a completely free material world.

However, Schopenhauer did not think of the Nibelung Ring or Tristan and Isolde. He did not want to know much about Wagner at all. His musical taste was much closer to Rossini and the Italian light opera. It did not impress him that Wagner made Germanic gods and heroes into symbols of will and imagination. Bruckner dedicated one of his symphonies to Wagner.

The Wagner couple, on the other hand, was so absorbed in Schopenhauer's thought that Richard and Cosima once adopted the aliases Will and Vorstel in the Munich period. It took some sense to find out that these were the abbreviations of will and imagination.

Wagner also broke new ground in the musical design of his works by avoiding most previously well-tended forms, smashing them and creating new ones. Wagner always avoided resolute arias, duets, and ensembles. Instead, he aimed at the setting according to the events of the drama. Certain musical forms remained preserved below the surface: Leitmotif and rhythm. He reached a more meaningful link with himself through the guiding principle that every actor and every symbol of action, as well as props of the game, such as spear, ring, etc., are given a musical motif, which reflects all the changes of the persons and occupations.

"If you could really play this music (ring) as Wagner heard it, you would have to ban it - by the state; It'll blow up the world. It is a fiery demise." – Herbert von Karajan

The reunion motif from Tannhäuser, the sword motif from the "The Ring of the Nibelung" and the theme from Parsifal accompanied and symbolized them. The Leitmotifs are well known to the visitors of the Wagner operas, even though a good understanding of these works do not require a "scholarly" approach, as was believed decades ago. Incidentally, there were already Leitmotifs before Wagner. Only they were not applied so consistently. Above all, none of his predecessors had the ingenious gift of creating such catchy symbolic language with just a few notes.

Friedrich Nietzsche did not say without justification that Wagner had done his best in inventing these smallest building blocks. Also, for his harmony, Wagner found role models in Weber, Spohr, and many others. Nevertheless, he had the essentials to go it alone. Especially in Tristan, he found captivating sounds full of pain and joyfulness. This work has, therefore, become the starting point of modern harmony.

Wagner made melody and rhythm serve his dramatic will to express its meaning.

In contrast to Beethoven, he composed so melodiously and linear vocal voicing that his operas combine the highest dramatic effect with consummate vocal quality. Wagner used the rhythm more naturalistically than ever. For example, he imitated forging, pattering horses with rhythmic imprints. Wagner's musical language is pathetique, baroque, brooding, and controlled through out. Wagner, for half his life, believed in the revolution as only some Frenchman believed in it. He sought it in the runic scriptures of the myth, and in Siegfried to find the typical revolutionary. "Where does all the mischief come from in the world?" wondered Wagner. "From 'old contracts' like all revolution ideologues." "The morals, laws, institutions, of everything German, on which the ancient world, the old society rests." - Friedrich Nietzsche.

Nietzsche's hated beautiful sounding music but at the same time reflected on musical language in symbols where it reflects all passions, impulses, ecstasies, and desires. Friedrich Nietzsche, however, claimed that he was doing this only in the manner of an actor. He called Wagner a mime among the composers. First Friedrich Nietzsche became enthusiastic about Richard Wagner, and then he hated him with the same obsession. Nietzsche suffered no less than Wagner under this tragedy of inner compulsion. One can explain this inevitable dichotomy had many good reasons. After all, there remains a twilight-like iridescence in Wagner's work as well as with Friedrich Nietzsche. On the other hand, today an impartial judgment is possible on the question of whether Wagner's plan of the Gesamtkunstwerk "all-embracing art form" has succeeded. To be sure, he wrestled with this old problem, which is that the modern world was more violent than ever, more than any other time. Though the music drama, in which music and drama unite in equal parts, did not exist. The music was, at times, tyrannical or in total control. Mozart was right when he said that poetry in opera must be an obedient daughter of music. Schopenhauer expressed the same view in the statement that music and word are like a "Wedding between princess and beggar."

But what remained of Wagner and why we still count him among the greatest is his music. In the musical and in the weaving of the notes, Wagner put almost everything he had in mind. We experience foreplay, love, and death from Tristan in the funeral march from the "Twilight of the Gods." Still, many performances are sometimes viewed with the content of dubiousness nature.

The Meistersinger of Nuremberg, maybe his best work, basically live on their incredible music, in which the brightest aspects of Wagner's humanity resonate. Wagner's path as a human being and artist was unique. Like his heroes, he always sought salvation in the eternal woman. Even when he had found his wife Cosima, this insatiable longing awoke in the idea of that character. As he attempted to enter eternal nirvana, he chased after the fulfillment of his dreams of a life like a fever. .

The many stations of his natural evolution cannot be enumerated. There were too many in his adventurous life. He was loved like no other and hated as well. To date, hardly anything has changed that outlook. He is still one of the most recorded on earth. Some blame him for all the musical misfortunes that he allegedly left behind, and others had to deal with his legend, to compete with him. Perhaps the ultimate meaning of those struggles we are carrying out now lies in trying to write the final chapter of the Wagner case. The mind of Wagner often denies him, and his followers, as there are monstrosities within. But nobody can escape the vitality and power of his music in the end. Wagner's music formed from overabundance, music from intoxication, and ultimately music as destiny.

Puccini – a problem here?

Hardly any other opera composer of the recent past is as popular and successful with music lovers around the world as Giacomo Puccini, and hardly anyone else has been so aggressively attacked by the critics and taken less seriously.

The naïve reader and opera lover may think it was precisely Puccini's extraordinary successes and popularity, combined with a certain apparent lightness and superficiality of his compositional gestures that made him a charlatan. The first attacks in his lifetime were made, strangely enough, by his Italian compatriots Fausto Torrefranca (1883-1955). He was a scientific scholar of the young Italian movement and supporter of art ethics, who led the way to the nationalist art movement.

Puccini's opera in 1910 'Girl from the Golden West' the critic wrote that it "reaches a low point in taste - mind you, a tasteful, not a musical one!" That's why Torrefranca was not the first. The Young Italians rejected the opera and demanded Italian supremacy in the field of independent instrumental music, referring to the history of Italian music before 1600. The opera, especially in the style of Puccini, has become international and cosmopolitan and it can never be regarded as the musical future of Italy. That sounds almost incomprehensible at first, for it was Italy that had cultivated the form of musical drama in a centuries-old opera story and made it exemplary for the whole of Europe.

Giuseppe Verdi's work was the incarnation of Italian music and at the same time the last artistic highlight of Italian opera before Puccini.

And he knew no more significant role model than Giuseppe Verdi, no higher goal than to write Italian opera. Torrefranca, however, appeared as the embodiment of all that he fought in theory and practice. Thus Puccini had to endure accusations in all its sharpness. Completely overlooking Puccini's Italianism, Torrefranca accused him of internationalism, decadent disunity, ill-disguised artistic impotence, feminism, and perversion. He was the "defamator of the artistic honor of Italy," who, like a musical "Volapük," collected his stylistic elements from all over the world and thus speculated on the flat, internationally leveled taste.

Even Torrefranca's operatic material was suspect, where Puccini's "morbid and perverted personality, could only use the romantic stories of fallen girls. Not ten years will keep his music!" Intimate stories told by enterprising publishers about his supposedly innumerable amorous adventures continued to undermine Puccini's artistic reputation. "Look at him, this Puccini," shouted his opponents, "this well-dressed gentleman with the melancholy cigarette in the corner of his mouth, who casually sets a stirring story in music every few years, making himself a rich man, look at him! He may have successes with the women and the uneducated audience, but never with serious scientists!" His easy successes also quickly made Puccini suspicious in Germany, and Torrefranca's arguments fell on fertile ground here.

Between 1920 and 1930, anti-Puccini literature evolved into more or less witty paradoxes that became fashionable in music journalism. Some examples may clarify this. Adolf Weissmann described Puccini's development as a "gliding path", although Puccini himself called a "most radical usefulness man" of "suggestive power." He only pretended power from "neurasthenic weakness" and especially among the woman he used "sentimental power." Mentality and piquancy flatters as a "great industrialist of the opera, for he knew how to distribute his effects in cold blood, but did not have the real means of musical depiction." Such claims, in which the fashion of psychoanalysis does not play the smallest role completely obscures the positive approach in Weissmann's work. In his "Opera in the Present" Julius Kapp wrote in 1928, Puccini pretends "what he cannot give…he renounces musical characteristics. Outwardly, it illustrates creepiness on the stage and in this way works on the tear glands of his audience. Puccini's art is inwardly untrue and tailored to audience appeal. It seeks to feign great tragedy with the light-hearted pleasing means of operetta. It is lacking any connection with the designed situation ... It becomes sweet and untrue in emotional outbursts and behaves completely hypocritical and theatrical with dramatic climaxes, which demand a coherent structure to which Puccini is incapable... "

Even Richard Specht, whose monograph appeared to Puccini in 1931 as an "atonement for the wrong done", did not come up with a clear and unified Puccini image. For him too, Puccini is a highly ambiguous and enigmatic artist whose success is predominantly based on superficiality.

"Actually, all this is horrible, but it is irresistible." His music, "poster art of the most screaming kind, but with painted subtle watercolor brush and often really with heart and soul ..., calls the mob in us to awake, but wrong with him as an aristocrat!"

About a decade after Puccini's death, musicologists began to deal in earnest with his work. German research relied predominantly on Italian sources and publications, and in this way arrived at a true and non-polemical Puccini image.   First of all, never forget that Puccini's artistic root lies in his Italian heritage. Like Verdi and Wagner, he too owes its universal validity and importance precisely to national culture. In his work, he continued the best traditions of Italian opera and increased Verdi's dramatic musical achievements to new and higher respect. Especially in opera, music, and language form an inseparable unity, and thus the German must by no means base his judgment on Puccini's German-language performances of his operas, often staged with inappropriate and modest sentimentality.

Puccini, to whom a Caruso and Gigli were still alive and available as singers, wrote exceptionally well for the Italian voice. It is also essential that Puccini's operatic art should never be measured by the standards of Wagner's philosophically founded music drama or even the stage performance.

From Schiller's view of the "stage" as a moral institution, Puccini was far from it. His heroes do not struggle for high ideals, but the middle class with their passions, longings, and weaknesses, even if they seemingly - like Gianni Schicchi or little Liù - come from distant times. He did not want to write music dramas or solemn festivals that, in their noble goals (as is usually the case with Wagner), go beyond the framework of musical theater. Puccini himself once said "the music of the little things," which was used for the simple man of our day is determined and wants of nothing more than to address, please, or even shake him musically.

As a typical child of the turn of the century, Puccini with his all-things-operas remained a problem of his time. Sometimes even slipping into being a sentimentalist, musicians of distinction with subtle feeling, he transfigured the obnoxious realities of everyday life with all the magic of his craft. He was a kind of naïve child, which ingeniously designed piloted the fates his opera characters. His artistic honesty and sincerity could not be denied to him. "I love the little things, "he said of himself. "I only want to do the music of the little things. If they are true, passionate, and humane, they will go to the heart." Puccini did not think of himself as a great master and was well aware of his artistic talents and their limitations. However, he was able to arrange "the little things" to really go to the heart.

Humanistic temperament speaks out of his music. If it does not know any intellectual difficulty and if it does not know anything about conflicts with the former, then it is an ingenious reflection of the waking reality: artistic exaltation of our earthly existence. And above all, Puccini's music knows about people and what can stir and move the heart. In this sense, we must now seek to understand Puccini's loveable personality with his work.

Puccini's opera style

The three factors that are decisive to operatic style are the libretto, all the musical elements, and their scenic application within opera architecture. For Puccini, who spent his lifetime with the dramaturgical and textual design of his opera scores took a sincere interest, character, and layout of the libretti.

Apart from two legends and fairy tales ("The Willis" at the beginning and "Turandot" at the end of his operatic development), all of Puccini's operas have real action where the exact moment prevails. Apart from Puccini's quest for style or the look of the opera, this realism differs from the naturalistic opera ideal. It is rooted in Puccini's extraordinarily clear sense of dramatic effects for example in "Tosca" and "The Girl of the Golden West."

Dramatic conflicts, usually resulting from an intimate love affair, far outweighed external intricacies, which is an essential difference from the conventional 19th-century opera in Italy. The bearers of this conflict formation are almost exclusively female figures, to whose fate Puccini's musical sense was inflamed. Only in "Gianni Schicchi" (an opera which, due to its comic character, occupies an exceptional position in Puccini's complete genre, where all others tend to the tragic), in which the main character is a man.

Puccini, as a born lyric poet, was more inclined towards the realistic arrangement of the intimate and female psyche than to a more robust external drama. It is significant that the formation of conflict, which focuses on the woman role, is an opportunity presented to a mundane life. The location and the time of the action play almost no role as Puccini's operatic figures embody passions and feelings of the everyday. It is not by chance that the outcome prevails here and it's usually tragic. The reason for this is not so much Manon's, Mimi's, Tosca's, Butterfly's, Georgette's or Angelica's character, which is incapable of a positive solution, but rather the social circle represented in the situation of the character. This results in a critical Puccini element, perhaps unconscious, where in the moment of his realistic opera design he takes a critical stance on the social conditions of the time depicted.

This may be seen as a reflection of his own social environment. His position is quite biased, in favor of the suffering and the oppressed. The fact that he makes a timely and socially critical statement both in choice and in the design of his operatic material is a fact that no director can get around today. In order not to give a false impression, it should be emphasized once again that Puccini was primarily concerned with the valid organization of private conflicts (which, however, were inextricably linked with relationships), and that as an opera composer. He never deliberately sought political expression, as is the case for example, Verdi did.

In his work there is only one opera that goes beyond indirect social criticism and concentrates on a highly political material; "Tosca," but that remains an exception. Puccini's operas navigate through the psychologically convincing depiction of the central conflict, stage like effects, elaboration of the main and subplot, and for his personal style one of the most important factors; loving the 'little things' like subsequent milieu drawings.

The singers follow the opera by obeying the laws of opera architecture within it's textual elaboration in scenes, pictures, and files. How much Puccini did with his personal creative concerns with the results of theater practice, the demands of text on the recitatives, arias, ensembles, choirs, and the length of scenes and images are adapted and testify to his outspoken talent for opera.

It has already been emphasized that for the musician Puccini the libretto was by no means of secondary importance. He saw the text as the main prerequisite for a successful composition and the majority of the time his work was already written. How much effort and work behind the apparent lightness, proves for example, that the final picture of "La Bohme" was rewritten fundamentally lyrically no less than four times, and even then Puccini was not yet satisfied. Such an intimate combination of text and music design naturally benefited from the uniformity of the poetic musical persuasiveness of his operas. If Puccini, and this is one of the nonsensical reproaches against his opera design, where only with the cheap and "slightly lighthearted means of operetta pretend great tragedy", would have been such careful effort alone to the libretto truly unnecessary!

The most important creative forces in Puccini's operas are, of course, his musical elements. Absolutely dominant among all is for Puccini the melody. He is a typical Italian in that his melody formation is unmistakable due to innate peculiarities. He avoids craggy boundaries between recitative and aria. An infinite melodic current permeates the whole, condensing at specific points into relatively smooth shapes, and around aspects of dialogue. One can see a particular influence of Wagner's "infinite melody," which is however turned into Italian, in that Puccini's melodies do not renounce cadence incisions and gradations.

Almost typical is his "Art of Transitions," which casually follows one melodic motif into another and still corresponds to the need for formal organization and musical unity. Thus predominantly (especially in the works since "Tosca") there is a melodic "mixed style" closely linked to the poetic word, to which Verdi's late work strove.

Everyday speeches and conversations, which Puccini always balanced between libretto and aria as no other opera composer could. He grasped as forcefully and convincingly into music as he could. In contrast to Verdi, there is no fundamental separation between voice and accompanying orchestra. Between both sound factors, a melodic thread spins alternately. Often, even at the beginning of an aria or an ensemble, the melodic lead is in the orchestra until the loosely interspersed speeches of the singers condense melodically, and an aria vocal sound flourish.

Singing voices and instruments are often coupled melodically at the climax, which is an atypical instrumentation technique by Puccini. The melodic idea is primary in the vast majority of all themes and motifs. It has an immediate, form-coalescing effect as the motif, and then attains the driving force in the unfolding aria. Wagner's "Leitmotiv" has been transformed into a "characterizing motif technique" that is psychologically tailored to the main characters and radiates a robust formal power through repetition and reminiscent.

Puccini's harmony is as distinctive as his melody. It includes a chromatic alteration style as well as exotic sounds of the Orient, parallel chords, harmonic fourths, and other tonal phenomena. From all these elements, Puccini created a very personal harmonic language whose main aim was to support and deepen the expressiveness of his melodic inspirations. His harmony is just as "characterizing" for people and the milieu as an opera's motifs. Puccini's style is his subtle harmonic restlessness.

His chord progressions are fleeting and unexpected, which lead to unexpected places for the ear. The timbre of his orchestration is also Puccini's whose ingenious instrumental choices and voicing is a singular hallmark of his craft. His scores are everlasting testimonies of the nuanced sense of sound. Dramatic events in his operas, ranging from the leitmotivs of special moments as day awakening in the third act "Tosca," dusk in the "The Cloak," or Moon choir from "Turandot".

From a rhythmic point of view, Puccini is restless, whereas in one single process he compensates with his melodic, harmonic, and tonal changes. This happens in the form of obstinate formations, whereby an underlying motive, which has been set up at the outset, is varied melodically, harmoniously and in terms of timbre, using a fixed basic rhythm. Dance influences are often unmistakable. The choice of time signature and tempo depends on the scenic progression.

Typically, scenes that can be broken down into exciting individual dialogues are often bound by a tense and intense broad Largo rhythm. Metrically, Puccini seldom adheres to regular eight-bar periods (especially with increasing age); Irrational formations of five, seven or eleven bars are often preferred (which of course has melodic consequences when most melodies are of even number bars).

The dynamic, with its subtle breakdown of all degrees of strength, is in some ways typical of Puccini. The dynamics are rapidly reversed, out of a seeming calm, along with fortissimo outbursts that seep into the piano. Puccini's dynamics are susceptible and excitable, which is expressed by very carefully set indications in the score. In almost every bar, one can expect a new dynamic. Based on which scene, there are decisive and triggering factors that determine the direction of the music.

There is an indication that all musical means are inextricably linked. Melody, rhythm and meter, harmony, timbre, and dynamics are intimately interrelated. They are essential and characteristic individual factors of Puccini's operatic style, which are a result of their complex interaction within the music that is ultimately dependent on the libretto architecture. Puccini's musical design is based equally on the psychological characterization of the actors and the subtle milieu. Both things cannot be separated from him, and one does not know whether in a work like "Turandot", which can be admired more.

All the musical components, solo, ensemble, and choral parts, as well as the orchestra, are subordinate to the primary purposes of opera design. In his musical gestures, Puccini tends predominantly to the 'little things', and can musically transfigure, stylize, and exaggerate the typical external and psychological moments. The love scene in the first scene of "Boheme" shows a striking example of how, following a previously relaxed contrast of the ensemble with Rudolf- Marcel-Schaunard-Collin, only small forms are lovingly joined together until the brilliant duet Mimi-Rudolf unites the scene is concluded.

Within all Puccini's means of musical melody, harmony, and timbre, the characters of Mimi and Rudolf are musically interpreted, and the utmost impulses of the soul are made audible. Especially impressive scene complexes are the key conclusions, which are historically conditioned. In the course of operatic history, the finals were first composed in an open sequence of individual "numbers" and effectively interlinked all the scenic and musical means.

In the first "Tosca" finale, personal and milieu characterization and contrast formations are musically realized simultaneously, a compositional masterpiece by Puccini. Perhaps his most personal gift is the musical drawing of an atmosphere, which through the characteristic melodic, harmonic and orchestral twists of "Manon" and "La Bohme," can give an unmistakable and unique character to operas.

How Puccini manages to charm the musical atmosphere in each of his operas with just a few dotted strokes will forever remain his creative secret. Typical of his operatic style is the structure of the act in action and mood contrasting scene complexes, the opposition also arises from the differentiated use of solos, ensembles, and choirs as well as from the different use of musical means in detail. Besides, Puccini especially loves such dramatic connecting tension creating contrasts in temporal juxtaposition.

Like no other opera composer of his time, Puccini knew how to musically trace the many scenic moments without falling into mosaic like detail paintings. The harmonious unions of close ties to the stage and at the same time the greatest possible musical independence and formal unity is characteristic for his technical ability, his sensitive theater sense, and his musical talent. However, Puccini's opera design and the main elements of his style are not always subject to continuous development. This is particularly evident in architectural terms.

In his first works, Puccini took up the ancient Italian principle of the numbering operas, which uses recitatives and arias, duets, ensembles and choirs as closed numbers in specific passages. But already in "Manon" and "La Bohme" the mathematical principle is mostly relaxed and adapted to the dramatic flow. Primarily through the influence of Wagner's through-composed music drama, "Tosca" becomes the turning point in Puccini's work. In front of number one; solo and ensemble, new forms now prevail; recitative, arioso, and choral and orchestral. These became ingeniously summarized as 'mixed style.' However, his Italianism and the associated Romanesque sense of form prevented him from unreservedly adapting to the Wagnerian style and did not allow him to forget his formal independence. In this respect, Verdi, the exemplary composer of Italian opera, became less of an influence on Puccini.

Puccini's operas not only undergo a development that spans forty years in musical and architectural terms, but evolved in their aesthetic point of view. Puccini's operatic development is not straightforward, but contradictory, and runs in two large ascending and descending curves. But this is not artistic weakness or lack of spirit, but lay the within change of the century that his opponents liked to accuse him of. In the course of a multi-faceted creative development process, successful and less successful works must necessarily coexist, with Puccini as with all other composers.

Puccini's operas prove the meaning of this conclusion is about his operatic style, not a product of an unscrupulous business mind or an artistically irresponsible concession, or an internationally diluted public taste, but the result of conscientious artistic work. They are the works of a typical Italian opera master, which stood at the end of a century-long development and elevated the opera of his time.

Admittedly, as an expression of the typical southern feeling for life, he tends more towards the shaping of the sensible than the spiritual, more the little than the large things. To use a word from Thomas Mann: "In the end, one should neither fear nor be ashamed of the sensuous." Is not the 'small world' of the eternal and human worthy of shaping? To understand Puccini's humanistic concern in his immortal works is the obligation of posterity to the great art of the master of small things.

Béla Bartók

Hungarian music and gypsy music

In 1859, Franz Liszt the great piano virtuoso and composer published a treatise on "The Gypsies and Their Music in Hungary." The publication of this work was a coincidence as it dealt with the subject of the unsuccessful attempt of the Hungarian people to liberate from the Austrian rule of the House of Hapsburg. This happened during the revolutionary events of 1848 and 1849 that affected all of Europe. The progressive thinking people were sympathetic with the oppressed.

In the spring of 1849 the Russian Tsar had been called to the aid of the Emperor of Austria to overthrow the Hungarian popular movement led by the lawyer Lajos (Ludwig) Kossuth. In a sea of blood and tears, the national Hungarian uprising had been stifled. The leaders of the army had been hanged, and many freedom fighters had been driven abroad, among them Kossuth.

In Hungary, the memory of Kossuth had remained alive as a symbol of the coming liberation of the country, and the Austrian part of the monarchy feared his name as an exterminator of feudal privileges and peasants' burdens. More than fifty years after the suppression of the Hungarian liberation struggle and nine years after Kossuth's death in exile in Italy in 1894, a symphonic poem dedicated to his memory burnt the national balance in a Budapest concert hall. The twenty-two-year-old composer of this "Kossuth Symphony" was Béla Bartók.

To fully understand Bartók as the creator of today's Hungarian style of music and as one of the leading composers of the 20th century, the knowledge of Liszt's writing on the Gypsies and their music is absolutely necessary. Surrounded by friends and students from all over the world, Liszt led the life of an internationally recognized, open-minded artist in Weimar. But despite his cosmopolitan nature, he had kept his love for his native land. Above all, understandably, the music attracted him, whom he remembered from his childhood. The instrumental music for the Hungarian noblemen was performed almost exclusively by Gypsies, and had also gained a foothold in the country, where they mainly performed for the wealthier peasant dances.

Hardly anyone doubted that the music was the authentic Hungarian folk music, and indeed, Franz Liszt agreed. Liszt was obviously amazed by the fact that the Gypsies never sang but mainly worked as instrumentalists, especially as violinists and cymbal players. At that time he had written; "My intention was ... to go alone and on foot with the bundle on my back to the loneliest parts of Hungary." He added regretfully, "But that did not work out." But we have to worry that his attention was focused on urban culture and its art.

His utterly unhistorical attitude made him come to no conclusions when he spoke in his treatise on the folk instruments flute, bagpipe and others used in isolated areas of Hungary. He was even aware that there were people who considered these instruments to be 'peculiarly Hungarian', and thought "that the melodies that had been sung only at first were played on them first." He also noticed that such instruments were never used by the gypsies and never crossed the area of their pusztas (steppes). Yet they still amused the loneliness of the diligent farmer or shepherd. Therefore, Bartók came to the following valuation; "The Hungarian songs, as they are sung on our steppes or mediated by these meager instruments, the honor of general Hungarian musicology and practice are today in spite of all reverence for the personality and the work of Franz Liszt opposite opinion. "

To enforce this other view is primarily the merit of Béla Bartók and his associate Zoltan Kodaly. It took a good hundred years before the call made in 1803 by the poet Mihaly Vitez; "Pay close attention to the singing village girl, the simple vintage!" Like in Germany, and in other countries, the reflection on the old folk song in the first half of the 19th century was an element to strengthen the national feeling. This was especially the case with people who had been oppressed for centuries by more powerful neighbors; Poles, Czechs, Slovaks, Ruthenians (Ukrainians), Finns, and not least the Hungarians. In their songs, they found the strength to resist the oppression.

However, it was first of all the philologists who collected and published texts of folk songs. "Of course, this is a very wrong procedure, because word and melody form an inseparable unity in the folk song;" this was Béla Bartók's opinion. It was not until the end of the nineteenth and twentieth centuries that musicologists were given the technical possibilities to record the song sung by the people both musically and lyrically.

In 1878, the American inventor Thomas Alva Edison, who constructed the first phonograph, helped to record the remaining music of early cultures. Bartók and Kodaly went to the peasant areas of Hungary to collect this music. Liszt foresaw its presence at the time, but was not stunned by the virtuosity and color of music played by the Gypsies and did not any draw conclusions from it. The result of Bartók and Kodaly was that music played by gypsies, that Liszt processed and imitated with abundant spirit, can by no means be addressed as Hungarian folk music.

Examples of this are Liszt's "Hungarian Rhapsodies" and melodies by Brahms in his "Hungarian Dances", violinist Joseph Joachim playing the violin concerto 'in the Hungarian Style'. Many of the composers of those tunes are known by name, but hardly any of them were of Gypsy origin. Bartók and his associates, among Bela Vikar, Emma Kodaly, and Laszlo Laytha acknowledged that throughout Europe the romantic legend spread that all Gypsies are musicians.

The Gypsies, who until now have been puzzling the ethnographers and supposedly come from India, have been known to be in Hungary since the 15th century. Usually, the Gypsies, despised by the landowning peasants, lived at the outskirt of the villages as tinkers or brick-burners. It was not until the eighteenth century when they combined into smaller or larger groups that they found their way to the village festivities. There they supplanted the original peasant musicians, or they entered the service of the landlords to whom public music making seemed dignified.

The gypsy musicians in the countryside also developed a vigorous activity as distributors of the 'Werberlieder' of the 18th and 19th centuries. This is a large group of their original and stylistic songs, not yet adequately clarified folk songs, used to recruit officers from the young peasant lads. From the villages and estates, the Gypsy bands finally invaded the cities and their places of entertainment. In the sociological and musicological investigation of this state of affairs, it was surprisingly found that there was little similarity between the gypsy tunes in the countryside and in the cities.

Instead, the environment in which they lived and the people they played with guided the Gypsies. It could be proven that those living in the villages or cities moved from place to place. Depending on whether they were active in purely Hungarian areas or in the regions of Hungary, which at that time belonged to Hungary but had Romanian population predominantly, musicians used different melodies.

Of these two types, there was the city gypsy music, which Liszt regarded as Hungarian music, and which is still presented to unsuspecting listeners as the epitome of "Hungarian," as well as in operettas, and shameless Hollywood-style kitsch films. Anyone who has the opportunity to hear such gypsy music in hotel halls in Budapest still gets a sense of the adaptability of these musicians.

In addition to the folk songs, which have dragged on for several generations, usually with feeble and painful emotional content that brings tears of longing and emotion to the quietly buzzing city people just as in Liszt's time, such gypsy bands also played modern dance hits.

However, they do not shy away from playing known and popular classical melodies, such as the cradlesong by Brahms, to their manner of performance. In this style, the violin of the Gypsy musician crying in the highest registers with a tiring tremolo is unbearable. One can then sympathize with the surprise and joy of researchers such as Bartók, Kodaly, and Vikar, when they discovered the real Hungarian peasant song is from the romantic, exuberant gypsy songs of the urban and feudal styles. "These melodies are classic examples of how one can most perfectly express a musical thought most concisely with the simplest means." With Bartók and the same goes for Kodaly, the great stroke of luck was a personal union of artist and scientist.

While looking back, Kodaly contemplated his life and was convinced that the composer Bartók would never have become what he had become without the scientist Bartók. But at times he even thought that Bartók's occupation with folk songs had kept him from his own work and having to deal with the tiresome necessity of earning a living through piano lessons.

In truth, it is regrettable that Bartók's collecting as a folkloristic musician during his lifetime was not recognized and given enough opportunity to evaluate and publish his finds. Unfortunately, many of his several thousand recordings containing phonograph rollers have not been transferred to the present. The limited life of the wax rollers makes such neglect almost incomprehensible. The word of kindred spirit, Bartók said, reminiscent of Beethoven's saying "folk song hunting is better than man hunting", was bitter; "If only the sum spent in armaments in the world in a year were available for research, then the people could collect music from all over the world."

Overall, the tunes found by Bartók, Kodaly, and the other Hungarian folk-song collectors may be around 16,000. Bartók's work turned the songs of his homeland, whose exploration was his heart and not just a hobby, is clear from a letter dated October 1938. He wrote to the conductor Paul Sacher in Basel; "I work almost ten hours a day, exclusively with folk-song material; but should work for twenty hours to get along reasonably well. Untenable situation. I would like to end the work before the new airborne world disaster. And at this rate, it will take a few more years! " His desire to organize, transfer, and surrender the raw material gained unfortunately did not come true. The catastrophe he had foreseen, the Second World War brought about by fascism, had interrupted his work and indirectly caused an early end to the Hungarian musician career.

It has already been suggested with which comparatively primitive technical devices Bartók and Kodaly tried to prevent the old Hungarian peasant songs from being forgotten. The researchers were aware that only the devotion of many Hungarians had kept the old songs alive. It was important that these songs were collected. In the economic conditions of the agricultural countries, which were changing as a result of industrialization, there was soon no room left for spinning rooms in which the women had sung their songs.

The improved transport links with the cities brought pop songs to the country, as well as the cheaper industrial production gradually pushed aside the remnants of ancient folk art. Kodaly says; "Around 1910, a rather sharp divorce from the song collections of the three primary life ages. The village folk of middle and advanced age not only did not sing the most popular songs of the youth of that time, but also mostly did not even know them. Still less did the children know the songs of the previous generation, which they rarely, if ever, used to sing. The village etiquette recognizes the right of the married man and the married woman to sing only for wedding ceremonies or other special occasions, and then only in a closed room.

An old man or an old woman who sing in public, necessarily for singing in the meadow is the prerogative of youth, the rigor of these unwritten laws softening into neighborhoods, but it is always a difficult task to get older people to sing. If there was any connection between the lore of the children and the ancients, the former were more familiar with the songs of their grandparents than those of their parents. The reason for may be found in the actual way of life of the village. In the case of the parents who work during the day, the grandparents often took care of the children, so that they could hear some of their grandparents' things they no longer heard from their parents. Another unique occurrence reinforces the music of children's games; it has probably changed the least since it tends to reproduce from child to child."

Only through the tireless educational work of Bartók and Kodaly did the youth again learn to appreciate the old songs again and to play the Hungarian folk instruments, especially the violin, instead of the improper plucking instruments and the accordion. Of course, the emergence of new folk songs is not excluded today. Bartók and Kodaly were able to ascertain a great deal from the period between 1870 and 1910. When Bartók and Kodaly appeared in the Hungarian villages with phonographs and wax rollers in the first decade of our last century, these apparatuses aroused mistrust. It required a great deal of persuasion to get people, especially women still educated in patriarchal dependency, to sing their songs without fear into the funnel of the strange device.

Bartók said of the various tasks, which such collecting activities pose to the musicologist: "The ideal folk music collector must have a genuinely encyclopedic or comprehensive education. Philological and phonetic knowledge is indispensable to him to perceive and record the subtlest nuances of pronunciation in the various regions; he has to be a choreographer to be able to describe the connections between music and folk dance accurately... too. He must be a sociologist so that he can observe the influence of disturbances in village community life on folk music. If he wants to draw conclusions, he needs historical knowledge concerning the settlement areas of the individual tribes. If he wishes to make comparisons with the folk music of other countries, he must learn the foreign languages concerned. At last, and above all, he must necessarily be a subtle musician and a good observer. A folk song researcher, in which so much knowledge and experience unite, has, as far as I know, not yet found and may never find."

Bartók soon realized that a comparison of the melodies found in Hungary with those of the neighboring people became necessary. With the same care with which he had proceeded in the individual landscapes of Hungary, he roamed the areas inhabited by Slovaks, Serbs, Croats, Ruthenians, and Romanians. Short before the First World War, Bártók even went to Algiers to get to know Arabic peasant songs in the Oasis of Biskra. In 1936 he made his way to Asia Minor, where he carried the inconvenience of bumpy peasant carriages and the tents of a barren landscape to examine the alleged similarity of the tunes of his Hungarian homeland with the music of oriental Turkic peoples on the spot. Except for a scientific treatise on the folk music of the Arabs, these studies, as well as extensive further collections of Romanian, Slovak, and Serbo-Croatian chants, are still unpublished.

Comparing his findings, Bartók noted a number of acquisitions of melodic material at the peoples' borders. Here the Hungarians appeared to him as giving part to the Slovaks and Ruthenians, which in his opinion, resulted from the different cultural heights of these three peasant cultures. On the other hand, he considered it significant that he did not feel any influence on the Hungarian song by the adjoining folk music of Styria and Burgenland, whereas the Slovakian music had in turn taken over the Syrian yodeler. However, Bartók's open-mindedness towards other peoples had not earned him any friendships.

Romanian musicologists accused Bartók of having diminishing the folk art of their country and in Hungary nationalist circles were angry with him, and that he lovingly gave himself over to the music of neighboring peoples. He was especially struck by this opposition when, after the conclusion of the Peace Treaty of Trianon, he refused to misuse his musical research for political vengeance. Bartók and Kodaly published their research results in a large number of journal articles in some of the German language books.

Bartók explains what he understands by peasant music and folk music: to mean by peasant music in a broader sense. "We are the totality of those melodies which, in the peasant class of any people, have survived or at some time lived on in greater or less temporal and spatial extension as a spontaneous expression of musical feeling ", and further: "Folk music is the totality of all the melodies that were used as a spontaneous expression of musical sensation in some human society at a greater or lesser extent over a certain period of time."

It does not detract from Bartók's greatness when we realize that these definitions are incomplete. They do not clearly distinguish themselves from hits and popular kitsch songs. In Hungary, the researchers found four musical dialects, which due to the landscape, revealed many differences in verse and melodic construction. As an underlying layer, they considered songs in the so-called 'old style', whose melodic material is based on the five-tone series (pentatonic), which was also used by the Turkish. Bartók and Kodaly spent many hours recording their notes down on the paper.

Folk music becomes art music

As a creative musician Bartók had soon turned away from the style of his early works, that is, the negation of German romanticism and the melting of elements of musical language in the style of Strauss. The impressionistically blurred imagery of Claude Debussy's music, too, was only in passing after he had recognized his task of comparable art music based on national folk music. However, it seemed to Debussy that Bártók and his friends did nothing more than edit those tunes of the people they had eavesdropped on.

Such arrangements take up a considerable amount of space in his life's work, but he strictly separates them from his own compositions. The more he got to know the folk melodies, the more intimately he penetrated into their depths, and the more he finally recognized the essential elements of folk music. That is why his works often sound 'as if' folk tunes were chosen as themes. In reality, they are creations of their own in the spirit of the folk song. Instead of merely materializing, "It is Hungarian, as far as it is determined by the country, the education, the ideas and spiritual currents of Hungary."

The path to the merging of the folk song already appears in the 2nd Suite for Orchestra op. 4, made between 1905 and 1907. At the same time, Bartók also collaborated with Kodaly collecting twenty original Hungarian folk songs for voice. The piano accompaniment was the original melody with nothing changed. On the other hand, for the accompanying part, the question immediately arises; what harmonic means must the composer of the present day use, in order not to support the chords? In the course of his many folk song arrangements he was struggling with this problem, be it singles, choral or piano pieces. Just as seventy years before him, the Russian composer Mikhail Glinka had been looking for the connection between the melody of his native country and the romantic embellishment of the church, which was opposed to the Western European major-minor harmony.

Bartók gradually strove for the style of Hungarian synthesis in his music. For example, it was necessary to find the unity between the edgy Hungarian melody and the shimmering colored fabric of sound that he had come to know in Debussy. In the end the simply cadences and accompanying forms that still satisfied Glinka were scarcely sufficient in the present.

In his arrangements and compositions he temporarily took over the technique of parallel shifted chords with thickening of the sound by added seconds, fourths and sevenths. "The music of our day strives decisively toward the atonal," Bartók wrote in 1920 and, like most of his contemporaries, in many of his works he paid homage to the exaggeration of Expressionism.

The nineteenth and twentieth centuries, in his opinion, had sharpened people's sense of equality for all twelve tones of the chromatic scale through Wagner's and Liszt's accumulation of altered chords, and Strauss and Debussy's increasingly freewheeling passages upon passages. Therefore, "the ultimate goal of our endeavors ... is the unlimited and complete exploitation of all the available, possible tonal material".

Without ever falling into the constructivism of the absolute twelve-tone composers of Schönberg's Webern and their followers, there are also twelve-tone formations in Bartók's violin concerto. However, they are melted down into a natural musicality so that they never impose themselves on the listener as sounding mathematical. Fortunately, Bartók's renewing contemplation of the rhythmic and melodic forces of Hungarian music saved him from losing himself in home-less egalitarianism.

He has also withdrawn from other exaggerations of his Expressionist period, for he had even expressed the opinion in the cited article of 1920 that the halftones would suffice as an agent for some time. Bartók was at first convinced that everything had to be done differently than the ears of jaded concertgoers.

He wrote piano music where his notation needed four systems to accommodate all the virtuosity and sound drama. He broke the last bonds to the traditional major and minor by altering the chords simultaneously up and down; he layered keys on top of each other, for example, E flat minor in D minor. Above all, he broke the fetters of rhythm, which had become a minor matter in nineteenth-century Western European music. Through his knowledge of folk music, and especially the Bulgarian, with its very complicated tactical formations, his sense of the old musical idioms seemed to be sharpened.

Forces of the primordial rhythm

Bartók referred to the creations of Igor Stravinsky, his ballet music; "Petrushka" 1911, the "Rite of Spring" 1913, not least because of the primordial power of their explosive rhythms in theaters and concert halls. It cannot be a coincidence, but the time was ripe for the fact that in those same years, the rhythmic forces of American folk music in jazz also gathered storm in Europe. Bartók, for his part, also made a famous work, which at that time earned him the reputation of being a madman, the 'Allegro Barbaro' for piano, in 1911.

Like all music that was first declared significant, this piece has lost some of its terror. The tonal basis has become clear again, and its rhythmic originality has helped to speed up the purification process in the music of our century. But people were mistaken if they thought the composer of such a hard-hitting tune was a bearded professor. He had still preserved himself as the son of the beloved mother and as a young father his child's heart and soul.

When his first son was born to him, he immediately thought of children as composers. It may be regarded as a feature of our century that the highest-ranking musicians create an open mind for the issues of youth and children's music, whereas in the 19th century a composer such as Schumann was an exception in this respect. On the other hand, Bartók, Hindemith, and Orff have recognized the necessity of introducing the younger generation to the tonal language of the present.

In the folk song and children's song, Bartók saw the mediators for the awakening of the natural musical sense of youth in instrumental lessons as well. Therefore, he worked in the years 1908 and 1909 with the same care the 85 piano pieces "For Children," as he composed them as works for adults. Bártók used Hungarian and Slovak melodies as models. He placed it, mostly unchanged, in the right hand of the playing child, enriching his melodious treasure. The frugal lines and chords of the left hand are intended to awaken the feeling for the harmonic, melodic tensions. Gradually, the children are prepared for linear listening, which later enables them to grasp even large concert and opera compositions.

Kodaly has transferred this idea for instrumental instruction, developed by Bartók, into a singing method. His demands for a trustworthy and pedagogically based music instruction in the general education schools, which are repeatedly brought before the responsible state authorities, are precisely what Bartók intended to do to introduce the young people gradually do spiritual deeds within their culture.

Kodaly, too, liked to design modest little singing exercises for the children in addition to his vibrant orchestral compositions and piano works. Bartók, anticipated this and continued to fulfill his pedagogical task with great enthusiasm. In 1913, he contributed to the piano school of Reschofsky by writing "Eighteen Small, Easy Piano Pieces." Earlier, Johann Sebastian Bach's, "Piano Booklet", Wilhelm Friedemann Bach, and Leopold Mozart, are examples of books and composers who had written music books for children.

Bartók's composed nothing less in the course of the eleven years from 1926 to 1937 for his two brilliant children. He had written material for his second son Peter with 153 piano pieces in progressive difficulty. Under the title "Microcosmos," they take a place today in piano pedagogy comparable to Bach's "Well-tempered Piano." The great Thomaskantor said in his own words about the "eager to learn musical youth", with its inventions, symphonies, preludes, and fugues that they conveyed "a strong taste for composition."

Beyond the technique, the pedagogical intention of Bartók's piano pieces always was the full-blooded musician with the goal in the player, especially in youth, to awaken the primal powers of making music. But not only did the children need to be educated. The adults to whom Bartók's concert works were technically unattainable, were to be further educated with a renewal in Hungarian music. The wealth of works, with varying degrees of difficulty has contributed to this breakthrough in music. It is precisely their national depth, which has nothing at all to do with the color or 'smell' that some of the composers of earlier times have attributed to their creations, that makes Bartók's art worthwhile for the music lovers of other nations.

Works such as the "15 Hungarian peasant songs for piano", 1914-1917, the "Romanian folk dances from Hungary" or the "Romanian Christmas carols" for piano from 1915, and the Piano Suite op. 14, 1916 are the synthesis of folk song spirit and personal expression. "Three Rondos on Folk Tunes for Piano", various notebooks with Hungarian and Slovak folk songs for one voice with piano, mixed voices, Choir with male choirs, are still far from being known.

Often the composer solves the problem of folk music art by introducing them in a new way. Bartók's ability to transfer vocal melodies to the instrument and to express them through an entirely new kind of accompaniment and depth is almost unlimited. Structures such as the "Village Scenes," and five Slovak folk songs with piano, 1924, are prime examples of the simple ways that nature becomes the personal expression of the composer. With a folksy supporting accompaniment, these highly elaborate creations, and the tonality of the sung melodies have nothing at all left. In the full force of his creativity, the thirty-year-old composer understandably wanted to compose for the stage.

In 1911 he created the opera character "Herzog Bluebeard's Castle." In the years 1914-1917, the dance play "The Wooden Carved Prince," and at the end of the First World War, the one-act pantomime, "The Miraculous Mandarin." He had little success with his stage works as the lyrics for the first two works were from the 1886 Szeged-born poet and journalist Bela Balazs, whose staunch approach to the socialism of Bartók's creations after the collapse of the Hungarian Soviet Republic and during the endless fascination of the country was very obstructive. It is too bad that Bartók was associated with the poet Balazes, who later became a member of the revolutionary government of Bela Kun.

In the composer's compositions, and especially in the educational literature of those years, the great unity of national style and personal style emerged had gradually found the value of native folk music. To advance to a text that remains trapped in the sphere of the individualistic, psychoanalytic, if not of illness and moroseness, what would we give if Bartók had made the stage design of Hungarian culture? As Kodály did in his incidental music to a play about the humorous folk form of 'Hary Jänos', or the atmospheric singspiel "The Spinning Room" which draws on national customs?

Bluebeard's Castle, a stage play for only two persons, Bluebeard and Judith, is profound to the point of almost symbolic incomprehension. "Bartók endeavored to preserve the natural language in the recitatives and to follow the behavior of the folk song in the more stylized sections, thus paving the way for a new path," says Kodaly as a friend and admirer of the composer. He goes on to say, "Only stubborn spirits can still ask if the work is an opera or not. The same amount! One may call 'symphony in pictures' or' drama accompanied by a symphony '- it is certainly a masterpiece, a musical geyser of sixty minutes' duration, a work of tragic power that leaves only one wish - to hear it again ... ". In the concert halls of the world, he seemed to be playing alone, unromantic, and very simple. But it was difficult to hear him breathe in the rhythmically moving pieces. He sought the sonority, the simplicity of a rigorous dramatic style, even with Mozart. Beethoven was oppressive, Bach even more colorful and expressive, Debussy, on the other hand, less poetic, but warmer, livelier in expression, almost expressionist. He did not play Chopin with the traditional pathos, although his waltzes sounded "very hot and passionate", says Denijs Dille of Bartók when performing on the piano himself.

This description is supplemented by the words of Basler's conductor Paul Sacher about the master: "Bartók's accuracy was astonishing. He always carried a metronome with him and controlled the tempi, even if he played himself. His scores contain the performance duration in minutes and seconds for each movement, often for certain sections within the movement". He also wrote… "Those who met Bartók in the thought of the rhythmically primal power of his works were surprised by his slender, delicate figure. He had the outward appearance of a fine-nerved scholar. The man, possessed of fanatical will and relentless severity and driven by a burning heart, was aloof and reserved of courtesy. His being breathed light and brightness. His eyes shone with glorious fire. There was nothing untrue and unclear in the rays of his inquiring gaze. When, for instance, a particularly daring and difficult passage succeeded in making music, he laughed boyishly, and when he was pleased with the happy accomplishment of a task, he was beaming. That meant more than non-binding compliments that I never heard from his mouth."

As a concert pianist, he led his way through the cities of the world. In France, Germany, England, people listened to the music of the man who, like Liszt, rejoined to take the name of Hungary through the whole musical world. In 1927 he visited the Soviet Union, then followed several concert tours to North and South America. Newspapers, picture reporters, and writers made him known, though his whole being was in no way eager for applause, much less for provoking sensations.

The purity of his pursuit unlocked his affection best and an influential artist of his time. He was acquainted with Paul Hindemith, with whose endeavors he had many things more expressionistic; wild times and like him, went through a process of purification. Special friendship connected him with the Basel Chamber Orchestra, founded and directed by Paul Sacher, and Switzerland's political oasis became more of a resting place for him in the fateful 1930s, overshadowed by the dark clouds of fascism abhorred by Bartók.

Several of the most significant works of his last creative section had been written for Switzerland, including the "Music for Strings, Percussion and Celesta" to celebrate the tenth anniversary of the Basel Chamber Orchestra, 1937. Next came the "Sonata for Two Pianos and Percussion" for the 10th anniversary of the Basel section of the International Society for New Music, and again in 1940 for Paul Sacher, the "Divertimento for String Orchestra". Under the conductor Willem Mengelberg he played with the New York Philharmonic Orchestra his effective Rhapsody, op. 1.

From the early period of creation in Paris, he performed with the Orchestre Symphonique under Pierre Monteux. Wilhelm Furtwängler conducted the premiere of the First Piano Concerto in 1927 at the Music Festival in Frankfurt am Main, the soloist of which was the composer himself. In addition to the works of Stravinsky, Schönberg, Hindemith, Berg, and Milhaud, to name only the most contested names of that time, Bartók's compositions were the focus of attention.

The blades of criticism were crossed, however. One side was enchanted by the Hungarian musician's pathetic, sometimes powerfully storming, super natural, dreamy language of sound. Others, on the other hand, wanted to deny him any musicality. Even a subtle and otherwise benevolent critic from Berlin commented on the performance of one of his two violin sonatas that "whose title can only be understood ironically" meant that it is in "formality and harmony destroying novelty."

Bartók's only piano sonata from 1926, a work in which the composer gives the Sonata a new content and reveals himself as the student of the late Beethoven, was called in Vienna "an atonal orgy that has a shattering effect on its primitiveness also by virtue of the undisguised ethical confession which undoubtedly is inherent in this musical flagellants".

It was part of Bartók's nature that in the years of political and artistic reaction he and other composers of the new direction took solidary despite all that separates him, for example, he distinguished himself from Stravinsky's persiflage and style copying, from Hindemith's purely motor polyphony and from Schoenberg's or Berg's twelve-tone constructivism. When the Nazi propaganda ministry in Düsseldorf carried out an exhibition entitled "Art degenerate", Bartók protested ironically against the lack of his works. In the meantime, the Hungarian homeland had not been able to learn about Bartók's world successes. In 1923 he was commissioned to contribute a piece of work to celebrate the fiftieth anniversary of the merger of the two cities of Buda and Pest, being the provincial capital of Budapest. With the solemn overture "Psalus Hungaricus", by his childhood friend Dohnanyi and

Kodaly, and together with his "Dance Suite for Orchestra" they were premiered. This great work has its raison d'être (the reason for existence), and since that day it has proved so. In Germany alone, it has been programmed more than fifty times soon after its creation during a single year. Nevertheless, the official political circles of Hungary were not at all proud of their internationally recognized compatriot.

Dohnanyi had been presented with an honorary gift of 50,000 pengo on the occasion of his 50th birthday. In those years 1 pengo corresponded to about 75 pennies of German currency, though the decency fell as a gift to Bartók's equal. A festive day occurred in 1931 with the performance of the ballet "The Miraculous Mandarin." At the last moment, regrettably "into the water, as a dancer, who had just been fresh and cheerful, suddenly fell ill." The composer had not forgotten that he had rather renounced the performance of his other stage works than to admit that the name of his librettist, Bela Balasz, on the index of the "unwanted" writer, should be omitted from the program.

Finally, in 1936, he felt morally compelled to become a member of the Hungarian Academy of Sciences. He expressed his old devotion to Franz Liszt by dedicating his first Academy lecture to this pioneer of Hungarian music. However, inner peace was no longer granted to the finely sensitive and seismographic reacting artist, and journeys into the countryside or into the mountains brought hardly any real relaxation. Especially after the invasion of Austria by the National Socialist Wehrmacht (armed forces), Bartók became more aware of the dangers threatening the world.

In a letter of April 13, 1938, he speaks of the "imminent danger that Hungary will yield to this robbery and murder system." He is already thinking of emigrating, especially as even in Hungary the so-called "educated" are inclined towards fascism and he is ashamed to be of this class. Also, his financial situation had become threatening, after its Viennese, publishing house, the universal edition, as well as the Austrian society for performance rights to which he belonged, "Aryanized," and he, like Kodaly, persistently refused to fill in questionnaires about ethnicity and racial descent. It is quite bitter in the letter mentioned; "... one could make pleasant jokes when replying, e.g., ... we are non-Aryan - because after all (as I learn from my lexicon) "Aryan" means "Indo-European"; However, we Hungarians are Finno-Ugric, and perhaps even racially northern Turkic, that is, not at all Indo-European, hence non-Aryan..."

Only his aging mother kept Bartók in his Budapest home, which he had furnished with valuable folklore objects. Only her death released the last bonds to the homeland. Paul Sacher in Basel supported him in his emigration plans to the best of his ability. Bartók wrote to him from Geneva in the second year of the Second World War; "We have arrived here happily from the unfortunate lands, have received everything necessary from Mrs. Stefi Geyer, and will continue through the unhappy country tomorrow morning. Maybe we go into the unknown, but we cannot help it. How long? God knows. - Thank you and your wife for your friendship and for your all the beautiful things you have given us; I wish you the best for the future - yes, what can I wish you to do for your country to be protected from being trampled!"

The last masterpiece in exile

"In my youth, my ideal of beauty was not so much Bach's, Mozart's or Beethoven's." Bartók wrote in 1930 to show the formal connections of his works with the creative forces of the German classic. But amid the sounds of his second, expressionistic period, the Bach experience had come. This is a process that is quite similar to the German composer Paul Hindemith, and the creator of unbridled stage works of the kind like the one actress "Sancta Susanna", and the brash and cheeky piano suite, written in 1922. The composer of serious operas like; "Cardillac", "Mathis the Painter", and the heartfelt song cycle "Marien-leben". Also the present day "Singing and Playing Music for Lovers and Friends of Music." Bartók made a new amalgamation of the polymorphic principles of design, whereby Hindemith had to come to other conclusions than the German composer because of his sense of nationality.

A new balance found between the chromatic and diatonic, even after Bartók's early years when he thought it might be replaced by the quartertone system. He often felt the healthy and unexploited vitality of folk music based on pentatonic and diatonic music. This new style, his maturity, within this era, is breaking through in compositions created since the middle of the fourth decade of our century. First we witness this in his fifth string quartet written in 1934. It is dedicated to Mrs. Elizabeth Sprague-Coolidge.

In the years following the First World War, this wealthy American took on the tasks posed to artists in the Baroque period by princely patrons and patrons. Schoenberg, Stravinsky, Prokofiev, Bartók and other musicians who were then among the first in contemporary composers, but who were not usually blessed with fortunes and wrote on behalf of Mrs. Sprague-Coolidge, also performed music festivals on which the new compositions were set for discussion.

Bartók created a total of six string quartets; the first being already highly significant, written in 1908. This compositional style of chamber music occupied him as his most distinguished genre throughout his life. In the quartets, all the stages of his development can be followed, starting with the experimental period around 1910, until the refining of his late style with the 6th String Quartet This was written shortly before the outbreak of World War II. Friedrich Herzfeld quoted; "These six string quartets probably show us most directly the true nature of Bartók. It cannot be overlooked that they behave similarly at least with Paul Hindemith and Arnold Schoenberg. His string quartets, too, are the core works of his work ... For him, the compulsion to abstraction imposed by the playing of the four strings seems grateful for the compulsion to gather in the composing with the essential. It must be booked as a profit that our time has mustered so much power to 'pure music.' Maybe that's what you'll call the hallmark of the New Music of our time." The "Cantata Profana ", 1930, Bartók's only large choral work with an orchestra, must not remain unmentioned, as it is an important creation of the transition to his late style.

His "Music for Strings, Percussion, and Celesta," composed in 1936, is today one of Bartók's most performed works and is considered by many of his admirers to be his most famous composition. In Bartók's music, the elements of his native folklore, which have been refined to the last detail, are adorably combined with the polyphonic construction principles of the highest art music to form an inseparable unity. He refined this in his sound contrasts as the instrument groups increase for the listener's charm. Dance rhythms and contemplation of the whole world, and even reminiscences of the rhapsodic presentation of Gypsy Hungarian music sets the outer framework for the profound sensations Bartók expressed in this composition.

Of similar importance is the "Sonata for two pianos and percussion" written in 1937, whose nonbinding nature of sound compared to the string, harp and celesta lengths of the previous work set easy listening limits for the average concert audience. The drum part should be regarded as the inclusion of eastern music practice, although the actual Hungarian folk music is more determined by the melody and mostly leaves the drums aside. However, Bartók's knowledge of Turkish and Arabic music seems to have found expression here in a certain way.

Incidentally, the composer also transformed this work into a concerto for two pianos with orchestra. He played the sonata with his second wife, pianist Ditta Päsztory in 1938, which premiered in Basel, Switzerland. In 1939, the Hungarian violinist Zoltän Szekely surprised the musical world with premiere of Bartók's concerto with the Amsterdam Concertgebouw Orchestra under Willem Mengelberg, which was dedicated to Szekely. In addition to the concertos of Beethoven, Brahms, and Tchaikovsky, this creation stands today in the repertoire of every violin soloist of rank. As soon as the first, powerfully melody drawn from the solo instrument rises above throbbing harp chords, there can be no listener, who can't find meaningfulness in this piece of music.

In the oppressive time of uncertainty, the Divertimento for String Orchestra, Bartók's last major composition, was his last composed on the old continent. Bartók had been provided a country house in the Swiss mountains. The reassuring vastness of nature seems to have entered the Divertimento. According to the letter addressed to the oldest son left behind in Hungary, an engineer, the composer felt like a musician of the good old days in Hungary.

In the United States of America, the famous conductor Serge Koussevitzky and the Boston Symphony Orchestra commissioned the 1944 Concerto for Orchestra and, on order of the violinist Yehudi Menuhin, the Sonata for Solo violin. This is a voluminous and extremely complicated work, in which Bartók flows through all the technical arts of the virtuoso solo violin playing, exploited in the earlier styles by masters such as Biber and Bach, and later again by Reger and Hindemith, with the hot breath of his personality.

Bartók himself could no longer complete his last two great works. Loving hands of friends and disciples have had to help to shape them into the form that is used today in every concert hall in the world. This is true of the concerto for viola and orchestra completed by Tibor Serly after Bartók's sketches, which the British violist William Primrose had requested and premiered in 1949 after the death of the master. Also, the third Piano concerto, which the composer dedicated to his wife Ditta, and was able to complete except for the last seventeen bars, which were also finished by Tibor Serly. There exists a record given by Serge Moreux in his biography of Bartók, that Mrs. Ditta Bartók, his second son Peter, who had volunteered in the United States Navy. Tibor Serly and his wife had surrounded the dying master and handed him the score sheets of the third piano concerto.

He believes himself to be reminded of Mozart's last hours and his composition of the Requiem, which was later completed by his pupil Süßmayr. A kind of requiem, a legacy to posterity, has also become Bartók's third piano concerto. His middle movement, a wonderfully moving adagio religioso, marks the ultimate perfection of the master.

Béla Bartók had reluctantly left the old country, but just as Schoenberg, Milhaud, Hindemith or Toscanini, to name only a few, Bartók preferred to accept the uncertainty of the stranger rather than to put himself at the service of a corrupt political system. When he had gone to America again in the fall of 1939, he probably guessed that he would no longer see his native Hungary.

The United States now included in the World War wasn't good ground for a pure man who wanted to live entirely on art and without personal concessions. Bartók and his wife gave concerts, which were poorly attended. His composing lacked inner leisure and relaxation. It was not his thing to provide lessons to students who were not gifted. He also did not like the advances from publishers and patrons for works he might never be able to do or finish. This is how Bartók has lived through difficult years when diagnosed with the life-threatening illness of leukemia. In place of the villa-like house in Budapest, he had been taken to a city apartment in a New York skyscraper.

Particular bright spots in the last part of the life of the soon dead Master were concerts for art-loving people, such as Washington University students and Columbia University honors. He was invited there to give scientific lectures. Eventually, a New York college fulfilled the decency required by all European teaching and research institutions to appoint Bartók the "Honorary Doctor." title for his services to musicological folk art research.

Despite some happy summer weeks with his wife at the beautiful Tanglewood, Serank, the physical power of the composer disappeared incredibly fast. On September 26, 1945, he had his last breath in a New York hospital. Once again, one feels reminded of Mozart's end. He had not enough money for his funeral so that the Society for Author Rights had to bear the cost of burial. A modest plaque in the Ferncliff Cemetery in New York marks the final resting place of the great master. In the meantime, many changes had taken place in the Hungarian homeland.

The shackles of fascism had been blown up, but the Hungarian people had to struggle under a new occupier. In his absence, Bártók was elected a member of the National Assembly and was asked to return to Hungary. Death thwarted this plan; thus, the homeland had to content itself with honoring him through scientific publications, stamps with his portrait and plaques, and above all through the loving care of his works. A proud series of well-known composers continues Bartók's work and also takes national folk music as a driving force for their own artwork, in the same way, that Viennese classical music was founded based on the German folk song.

Today in Hungarian music schools there are pictures of the two great composers Belá Bartók and Zoltán Kodály, who have written an important chapter in world music history. At a memorial service in honor of his deceased friend, Kodály particularly admonished the growing generation, and to pay tribute to Bartók's legacy, "We have missed the never-to-be-missed historic opportunity to make direct contact with his genius, and the love that surrounded him which would make our life more livable. We remain in his debt. Today we cannot give him anything anymore. But today we owe it to our self to embrace Bartók's work and to create a better, happier life for ourselves".

Kurt Weil: Threepenny Opera

The Three Penny Opera deals with popular ideas not only as a vehicle to present them but also represents them. It is a kind of presentation about what the viewer wants to see in the theater of 'life.' However, the viewer sees at the same time some of what he does not want to see. Since one not only sees his wishes, but also criticizes them as well, he sees himself not as a subject, but as the object. This gives the theater a new way through innovation.

The Threepenny Opera is adapted from an 18th-century ballad opera called the "Beggars Opera" written by John Gay. It was premiered in 1728 and revived and revamped 200 years later in Berlin by the duo Brecht and Weil. The revival was premiered in 1928. The composer is Kurt Weil and the text of the play is by Bertoldt Brecht. Since the theater itself opposes reorganization, it is good if the spectator plays dramas that are not only intended to be performed in the theater but also to change it through the singing parts.

When the actor performs this new function and sings as well, nothing is stranger than when the actor pretends that he does not realize that he has just left the ground of sober speech and is performing. The three levels: sober speech, eloquent speech and singing, must always be kept separate from one another, and in no case does elevated speech mean an increase in sober speech, and singing is one of high-minded speech. For this purpose, Brecht uses the brash language of everyday life, through the words of the text in rehearsals; common text, profane types of poetry, and expressing something similar to the original intent.

As for the melody, Weil does not follow it blindly. There is speaking that is counter the music, and has a significant effect, emanating from stubborn sobriety, indifferent to music and rhythm, and is incorruptible. If another singer joined the melody, it must be an event to emphasize that the actors could reveal their own enjoyment of the melody. This epic drama set in a materialistic and mundane time exemplifies that there was little interest in the viewer's emotional investments of the characters.

The dynamic and ideologically directed (for example in the Elizabethan women), in all decisive points more radical than 200 years later in the German pseudo-classics. The dynamics of representation with the dynamics of the person in question have been confused and his individual already "ordered." The whole force of this drama comes from the gathering of resistance. Yet the desire for a cheap ideal formula does not determine the arrangement of the subject matter.

Here lives something of that Baconian materialism, and even the individual is reluctant to use the formula. Wherever materialism exists, epic forms emerge in drama. Today, where the human being must be understood as "the collection of all social relations," the epic form is the only one capable of grasping those processes, which serve a dramatic comprehensive worldview. Humans too can only be grasped from the processes in which they stand and through whom they stand. The new drama must methodologically accommodate the 'attempt' in its form. One must be able to use the contexts on all sides of the drama.

The Threepenny Opera gives a representation of bourgeois society (and not just "proletarian elements"). For its part, this bourgeois society has produced a materialistic world order, that is to say, a quite definite worldview without which it cannot manage. The emergence of the 'king's mounted messenger' is where the bourgeoisie sees its world represented, completely inescapable. The character Mr. Peachum, if he makes good use of society's bad conscience, will do nothing else.

Theatrical practitioners might wonder why nothing is more stupid than embezzling the horse of the mounted messenger. One sees how tactless it is to make the audience laugh at themselves by revealing the emergence of the riding messenger of serenity? Without the appearance of a messenger riding in any form, bourgeois literature would sink to a mere representation of conditions. The riding messenger guarantees a truly undisturbed enjoyment even of untenable states and is thus a sine qua non for a literature, whose condition sine qua non is the consequences.

Writing in 1929, Weill wrote "With the Threepenny Opera we reach a public which either did not know us at all or thought us incapable of captivating listeners [...] Opera was founded as an aristocratic form of art [...] If the framework of opera is unable to withstand the impact of the age, then this framework must be destroyed...In the Threepenny Opera, reconstruction was possible insofar as here we had a chance of starting from scratch."

Stephen Hinton a noted Weill expert wrote "generic ambiguity is a key to the work's enduring success", and points out the work's deliberate hybrid status: "For Weill [The Threepenny Opera] was not just 'the most consistent reaction to [Richard] Wagner'; it also marked a positive step towards an operatic reform. By explicitly and implicitly shunning the more earnest traditions of the opera house, Weill created a mixed form that incorporated spoken theatre and popular musical idioms. Parody of operatic convention – of romantic lyricism and happy endings – constitutes a central device.

History of Brecht's 'Threepenny Opera" performance

Bertolt Brecht wrote his "Threepenny Opera" lyrics after John Gay's "Beggar's Opera." The John Gay opera had its premiere in 1728. Two hundred years later, in 1928, it was reworked by Kurt Weil and Bertolt

Brecht. The original was the most successful English play of the eighteenth century, and it promised to be the most successful of the twentieth century. And contrary to the critic's prognoses; the two theater directors, John Rich at Gay, Ernst Josef Aufricht at Brecht, feared scandals. The "Threepenny Opera" turned out to be an attraction, with all the real consequences.

Encouraged by the success of the 'Beggar's Opera,' Gay wrote a second part of "Polly," and after, this was forbidden by censorship. The character "Polly" falls quickly in love with London's greatest and most notorious criminal. The "Threepenny Opera" brought Brecht a film deal. He modernized the material, sharpened the satire, and hoped for a successful scenario. The film company rejected it. Yet both times he tricked the censorship. John Gay was not allowed to perform his "Polly", but he did print out the textbook, so his play spread through reading. Bertolt Brecht could not realize his Threepenny Film, but he did a 'sociological experiment'. He sued the film company, lost the case, and proved that the exploiters society, film industry, and the judiciary were corrupt. Even John Gay also criticized the corruption.

John Gay belongs with Alexander Pope and Jonathan Swift to the most famous English moralists and satirists of the 18th century. His ascent was steep but troublesome; he was orphaned early, came to London as a merchant's apprentice, then became Courtmaster Duke, wrote Parallels of Parallels, and approached the party of the Tories. Then as one of their opponents, the Whigs Government came, renounced a brilliant court career, and one offered him only a post as chamberlain of the two-year princess, which struck him as an indignant insult.

Surely the 'Beggar's Opera' was stimulated by the degrading court offer, but not only. The idea was already as old as Swift had suggested, for in 1716 that Gay was writing a pastoral of prostitutes and thieves. A decade later, Gay took up the plan, but the pastoral story became an opera. When the play was made, Gay was staying with Pope in Twickenham. He also visited Swift and the trifecta of the most famous English satirists was complete. This was also the reason for the later suspicion that Gay was not the sole author of the "Beggar's Opera," and that the social critical passages came in particular from Pope and Swift. Pope himself refuted that Gay had indeed shown them the designs, they had also discussed it, here and there and proposed changes, but not lend their own ideas.

Gay was also accused of plagiarism, for no good reason as he stole his play from Christopher Bullock, and then from John Marston. But all targeted intrigues missed their target. The 'Beggar's Opera' had been premiered in London's Premier Theater with sixty-one repeats in the first season and spread rapidly in England, Ireland and America. The European mainland, however, could not be conquered. The reasons for this were the intolerance of the French and German censorship authorities, the difficulty of illuminating the many local allusions, and the incomprehensible to the foreigner.

Although French and German translations were printed it did not appear on stage. In the English speaking world, the "Beggar's Opera" was always in the repertoire. Although the curve of success declined in the 19th century, it rose in 1920, when Frederic Austin and Arnold Bennett presented their new work to the Londoners. The Hammersmith Lyric Theater had included it in its repertoire for years to come and it became a theatrical sensation beyond comparison.

In Germany, they became aware of its success, but the old difficulty arose; the strong local culture restricted the effect it had abroad. The German adaptation, which, based on the Hammersmith version, appeared in 1928, and failed. Only the adaptation of Bertolt Brecht and Kurt Weill, premiered in the same year, helped the "Beggar's Opera" which is now called the "Threepenny Opera," to triumph in Germany, and soon went across the borders.

Brecht got to know the "Beggar's Opera" through Elisabeth Hauptmann, his colleague. She did a translation what Brecht had edited, and evaluated it creatively; for he not only deleted or supplemented, he introduced new motives for action and changed characters. Above all, he criticized, from the perspective of another century, armed with Marxist knowledge, the bourgeoisie more precisely and sharply.

The original title was intended to be preserved, and was already on posters. Just before the premiere Brecht changed it to the suggestion of Lion Feuchtwanger, the "Threepenny Opera." Ernst Josef Aufricht, a daring young theater director, opened the Berlin Theater, which he rented on August 28, 1928, with the "Threepenny Opera." Stormy weeks of rehearsals preceded them; various actors dropped out, others did not fit their role or the piece, they announced special requests, the general rehearsal lasted until the morning of the first day and the theatrical gossip produced wild rumors. The theater director Aufricht was already looking at bankruptcy and he was desperately looking for a 'rescue anchor', a new play, but the premiere was, to the astonishment of those involved a success.

Yet another parallel exists between the work of John Gay and the Bertolt Brecht. The "Beggar's Opera" established a new dramatic genre; that of the "Ballad Opera." They used the newly found resources to portray the society of their time in repugnant but instructive carica- tures. The "Three Penny Opera" also resulted in a type of theater with historical consequences, with their beginnings as a new way on stage to the epic theater. Brecht coordinates from the action and narrative, the dramatic level as opposed to the reflexive. It developed a new type of drama, which was soon imitated. The "Threepenny Opera" moves the action of the "Beggar Opera" into the Victorian era.

This proved to be the desired alienation effect, current problems should, historically disguised, curious examines and ultimately better be recognized as beneficial. Brecht said, "There are some things to know about the Victorian era, but at the same time it is remote enough to judge critically by a long way, so that viewers can easily find out what they are looking for. From this time the piece was easier to transport to Berlin than from the time in which it has put John Gay. "

In the "Threepenny Opera," Brecht shows relatively old- fashioned forms of capitalist business conduct. The forms have changed and their content has remained. By comparing the robbers of the past with those of today, one becomes aware that they are not so different from each other. One can recognizes the essence of the modern, often mysterious capitalist tricks more precisely, if one sees their archetype, the naked crime. The "Threepenny Opera" deals with this concern with discrediting the modern exploitive society that is unlike the "Threepenny Novel", yet no less effective.

Brecht brings a new, paradoxically, but just as true-life final version. Peachum gets ready to mobilize the masses to enforce his demands, but he gets scared of his own courage, rightly; for the anger of the masses could overshoot the intended goal. It could be dangerous to the prevailing corporate order, and could thus also be directed against the one who kindled it. When the bosses agree to throw an innocent, and not the criminal 'under the bus' so to speak, law and order would be shaken. In the "Beggar's Opera", the author formulates the doctrine the beggar wanted to convey: "In the whole piece you can see how the manners of the higher and the lower classes are so completely the same, that it is difficult to decide whether the nobles, in their crimes, imitate the gentlemen of the street, or conversely, the gentlemen of the street the noble gentlemen."

The play's original intent contained a most instructive morality. It would have shown that the poor have the same vices as the rich, yet the poor are punished for it. That means that the distinguished gentlemen are robbers, but that they have privileges, their possessions - which they possess, and protect against punishment. So the question of the legitimacy of privileges is provoked. Thus, ultimately, the injustice of the dominant social system is unmasked. The criminal milieu is therefore not an end in itself but a means of satire. Nevertheless, it is a historically guarantee as London was an underworld 'nest' for John Gay's time.

Jonathan Wild (real criminal in old London) was robbing and murdering according to modern business methods, a rationalizer of crime and at the same time an informer in the police service. It was easy to see he was the inspiration of Jonathan Peachum. To show the double meaning, Brecht said about the "basic idea" of the "Threepenny Opera": "Beggars are poor people. They want to do a grand opera, but they do not have any money and they do it their way. How do you show that? With the help of a sumptuous entertaining performance (which, however, must reveal the circumstances and circumstances of the time) and at the same time, by showing the efforts which do not lead to the intended goal, but often turn into the opposite. For example, beggar actors do not succeed in portraying the respectability (for whose depiction the Victorian era is particularly favorable); instead, there is a constant derailment, especially in the songs. Great aspirations fail and suddenly everything becomes tedious. "

The London beggars frequently appeared as street singers during John Gay's time. They offered 'ballads'; old English folk tunes, under laid with new, often politically colored text. Such parodying, still common in cabaret today, ensures the popularity of text and melody. The "Beggar's Opera" takes the form of the parody ballad into drama. The piece is interspersed with sixty-nine songs, in which new lyrics are imparted in the manner described as 'borrowed music.' Special fun often results from the disparagement of the old words compared to new ones. The original text, so to speak, forms the sub text, and one draws comparisons with it, thus fulfilling the commentary function. Often a comparison is provoked by the fact that certain phrases of the original text recur literally. Remembering the identity of a beggar and a ballad singer, the "Beggar's Opera" could also have been titled the "Ballad Singer."

It was not fundamentally new in form. The vaudeville comedies of the Parisian carnival theaters mixed the 'hits,' re-edited to fit the action of the drama. John Gay got to know such plays while traveling to France, and he was also able to see them in guest appearances, as in the Comedie Italienne (which had created the vaudeville drama) in London. He was also able to build on national traditions. The so-called "jigs," that flourished in the 16th century were vocal spoirs (vocal ancestry) based on parody. The "Rehearsal" (1671) of the Duke of Buckingham, modeled for many burlesques of the Restoration Period, seems to be a later jig descendant, because it contains several ballads (which reinforce satire, as in the "Beggar's Opera").

In the beginning of the 18th century, the burlesque was evolving in London, with a growing number of ballads. It is suggested that John Gay created the new English genus type of vaudeville and burlesque. Ballad operas became fashionable, and inspired by the mainland, they returned to the mainland, rooted in the German Singspiel. The ballad operas, as well as the vaudeville comedies, are national, even local. Their popularity is based on familiarity with the music, and the many allusions to the "subtext" can only be understood if one knows it. For this reason, the first German editor of the "Beggar's Opera" has partly transferred the ballads very freely, sometimes even with new ones. The "Threepenny Opera" neither quotes textually nor, with one exception, musically the old "arias." It also renounces the parody procedure; the music is not edited, but newly composed.

According to Brecht, the "Threepenny Opera" brought a "first use of stage music to newer aspects." When the actor sings, they perform a change of function, where they step out of action and turns directly to the audience. No more persona dramatis, if he no longer needs to convey their views, he can become the direct mouthpiece of the author. In the first three-penny finale, the Peachums complain that social conditions are inhumane and prevent them from falling out of their role.

They formulate a knowledge that exceeds their consciousness. Moreover, they would never utter cognition, but would rather behave hypocritically; because they live in adverse conditions. The cognition comes from the author, but it is incomplete, and the viewer has to add it. If the prevailing social conditions do not allow kindness, they must be changed. In the Salomo song, a Moritat, recited with a hurdy-gurdy music box in front of the curtain, Jenny shows examples that virtues such as wisdom, audacity, and thirst for knowledge lead to destruction, so she concludes: "Envies, who is free of it!" Here she becomes the medium of the author, submits his teaching, but is cleverly concealed.

By offering the public an obviously false morality, the author suggests that he thinks about perverting the concept of virtue. Not to renounce virtue helps, but to create conditions that do not punish virtue, yet reward it. Also in relation to the commentary function of the songs, parallels between "Beggar's Opera" and "Threepenny Opera" are conveyed. John Gay's "Arias" may also be quite casually deduced from the plot they nevertheless form foreign bodies in the sense of Aristotelian dramaturgy. Well-known melodies, and new words with allusions to the 'subtext'; that is, the audience cannot empathize that it must draw it's comparisons, criticisms, and determine the lessons. In short, they must participate as an independent partner.

About Weill's music

The commentary function of the ballads is corroborated by the fact that the rewriting often causes a caricature disfigurement. The rewriting of the musical parody combines with the comically critical musical parody. The social criticism of the "Beggar's Opera" includes art criticism.

The main theme of the polemic is Italian opera. Since at the beginning of the eighteenth century, native to London, critics had already challenged many attacks on the national-minded bourgeoisie. The attacks were partly essayistic, partly in an artistic form: as an opera parody. It may have already been suggested by the French, as a role model in the form as opera.

Parodies included both the repertoire of the Comedie Italie and that of the Parisian theater. The "Beggars Opera" was not the first English opera parody, but the most effective one. The Royal Academy of Music and the nursery of Italian operas had to close for a year due to the sharp, blasphemous competition.

What becomes parodied is the result of the conversation between beggar (author) and actor, the scandalous, open-ended dispute between two rival prima donnas, the far-fetched, often discordant metaphor of the texts of the Aria, and the obligatory, though highly unlikely, happy ending where the established criminal receives a pardon from the Queen of England. Also the taunting of Gay against Handel, the head of the Opera Academy, he quotes a march from his "Rinaldo," but at the same time transports him and gives him a new function; if a heroic army moves past his commanding officer in Handel's case, the gang of criminals in front of their chief goes by too.

Already in the title "Beggar's Opera" lays a parody: he promises an opera, with arias and recitatives, but is offered a criminal piece, with ordinary, choking speech dialogue. Of the sixty-nine songs, the majority are English, Scottish, and Irish ballads, which can be found in collections in Zeiss; but also quotes borrowed from Purcell, Barret, Clarke, Carey, Bononcini and others. Johann Christoph Pepusch, the musical collaborator, composed the overture and arranged the songs.

That he, a German, determined their choice seems unlikely; for that required accurate knowledge of the ballad repertoire. Moreover, only the poet could find out about their dramaturgical usefulness. The music of the "Threepenny Opera" came into being in close contact with Brecht and Weill. Certainly, it also contains many ideas of Brecht. Weill took his suggestions and they often went down to its musical details very accurately.

From the "Beggar's opera," only one way has been taken over by Peachums morning chorale. Opera parody only offers the beginning and the end. But parody was not neglected, it chooses other objects; popular music in operetta, jazz, & hits. The musical style was subordinated to the content refreshing itself. Brecht writes: "The music thus worked on the revelation of bourgeois ideologies, just by being purely emotional and without giving up the usual narcotic stimuli. It became, as it were, aroused, provocator, and penunciator."

In the beginning, the three beggars complain of the poverty of the world and the wickedness of the people, but to operatic music of carefree merriment. The discrepancy between word and sound points to the (ideologically calculated) whitewashing of the operetta: the freshness is only make-up. Digestible music makes itself questionable by criticizing itself. It dislikes the tastiest gestures of popular music and, as it were, elevates it to the point of being oversized, thus revealing its whole hollowness: the sweet: is denounced as sweetish, the sentimental as sentimental, the cheerful as silly.

Means of criticism is not only the exaggerated, self-devaluating expression but also the 'last word.' Interspersed with obvious "mistakes," it undermines the pretended security. There are sounds, delicately tainted by a tiny dissonance, a discord, not a color value. Courses of harmony that do not unfold logically (one from the other) but diverged, poorly cemented and string together. Melodies, made out of simple phrases, collecting quotations, at the rubbish bank of music history. The whole defectiveness is highly artfully disposition, and thereby, in an aesthetic sense, is eliminated. Yes, it only lends music its artistic value: banal popular music is not merely imitated, and criticized, its banality is shown, in musical and artistic creation.

Fashionable mingles with long stale ones: jazz and bar songs, shimmy and waltz. The anachronisms point to the transience of fashion, including the present. Yes, they even call present day fashions obsolete. In fact, fashionable popular music, even if it is up to date, is not a valid time mirror; they beautify, transfigure, whether in 1728, 1928 or 2028, their styles may change, their lying content remains the same.

(Strawinski, 1920s parodist of popular music, here Weill's role model, achieves a similar effect when he uses the cimbalom in his "Ragtime for Eleven Instruments." Gypsy chapel jazz props: a break in style, but of profound importance is fashionable and outdated. Thus, the modernity reveals itself as a mere fake.)

The overture strives for dignity, but it remains at the stake; the desired nobility fails and makes a clumsy pose. The ideas, baroque items, are soon being used up: no spinning out new motifs, but continuous sequencing. Even the schoolmasterly fugue as form frozen to a formula.

Like an orchestra, a jazz band becomes a stunning baroque style and time fashioned song meets each other, devaluing each other. The "jealousy duet" - Polly and Lucy quarrel over Macheath, and are caricatures within the silliness of operetta music. The fullness of form, yet entirely unspiritual, unrelated, and contain no development, but mere assembly; chatty with alternating chant, pressed in stubborn rhythmic patterns, partly rousing, sometimes tenderly teasing, and always worn out motifs; Kitsch.

The "love song" between Polly and MacHeath: salon music from great-grandfather's time. As if an oath of loyalty, immersed in thick sentimentality, candied saccharin sweet. He begins with a romantic vocabulary: "Do you see the moon over Soho?" He then loses his tonal orientation. The inability of musical dressmakers to beat far sweeping melodic arches, develop the harmony dynamically and at the same time logically, here it is purposely calculated. The parody reveals musical ignorance.

Musical brutality reflects human brutality: a cynical hymn to the slaughtering colonial soldiers, but one that must repel. The Mack-the-Knife song, composed only during the rehearsals, has the character of amorality. Seven repetitions of an elementary motif formula, always rhythmically identical, only intervallic variant: Simplicity combined with refinement that is mastery. The result is a melody that bore itself into memory. It is repeated eight times in the manner of a stanza song, with the barrel organ playing.

Again, Weill achieves the deepest effects with the simplest means. He preserves the monotony, and yet he enhances the form, through tonal development and imitations, through countervailing and sound paintings. (The whole skill of the accompaniment only becomes fully aware when the song, which became a world hit, is heard in modern arrangements that preserve the melody but change its garb, leaving out the ancient style that led to the escape of art.)

Brecht has emphasized that the music of the "Threepenny Opera" serves social critique. "The romantic songs," he says, "should be sung as nicely as possible, but the false nature of this attempt at a romantic island, in which everything is still correct, must be particularly supported." The singers must therefore not blindly entrust themselves to the content of the songs, identify themselves with them or they should rather criticize them. It does not depend on bel canto, but on the elucidation of the underlying meaning. The music only reflects sentiment, cheerfulness, and beauty, for music wants to cover despair, constancy, and meaningless with calculated callousness. The poverty is calculated and the resulting dizziness is revealed. The exposure continues on bourgeois ideology, which takes precedence over materialistic reality. The equation that Brecht set up therefore dissolves and the bourgeois is a robber. Perhaps the conclusion is that there is no way to stop this ending.

Marlene Dietrich: Chanson

Marlene Dietrich is a singer with a distinct world sound, inscribed in film and chanson music history from our last century. The list of her films includes half a hundred titles; the directory of their songs and chansons, without searching for completeness, three times as many titles. For more than forty years, Marlene Dietrich, apart from the few years on the stage of the theater and the revue in Berlin and Vienna, was almost exclusively on the screen. For the last two decades of her artistic career, she presented herself to her audiences live on stage with songs and chansons, many of which have long been world-hits or have become new through her.

Cheered from Paris to Moscow, from London to Warsaw, Las Vegas to Monte Carlo, Rio de Janeiro to Tokyo and Sidney, Marlene Dietrich was able to renew her world fame, which had once begun with the film the "Blue Angel" in her native Berlin. The artist, born in the theater city of Berlin, with her American passport and residence in Paris, gained international fame and sang to the understanding of peoples and nations at a time when the wind of the Cold War blew icily. The names of those who have described and praised Marlene's personality and artistic fascination are grand and sonorous: Ernest Hemingway, Jean Cocteau, Noël Coward, Erich Maria Remarque, Maurice Chevalier, Alfred Hitchcock and Elisabeth Bergner, Margo Lion and Hildegard Knef and others who were on stage with her. Marlene's colleagues who worked with her in film also wrote or re-wrote songs for her.

Marlene Dietrich's way to becoming a chanson singer was via musical training as a concert violinist in Weimar and Berlin, and had acting training based on the principles of the Max Reinhardt School, through revue and drama to film; in 1953 to the one-woman show as Entertainer in dress and cylinder, with dance girls and chansons on the stages of great music halls and variety theater of world renown.

Marlene Dietrich had grown up on the musical soil of Berlin, her love for pop and chanson had received early sustenance, and she sang in three world languages: German, English and French. Her commitment to the humanist, unifying role of her Art gave her the reputation of one of the greats chansons artists.

With the melodies from the "Blue Angel" in 1930, Marlene Dietrich inaugurated the era of film audiences, which replaced the chanson of literary cabaret in Germany and more than hitherto gave folk music to pop music. With the song of Friedrich Hollaender "I am set to love from head to toe," she had given the world a hit song and form, so uniquely perfected, that from then on the world equated Marlene Dietrich with Lola. Life with your own legend became her destiny.

Friederich Hollaender was a music composer for film and theater. German but born in London moved to Berlin in 1899 where he started to write music for Max Reinhardt productions. His breakthrough happened when he wrote the film music for the 'Blue Angel' (1930) which contained the song "Falling in Love Again (Can't help it)" sung by Marlene Dietrich. His path was very similar to Marlene's, moving to Paris and then to Hollywood for similar reasons.

Hollaender composed much of the film music and songs that projects Marlene was involved in. Marlene Dietrich carried it with the grandeur of the Hollywood star and the humor of the Berliner. Her repertoire included over 160 songs, hits and chansons. Traditions of the Music Hall, the Song, the Chansons d'amour, the Popular films, and the Berliner Berlin's Cabaret have flowed into their art and vocal style. The international fame of Dietrich is based on the fact that she sang her songs in several languages and was not satisfied with her traditional film hits. Her repertoire also included children's songs, German folk songs, American folklore, Brecht-Weill songs, songs from Gilbert Becaud's repertoire, Edith Piaf's, Jacques Brel's, Charles Trenet's, anti-war songs, Cole-Porter songs, and musicals: models as well as Old Berlin songs of the Jean-Gilbert and Walter-Kollo period.

When Marlene Dietrich stopped filming as her main job, she took the song of love, the song of all her songs, out of the scenes of the film and put it into real life. This added a new dimension and added qualities to it that made it stable over the changing daily fashions. She has thus become the creator of a new song genre: the Marlene Dietrich chanson, for which there is no definition of music history or literary science.

The style of her concert tours to all five continents of the world has been shaped by such great world hits as "Honeysuckle Rose", "La Vie en Rose", "Lili Marleen", "Moon River", Candles Glowing, "I've Grown Accustomed to Her Face" and "Tell me where the flowers are". There were many tunes that belonged to her alone, such as "I'm set to love from head to toe," "I'm the smart Lola," "Beware of blond Fraumy, "Alone in a big city ", "If I wish for something "," The Boys in the Backroom" or "I do not know to whom I belong". Even today some voices attach more importance to the monologist Marlene Dietrich than the actress and argue that her film fame is already outshone by her stardom as a singing actress. Film actress Dietrich has not been a competitor to singing show star Dietrich. People will always like to watch their old films while there is cinema and television, and they will also like to hear their songs from records, just because you cannot listen to them all in the movies and because you know that her way to the chanson would never have been possible without her films.

So far, it has always been the same story when an article appeared in the newspapers and magazines on Marlene Dietrich's birthday. Letters were sent to the editors saying that the year of birth was wrong. Readers referred to the information in their lexicon, which mentioned a different date than the newspaper and wanted to know what was right. If several encyclopedias were on hand, several years might have come up, and this jumble, strange as it is, has the public, claiming to know everything about its stars, but also everything in detail deranged.

A gallant and courageous journalist once responded to one such letter when they became too much for him that such a beautiful and eternally young woman as Marlene Dietrich did not need to engage in such a trivial debate for a ridiculous three years. This attitude was absolutely in the spirit of Marlene Dietrich, who is said to have blamed the "bad habit" of recounting her years: "Do not my friends have anything more valuable to count than my years?" In the meantime, the parties have come to an agreement. On the part of Marlene Dietrich, December 27, 1904, is the sole date of her birth. That's how the authorities get it, it's in their passport, and everything else is wrong, she says. For the rest of the world, however, it is December 27, 1901, evidenced by the birth certificate, which was rediscovered at the beginning of the sixties.

It was in the German town of Schöneberg in the winter time, when the light of this world illuminated little Marie Magdalena for the first time and thought that she was a very pretty child. The little Dietrich was born in Sedan Street No. 53, today's Liver Street. Her father was the Prussian police officer Louis Dietrich, her mother Josephine, born Felsing, the daughter of Conrad Felsing, owner of the renowned watch and jeweler shop Felsing, Unter den Linden 20.

Marlene Dietrich grew up under conditions that are considered bourgeois, by which the reader can understand certain prosperity and material independence of the parental home. The family of the Dietrich's included businessmen, civil servants, and officers with maids, cooks, and coachmen in the house. This meant for in those days a proper education of children, obligatory school attendance with private teachers for individual subjects, and the ability to pay a governess. This also meant enough to finance the professional career of the sons and to raise a reasonable dowry for the daughters. Incidentally, Marlene was not the only child of the officer family Dietrich. She had a sister, Elisabeth, who was almost two years older, who later became a teacher.

The two girls were brought up together and lived until shortly before Marlene's marriage. Marlene Dietrich lost her father very early, resulting in financial difficulties for her mother and her two children. Her mother then took a position as a housekeeper with the family of Losch, where she met her second husband Eduard von Losch, who adopted the two girls and thus became Marlene's stepfather. Many publications on Marlene Dietrich mention the "Prussian officer's daughter Maria Magdalena von Losch," while repeatedly stressing that Marlene Dietrich is her "real name."

She cannot tell you anything about her early childhood. Her memory does not begin until school, so that part of her life remains in the dark. One only knows that her father was once transferred to Weimar as an officer for a short time and that the entire family was there for the duration of the transfer. That was before Marlene started school. The conscious encounter with the city of Goethe, the work and the intellectual world of this poet, which had a lasting influence on her upbringing and her attitude towards life, came only in later years.

Weimar was to play a role in her vocational training as a concert violinist after graduating from school. Then, she was still the child of Sedans Street, playing with marbles, walking in the hand of her governess, loved by her family and cared for, while strictly trained. As an officer's child, she was probably relocating often and used to changing garrisons. As Franz Hessel writes, "always at home in the city of sober bright day colors and long twilights, the tender winter blues and long summer evenings that nobody forgets who wanders around Berlin."

Her birthplace, Schöneberg, which had become a city just before 1900, and had grown together with Berlin in its streets, had its prince. Heinrich-Gymnasium (high school), his Kaiser-Friedrich-Strasse (street), and Emperor Wilhelm I, cast in bronze in front of the town hall. Not far from the Sedan Street, where incidentally the actress and Marlene's friend Hildegard Knef spent their childhood, was the city boundary to the east, a military station and a shooting range. In 1900,

Berlin Under the Linden Street, was the watch shop of grandfather Conrad Felsing.

One house further, No. 21, opened the first permanent cinema theater in Berlin in 1905: "Meßters Biophon" The few civilian additions to the villas and streets in the founding style of Schöneberg at the turn of the century were the Old Botanical Garden and the Matthew Church, where important men of the arts and sciences were buried, among them the Brothers Grimm.

From her parents, Marlene got solid, Prussian virtues such as thoroughness, perseverance, a sense of duty and of justice. When she was living in Hollywood, she was often admired for her self-discipline and perseverance. For her environment, she was generally "the Prussian," the proverbial German housewife who cooked and scrubbed with enthusiasm, a pattern of thoroughness and solidity. These features were also noted by Charles Higham, who became acquainted with her: "If one observes Marlene Dietrich in action, she gives the impression of north German straightforwardness: cool intellect, precision, discretion, and an iron discipline that does not tolerate distraction, and as a counterweight a very sensitive, self-critical and never entirely satisfied personality."

Remarkable for the reader of her memoirs is the fact that she associates nothing more with her father than the memory of "a great imposing figure, leathery odor, shiny boots, riding, and his horses," while her mother, an absolute reverence for her, is brought out of the memory with love. "Her appearance was as perfect as her features. Her mind, her heart was noble. She was like a good general. She followed her own rules; she was the example we needed." The mother does not appear only as a beautiful woman, but also as an intelligent woman who was educated, strict in this respect.

She sent her youngest daughter to school at the age of six. It was the girls' school in Nürnberger Street. The principal was an elderly lady, presiding in a sumptuously furnished salon, and above the fireplace was the portrait of Empress Auguste Victoria, after whom the school had been named. Marlene Dietrich also remembers the heavy iron gate, only opened if one pushed hard against it with your back. As you know, these old schools did not have much friendliness. They were more akin to barracks in their sober atmosphere, designed to keep their imagination and their dreams short.

Her guardian angel at this school was her French teacher, revered and loved by her. Because little Dietrich was younger than the others in the class, she felt excluded from the girls and their confidences. That was the reason for her sadness. Breguand, that was the name of the teacher could give her the joy of school because she took the frightened girl's sorrow seriously. "She frightened my loneliness, my childish worries, my sadness. It was desire and fulfillment. I spent every morning figuring out what to give her: blue, white, red ribbons that my mother had worn in her hair at the German-French ball; French landscapes, cut out of magazines and put away by my mother, a bouquet of May bells on the May 1st or I tied together a cornflower, a daisy, and a poppy and sent it for National Day on July 14th. I bought French Christmas and New Year cards and dreamed of French perfume for them. But my mother said that such expensive gifts would embarrass Mlle. Breguand."

The French Miss waited with her outside the school when the governess was late and sometimes went with them for a while. "On the last school day before the holidays, she never forgot to give me her address, which she had written on one side of her notebook. It was clear: She knew my shy hopes and the cure for all my pain." This is how Marlene Dietrich describes in her memoirs her affectionate and child-like relationship with the French teacher. She had found in her a clever person to cling to in her school days.

Marlene's progress in French was also an incentive, especially since she already had a good command of the language thanks to her mother, and so she felt the teacher's affection as an added distinction. The bond of this love was torn abruptly when World War I broke out. In those days Marlene saw the retreating regiments, flags hanging from the windows, military music playing, and she did not understand it: flowers on rifles for a war against her beloved France! Your teacher no longer at school! This loss has given the thirteen year old the first deep pain of her life. Only her feelings, which told her what was right and wrong, gave her security. "I loved Marguerite Breguand and loved France. I loved the French language. I was the first one robbed! The first victim! Nobody could force me to go to war with France."

"The children now have to knit socks, wrist warmers, and sweaters at school, which is a patriotic duty. Anyone who uses French words, the language of the enemy, must pay ten pfennigs to the school collection box as a punishment. Marlene pays the ten pennies despite all this.

Marlene Dietrich loved the Berlin of her childhood and adolescent years, and always kept a grateful memory of it. Here she heard and learned the songs of her childhood, the old Berlin hits, which became favorite songs for her. On her long-playing records, more than forty years later, she sings of what she meant by these street songs of art: memory, joy, and yearning for childhood. That was in Schöneberg in May.

A little girl was also there that often and gladly kissed the boys, as is so common in Schöneberg. These recordings of Old Berlin songs, which she made in the sixties, she described in 1983 to the actor and director Maximilian Schell as her best records. The songs of her youth deeply influenced her. She preserved the sound of these melodies, which allowed her to find a lovingly personal artistic interpretation of this experiential world. The fact that this musicality developed owes not least to those favorable living conditions under which she grew up. In her autobiography, she says briefly in a nutshell in Berlin: "My family had money, and I got the best education."

As her musical talent showed up early on, she was supposed to embark on her musical career and become a concert violinist at the request of her mother. This professional goal was served very early by private music lessons in violin and piano, which ran alongside the school. That meant a lot of practice, usually under the supervision of the mother, who herself played the piano very well. The works consisted of Mozart, Bach, Beethoven, and Chopin; sonatas, études, waltzes. Practicing for lessons and during family music evenings, and when any leisure time was left, it belonged to books and poetry.

It was they who aroused her the love for the German language and the longing for great feelings, romance and worship. Together with her mother and sister, she proclaimed poems by Goethe and the classic ballads, read the books of Dostoyevsky and Knut Hamsun. Although she also worshiped stage stars like the Duse, whose picture she had set up in her room with a candle, there is nothing to be said about her passion for theater, the urge for limelight and fame.

She seems to have been more dreamy than coquettish, said Franz Hessel, at least she has not consciously perceived or even play out the abilities that lie dormant in her mind. A classmate even described her as nervous and insecure. "Marlene was the shyest girl in our school, nothing seemed fun to her." She'd liked to sit on the benches, was always nice and friendly, and had the girls copy her French essay homework. The impression remains that she did not want to be better, although it was clear that she was something special.

What was unique about her can be seen in the photo of her class, where placed in the foreground, she attracts the eye of the beholder. She sits in a relaxed, restful posture, straight as a candle, photographically aware of her gaze on the apparatus, which seems to have a deep meaning for her. The big butterfly loop in her lush, beautiful hair creates a background and completes the picture; a phenomenon that fills space in every view of her.

On her own, Marlene Dietrich gives a very understated description: "I was skinny and pale as a child, my hair was reddish-blond. This reddish-blond hair gave me a white complexion, a transparent skin that is peculiar to the red-blond. I looked pretty ill. " As serious as the training in music, the children were led to other sides of popular bourgeois culture. "I grew up with Goethe, he taught me everything I know." This is a sentence she continually repeats. From her parents, especially her mother, Marlene Dietrich has learned that one has to fulfill one's duty, according to Goethe's maxim: "But what is the duty? The demand of the day!"

Despite governess and maid, she worked in the kitchen and participated in all domestic matters. Stooping to useful work, she was equally fond of sewing, cooking, and embroidery, in which she had inherited her mother's talents as well. Sitting around and idleness was not tolerated. Her parents taught them to "never give up or share my responsibilities." To Kant, the philosophical teacher of the categorical imperative, that guiding principle of morally right action, is found in the "ABC" of her life, a forerunner of her memories, the enlightening sentence: "His laws - my roots!" To the term "self-discipline" means: "The most useful of all disciplines."

The careful education in the cultivated parental home favored the development of their musical skills and interests. As a high school student, she is most talented in music as she played the first violin in the school orchestra. From those years, a photo of a music pupil performance has been preserved, which shows her in the Spanish folklore costume with the violin, and four classmates dressed in traditional costumes, who perform dances to the tambourine. This performance was supposed to have been a memorial service for the occasion of the shooting of Emperor Maximilian of Mexico, for which the "La Paloma" school orchestra rehearsed the violin solo played by Marlene Dietrich.

At that time, she also practiced individual pieces to pay homage to movie star Henny Porten. This woman, the silent film incarnation of the German ideal of women and mothers one day, became her great love, so powerful that it urged her to show her adoration. After school, she waited in the Zoo district where Henny Porten lived, to see and speak to her. Henny Porten says it like this: "Whenever I came out of the house, there were some girls down in the street, trailing me, who made a curtsey, said hello, and hurried away. Once, however, when I had reached the corner of the street where there was an advertising column, suddenly a very pretty blond girl came rushing out from behind the pillar - she must have been standing there for a long time waiting for me - hardly said in embarrassment "Hello, and with a stuttering" Here, please! "Put a painted postcard in my hand. Before I could say anything, let alone thank her, she had already run away and disappeared around the corner. I looked at the map; it was a so-called artist's postcard with my picture, but the photograph was painted with great care, so clean and fine, that there was not a single spot or just an edge, and it almost looked like an art print. Too bad I wanted so much to thank the kid and tell her how happy I was about her gift, but - she was gone, nowhere to be seen."

"Soon after, I had my birthday, and in the morning, in my room, I heard a mysterious whisper in the hallway outside. And immediately afterward there was music, violin playing, a lovely little song, the Angelic Song of Braga. Wow, who brought me a serenade? I stepped into the adjoining room - and there she was, well, it will not be hard to guess that, just the same little cute girl with the blond curls and played. I thanked her very much for the lovely surprise and asked her to stay a while and have a piece of birthday cake with me. And she did that too. But she was still terribly embarrassed, said very little, only now and then: "Now I have to go" - and yet we were good friends from day to day. And she soon confessed to me that she had been the one that gave me such splendid cream slices and even a self-made tapestry pillow."

"A year later, I was in the town of Garmisch, and one morning, when I woke up, violin playing resounded to my ear. I step to the window to look out into the street, and there's the little girl downstairs again, bringing me the second serenade. She had discovered my name on the Garmisch residence list. I did not know what to say to it with joy and emotion."

The first painful break in Marlene Dietrich's life was the First World War. The war brought a lot of sad things for the family. Her stepfather fell on the front line in 1917, her mother was alone with her two children again. In the war years, there were only women around the slowly growing Marlene, mother, sister, grandmother, and aunts, so that once she referred to the peculiarity in her biography that she grew up in a women's world. Despite the war and deprivation that all families experience, the music lessons continued. For the magazine "Esquire" she once described in detail how she spent the evenings at war with her mother at the piano and earned the pleasure of playing a waltz by Chopin with the endless practice of Bach and Handel. She loved her violin and the mournful sound of strings above all else. The monotonous exercises, on the other hand, she liked less. She also loved Bach, but after the lessons, she wanted to play the Toselli Serenade or Godard's "Berceuse," into which she could let her feelings flow, corrected by no one.

Her violin teacher Bertha, who looked with her reddish-brown hair "like a fox called Bertha," she received the necessary encouragement. The words always saying 'work, work, and only work pave the way to stage fame.' "If I had learned piano instead of violin," she said, "I might have become a pianist. But although I learned to play the violin and got along with all the difficulties more or less, I could not imagine becoming a professional violinist."

Her piano teacher especially loved Chopin and Brahms. Marlene spoke of her as a chubby and comfortable person, who threw her head back in delight as she played waltz with Marlene. Mother and daughter received Christmas presents from her self-made scarves, on which the first bars of a Chopin waltz were painted. "They were terribly stiff, and the color fell off from one Christmas to the next, leaving holes in the melody." Her third teacher, whose name was Marianne was a young, funny person with straw-blonde pigtails. She gave lute lessons and impressed the Losch daughter with her clear, powerful voice as she sang folk songs. Inspired by Marianne, her teacher, she started collecting music for her lute and singing little Bavarian and Austrian songs with instrumental accompaniment. At the same time, she let the chords ring to give her what she thought was a weak and breathless voice, the necessary support. Gradually, she loved her lute more than her violin, which made her feel guilty.

The end of the First World War coincided with the end of Marlene's schooldays. In 1918 she left the Auguste Victoria School with a high school diploma and went to Weimar to study music. The strange environment around her initially offered her little warmth. The school was cold, the streets seemed odd to her and smelled different from the ones from the big city. She missed her home, as there was no mother or no one she knew. But because she had this chance to be in Weimar, where her idol Goethe had lived, she felt her existence filled with overabundant enthusiasm.

Goethe's house she writes. "We went there daily to purify our souls." She shares her room with six other girls as a student of the conservatory. At first, she lived in a boarding school but then moved to a pension that gave her more freedom. She also had access to the work of Rainer Maria Rilke, a poet, whom she adored for life. She fills her free time with concerts and theater visits. Every three weeks, the mother arrived from Berlin by long-distance train to check on her and once again to do the hair washing.

In the circle of girls, Marlene had settled down. One of her friends writes her in a poetry album: "The Marlene came from Berlin.. and we like to see them here… To be funny is their Plaisir,.. and that's the main thing here. " There are no more records available about her education at the conservatory in Weimar, for example, exactly when she began and finished her studies, who her teachers were and how her abilities were assessed. One witness, a Bauhaus painter, wrote about Marlene, "a gracious, stylish young girl we all liked. She lived in the house of Frau von Stein ... and liked to play with our little son. She was very musical." By this Schreyer meant that she was devoted entirely to her music, but also in her attitude and movement, she had been a model of elegance and grace.

A second statement about her studies in Weimar comes from her fellow student Wolfgang Rose, a nephew of the composer Gustav Mahler. Rose says she was very modest and timid and did not seem to be aware of her charms at all. "By the way, she was by no means an outstanding student, and I doubt that being a violinist would satisfy her. Indeed, if she had continued to work with the passionate zeal she displayed, she might have found her way to the concert stage."

Her training in Weimar could not be completed as her mother appears one day and brought her back to Berlin. The reason for this is not known. Nevertheless, her study in music will then be continued in Berlin with a well-known violin virtuoso Professor Carl Flesch.

Unfortunately, it all came to an end after a tendon inflammation in her left hand, caused pain by much practice. This makes it not possible to play the instrument continuously. The inflamed hand must be plastered. Fate had thus decided against the violin career. "It was a big blow for me. I knew that I would never become a first-rate violinist and never a "concert artist." "

Her mother said, "Do something!" when Marlene, sitting at home, tried to get over the crisis of her young existence by reading the works of Rilke and Goethe. Her mother did or could not tell her at the time: "Go to work in the theater or to the movies!" because the family's consciousness of the class, even in 1920/21, would have stood in the way of this profession.

Ms. von Losch seems to have left no doubt about this to the daughter. What was better for a beautiful, romantically minded, realistic girl from a fine family than theater if she did not have a completed education and wanted to earn some money? Marlene decided to try the theater, especially as she considered it an appropriate place to bring out the beauty of the language. Besides music, literature and recitation was her great passion.

The first attempt on stage ends without result. When she appears for an audition in the drama school of Max Reinhardt, in the vague hope of being accepted as a regular student, she did not leave a unanimous impression with the role of the girl from Hugo von Hofmannsthal's play "The Door and the Death ", even though she rehearsed the text carefully.

The director Carl Heine and Berthold Held as head of the school were impressed, but Max Reinhardt was not convinced of her talent.

She was not given accepted into the school. However, Berthold Held agreed to provide private lessons to the beginner, together with another student named Grete Mosheim, the same Mosheim, who was soon to become the female celebrity star of the Reinhardt ensemble. In retrospect, Grete Mosheim doubted the quality of these private lessons and said in an interview for the Marlene Dietrich book by the American Charles Higham: "After less than a year, we stopped without having learned anything. But that we had lessons with him justified us in getting some work at Reinhardt's theater." They received roles, and that was all that mattered.

Grete Mosheim gives the following description of her friend Marlene: "I always noticed that she wore the most elegant stockings and the shy high-heeled pumps while I was walking around in socks and half-shoes. How she could afford it, I do not know. But she managed to be gorgeous in the morning at seven."

After the end of the war, Marlene Dietrich took on various jobs to keep herself financially afloat. She sold gloves, entered cabarets, and asked a dancer, if there were any attractive pairs of legs missing. Her knowledge in violin playing helped get her work for a short time with a position as concertmaster in the silent film music orchestra of Giuseppe Becce. As Becce remembers, she had only asked a small fee, but she wanted to be so placed on Henny Porten films that she could always look at the screen while playing. Orchestra boss Becce would have liked to keep her longer, but after four weeks he had to refrain because her "unusually beautiful legs " had the entire male orchestra missing the beat.

The participation in the cinema orchestra at Becce remained a fleeting episode as it was mainly the stage and the silent film that determined the artistic development of Marlene Dietrich in the early 1920s. For aspiring actresses, it was not difficult to get a role somewhere in a play or movie around 1920-21. With the end of the war, the theaters were looking for extras, girls, and choristers. They only needed the required quality of voice and figure for a role. Many innumerable private film companies were being founded and there were many chances for interested applicants. But because of the high capital investment, many film companies often declare bankruptcy. A potential actor or singer could just ask in the occupation office for another company for a role.

It was not much different at the theater where it would be easy to find a job as a 'fellow' if you had a good friend there. Marlene Dietrich herself tells how she came to her first roles as a minor actress. Her friend Anni Mewes, who was at the beginning of her career, called her several times a week and asked if she could take over her role that evening. "It's just a sentence, my dress will fit you. But do not tell anybody about it, just go there, take your cue, take a pencil, and write it down!" Marlene took the pencil, noted it, got the dress, and went in the evening, speaking the sentence or the two sentences, while Annie Mewes amused herself somewhere in private without anyone at the theater even noticing that the words were being spoken by someone else.

Judging by the plays of Shakespeare, Björnson, Shaw, and Sternheim, from 1924/25 onwards provided only supporting roles for them. In pieces of literary substance that could be proud of a literary education, the tasks were entirely inconsequential before. She usually just stood there silently, walking a few steps, talking a few words that might as well have not been spoken. Being a theater actress, of course, was valuable in that she grew through the experience.

In 1923 Marlene married the film producer Rudolf Sieber in Berlin. Marlene was still unknown at this point. Together they had a daughter Maria. They both went their separate ways in the 1930s, but stayed married until his death in 1976. The breakthrough film, the 'Blue Angel,' gave Marlene her start and recognition as a singer and actress in Germany. Her screen test for the 'Blue Angel' showed a young, ambitious, and talented young lady. Her ability to speak some English also gave her the edge to win the role as it was to be filmed a second time but in English for the American market. The role of 'Lola' in the film along with the songs she sang would be a benchmark part that would accompany her the rest of her life.

The pairing of Marlene and the composer Friedrich Hollaender in the film would be one of many musical collaborations to come. The film brought her practically overnight success and a contract offer from Hollywood.

America & Hollywood: film and music

Marlene Dietrich took the night train to Bremen, from where she should board the fast passenger steamer of the same name to the US, as there were no transatlantic passenger flights yet. You traveled a week by ship from Bremen or Hamburg to New York and from there by train via Chicago at a speed of one hundred kilometers across the continent to Los Angeles: a trip from the east to the west coast of America took five days.

After some hesitation, Marlene Dietrich decided to sign the contract with the American film company and leave Berlin. Between her and the UFA was an option contract, as was customary in the film industry. Now that the "Blue Angel" had been filmed and presented, UFA did not take up the option, that is, it did not make a new offer. Marlene Dietrich had to assume that the film was not considered promising by the UFA group's leading people and that's why she said she accepted Paramount's offer. What else would you have left to do than wait for new film or recording offer?

It was an uncertain time with an economic crisis in which even big-name actors were not fully booked, and two thousand Berlin musicians, actors and artists were unemployed and on support with social assistance. The knowledge of the misery of joblessness may have had a decisive influence on her decision to accept the offer from Hollywood, especially as it was long term and generous.

She would be obliged to film in Hollywood for 26 weeks with the remaining 26 weeks able to spend in Germany. The duration of the outward and return journey would be included in the 26 weeks of work. Although the contract with Paramount regulated everything, there was one more obstacle to overcome before Marlene Dietrich could make the trip.

The contract between her and the director Robert Klein still committed her to eleven months for his Berlin theater. The next production was the play "Sex Appeal" by Lonsdale, with Mady Christians in the lead role. Director Klein did not want to release Marlene Dietrich and complained about compliance with the contract. Both parties appealed to the stage arbitrator to declare that she was not allowed to leave, but Marlene Dietrich claims that she was allowed to leave citing the clause that gave her one Holiday for the purpose of filming. If a settlement is reached, Director Klein demanded payment of 60,000 marks, "and I do not want to pay anything," argued Marlene Dietrich. Since a settlement could not be concluded on this basis, it was finally agreed to a penalty of ten thousand marks. With that, she was released from the contract. The "Sex Appeal" had to take place in Berlin without her.

Legally, nothing was in the way of departure. After a five-day crossing on a stormy sea, Marlene Dietrich was able to go ashore in New York. She traveled further from the east to the west coast of the United States and eventually reached Los Angeles with the Hollywood movie suburb.

Los Angeles, the largest city in the United States in terms of Hollywood, stretched across plains, mountains, and hills from the Pacific Ocean to the desert and the Rocky Mountains, loosely pieced together and with such vast undeveloped areas between the neighborhoods that the car has long become a matter of course. There was no other way to reach the workplace from another district. Observers and connoisseurs describe the city or suburb of Hollywood depending on how the observer views it; as neither typically American nor truly international, neither as a large city nor as a small town, at least as a city without a real boulevard.

The city center was a new west American main street with magazines, bars, hotels, and movie houses. If the artists and film people did not prefer to have an even greater distance between themselves and the studios, they lived in the edge settlements.

Hollywood, this eternally sunlit place in California, with its infinitely mild, warm air, the paradise of citrus fruits, was for the time being Marlene Dietrich's new circle of life. She found one of the usual rental villas with agaves, palm trees, garden, and swimming pool, and so, as a newcomer to the industry, she began the ordinary film routine.

At nine o'clock, the actors had to be ready to shoot in the wings. That meant arriving at six o'clock in the morning for makeup, hair washing, and styling. The studios worked with the same organizational methods as large-scale companies in the industry. You punched a time clock early in the morning that watched over punctuality. As much as the companies spoiled the stars, they still demanded precision and conscientiousness from them in front of the camera. For the little pleasures outside, you had to pay in the studio with hard and disciplined work. As far as that was concerned, Marlene Dietrich never had any difficulties with that.

Of course, she had to switch to the American movie company so she was expected to follow the rules. However, she soon set her own rules; and as her fame grew, she was regarded as the "reigning queen of Paramount," and was left alone. She was very fortunate to find the Sternberg Agency to represent her. "I had a beautiful house with a garden, the blue sky above me and a real friend who told me what to do. What more could one wish for? When I think back to it today, it feels like the quietest time of my life."

In the beginning, Paramount had their biggest fears, as their boss, Adolph Zukor later admitted; that the Newcomer from Germany could be regarded by the millions of moviegoers as a Garbo imitation. How should one avoid this? After her arrival in Hollywood, Marlene Dietrich already gave a detailed account of her child and her husband, Rudolf Sieber, during the first interview.

The studios perceived this as not right for the film company, so they considered how further interviews could be avoided. But that would have made her the Garbo imitation because the Garbo was famous for her silence, which formed her image promoted and maintained by the film company. And because Garbo was silent, Marlene Dietrich was now allowed to chat frankly about everything that concerned her. The main thing was that the film company should not suffer any damage she might inflict on it.

Marlene Dietrich repeatedly said she has never had much influence on others. But she is the reason why millions of women started wearing trousers in the early 1930s. It all started in America, a photographer from Paramount made new advertising photos of Marlene. When she arrived for the photo shoot, she said she was only running around in pants at home. If he wanted to photograph her that way that was okay. After the pictures had appeared in the newspapers and magazines, all the women poured into the shops for trousers. This new fashion has taken hold.

The actress Louise Brooks, wrote about Marlene Dieter. The first Hollywood year: "Marlene Dietrich came in a time to Hollywood, as there the entire film industry Greta Garbo idolized - unacknowledged, but so unmistakable that it was laughable. Garbo imitations were introduced from all over Europe. Directors (among them von Sternberg) told actresses how to play Garbo. Male stars asked for less money and name credits in second place if they were to work alongside Garbo.

Small, dark-haired actresses were no longer in demand; others blanched overnight, eyebrows drawn in thin sheets, and wore false eyelashes. In front of the camera, they had a mysterious look in close-up shots, unexpectedly throwing their heads back and falling back onto unsuspecting beds and sofas. When I first met Marlene Dietrich in 1930, no one would have been less like Garbo in appearance and appearance. I went to a party with Irene and David Selznick, unaware that the nightclub had been turned into a gaming room for charity. Any kind of gambling is an abomination to me, so I crumbled into an empty adjoining room almost empty, on a round bench, her head leaning against the pillar, sitting alone a pretty blond. It was Marlene Dietrich.

Her beautiful blonde hair was tightly wavy, she wore a sky blue chiffon dress and her remarkable legs were in heavy German silk stockings. To my surprise, she greeted me in a warm, friendly tone."

Faithful admirers still claim that nothing better could have happened to Dietrich than the transformation into a sophisticated Hollywood glamor girl. And with her first Hollywood film 'Morocco,' Marlene Dietrich created a type of woman with whom she began to identify herself as the woman who only follows the laws of her love and takes full advantage of her freedom.

The cinemas were particularly enthusiastic about the final scene, with which the idea of the film is once again set in a grandiose painterly picture. You can see Amy Jolly following a troop of soldiers into the desert sands through a Moroccan gate, determined to share the fate with her legionary (Gary Cooper), all the other man (Adolphe Menjou) the well-kept little beard and all its riches and offers, which would have belonged to her, leaving them behind.

Lola-Amy has remained faithful to her cinematic purpose: she can only love, and nothing else. This first American Dietrich film, a film of pure visual language, impresses with the atmosphere that Sternberg gave to the individual scenes, especially those in which his star has to sing the songs that belong to the nightclub performance. One of them was: "What Am I Bid for My Apple" and "What can I get? She goes from table to table with an apple basket, and turning her head around by the mysteriously seductive way she smiles, emphasizes and stretches the words of her songs, and beguiles men and women. One of the thrills of the film was the scene that was unusual for the time when Marlene Dietrich kissed another woman's passionate grace on her lips after the performance of her French song "Quand l'amour meurt".

The film "Morocco" was a success, the cinema owners registered full cash registers. It was noteworthy that in this early film of 1930, in her later artistic career she appeared in nightclubs, with this gentlemen's craze of English and French songs.

The work in this film was a difficult phase for her. Marlene Dietrich could barely speak English, and she had to poke the text into phonetic transcription and had difficulties with the exact pronunciation. The malaise with the English pronunciation had already appeared in Badelsberg (film studio in Berlin) when the English version of the "Blue Angel" was made. In the chanson with the line: "Men cluster to me like moths around a flame", the moths gave her enormous difficulties. It is said that she had to repeat the chanson 235 times in two days of shooting. The famous Weintraub overdubbing company always had to break off and re-insert sound at this point. It was no fun for an accompaniment orchestra. Sternberg managed at that time, placing him at the place with the moth word, a voice came from the crowd. It was the orchestra musician Horst Graff, who let out loud: "A beer! A beer!" The appearance of Lola in the "Blue Angel" was thus saved technologically.

This incident of 1929 still had an amusing aftermath. In 1960, Marlene Dietrich also gave a concert in Australia on her tour of the world, where the Weintraub musicians had emigrated in 1939. Of course, her song "From Head to Toe" was in the program, and of course in perfect English! When she came to the line with the moths, the presenter Horst Graff shouted loudly into the hall: "A beer! A beer! "She could not hear it but laughed a lot when she heard about the idea. Many small episodes that seemed to be edgy, were just a picture of the difficulties that Marlene Dietrich had to overcome on her way to chanson.

Before Marlene Dietrich was able to return to Germany to her family in 1931, she had to work on a second film in the studios of Paramount called "Dishonored." Again, under the director Sternberg, the espionage affair film provided even more mystery. She is the secret agent of the film; beautiful, clever, and in the end, she is executed. Alone with her voice she could, perhaps because she had very few lines, create an aura of mystery, that makes many of her later chansons so valuable to the connoisseur of voices. The film "Dishonored" from 1931, as well as the following "Shanghai Express" from 1932, remained without significance for the repertoire of Marlene Dietrich, since they remained without song.

She then returned to Europe for five months, attending the premieres of her film "Morocco" in London and Paris, taking care of her ill daughter in Berlin until she was in good health. Before she went to Hollywood, in February 1930, all titles from the "Blue Angel" had been recorded for Electrola in Germany, two of them in the English version. Anyone who already collected the songs of Marlene hastened to acquire even the most recent record titles from the movie "Morocco" on Odeon.

In May 1931, Marlene Dietrich returned with her daughter Maria to the United States, accompanied by a friend. She took the child with her because Sternberg and Rudi Sieber had decided that it was best for them and for the child. On arrival in Hollywood, she interviewed with the press, and the headlines promised nothing pleasant. There was talk of her and Sternberg's divorce. This topic was the talk of the day, nourished by speculation and sensationalism because Hollywood was not only a metropolis of the film, it was also a metropolis of gossip, from which many newspapers and journalists lived.

It was true that Marlene's husband had been living with actress Tamara Matul for some time. He had moved in with her in 1932 to Paris to work in the local studios of Paramount. Marriage between Rudi Sieber and Marlene Dietrich, although both went their separate ways, formally continued to exist in the agreement of both partners. This comradely and close alliance lasted until Rudi Sieber's death in 1976.

As soon as Marlene Dietrich left the ship in New York and read the first "scandal news," two lawyers brought her a claim for damages from Sternberg director Riza Royce, who lived in New York, amounting to a total of $ 500,000 for alleged slander and disorganization of the Sternberg marriage. Mrs. Dietrich told a Viennese newspaper that Mrs. von Sternberg was a "dutiful wife" and that Sternberg wanted to divorce her. In this precarious situation, Marlene Dietrich asked her husband Rudi Sieber to come to Hollywood and attend a family reunion for several weeks. As a trusted friend and gentleman, he, of course, did this. Sternberg was thus given decisive help in his divorce proceedings, and Marlene Dietrich made it known that she would much rather enjoy the publicity of the Sternberg divorce than the idea that she would pay even a penny for absurd, outrageous and unjustified allegations against her and others.

At that time reporters swirled around them like moths, and when they became too bold, she said with a slight emphasis in her voice, "Gentlemen, you forget that I am a married woman!" To her star director and his work, Paramount paid Mrs. Sternberg a sum of $ 100,000 to settle the matter. For the society's cash register and the revenue of the cinema owners, it was essential that the next Sternberg-Dietrich film "Shanghai-Express" arrive punctually. Everything else was unimportant.

In this new film, she has been stylized into the fascinatingly exotic Shanghai Lilly, an adventurer who has left far behind the comparatively benign living conditions of the Tingel-tangel Lola. The film "Morocco," and "Shanghai Express" are of extraordinary visual impact, for which Marlene Dietrich's face gave the object that was constantly reimagined by Sternberg's eye. In her black-feathered dress, she looked like an exotic bird. She had no songs to sing in the film, only slow speech "almost like a talking turtle" to provide the mysterious flair.

In the opinion of the critic Charles Higham, Sternberg's art and the beauty of the leading actress, have produced a fantastic and bewitching film that none of their other films have surpassed. Hollywood successes and personal upheavals continued for the rest of the year 1932.

Shortly before filming the "Blonde Venus" gangsters tried to blackmail them with a massive "kidnapper threat." The life of her daughter Maria, then seven years old, was at stake and had to be protected. That meant bars in the windows, reinforced door locks, and installation of an alarm. The child was always with her, even in the film studio, sleeping on the floor at night, engaging bodyguards, also arming the nanny, a police dog in the hall, sleepless nights, sorrow and worries.

Everyday life no longer took place in the warm light of the Californian sun. There were serious differences between Sternberg and Paramount, which unsettled Marlene Dietrich. Only after lengthy settlement negotiations was it possible to start filming the "Blond Venus." Marlene Dietrich said the new film had not been "a particularly good film." The storyline is quite absurd. All out of love for her little Johnny, the film is about a woman who lets herself suffer for the sake of her husband and becomes a prostitute for her child. The critics did not unanimously accept this.

The words "manicured," "Sternberg's low," "lemonade," never saw anything less needy and "Hollywoodian" than this story. But the main actress was the winner as always. "What she does, says, and sings, is unadorned, as if she did next to nothing, said or sang nothing. An admirable achievement," said the Berliner Tageblatt on 19.11.1932. And the "Cinema Quarterly," Edinburgh 1/1932, wrote: "As in" Shanghai-Express," Marlene Dietrich is in the center, and just like in this film, each of her poses is photographed grandiose. As a matter, of course, she takes the film for what it is a background for her ego." Noteworthy are the English songs and nursery rhymes that Marlene Dietrich sings in the movie: "You Little So-and-So," "Hot Voodoo" and "I Could Not Be Annoyed" that show her from a new side.

The holiday Marlene Dietrich spent in Europe after filming was more than deserved after the hardships and tortures left behind her. For a short time, she came to Berlin to meet with acquaintances and actor colleagues. It would be the last time she would be in Germany for the next thirteen years.

For Berlin, she had become the world's number one. She was so popular that there were already cabaret and variety parodies such as the Comedian Harmonists who profited from Lola's fame. There was also something unpleasant for Marlene Dietrich in Berlin when she opened the newspapers and read the following reports: Henny-Porten-Film-Company opens bankruptcy! - 6500 cinemas closed in the US! - The Metro movie cuts the fees by 35 percent! This was just a few months before Hitler seized power and Hermann Goering was elected President of the Reichstag.

The crisis in the political situation encouraged her decision to stay in Hollywood, although she had always toyed with the idea of returning to Germany. When she said goodbye to her friends and acquaintances in Berlin, she did not suspect that barely a year later, the first of them would arrive as political refugees in Hollywood.

When she returned to the Hollywood studios, the film company demanded that she work with another director. She refused and found herself being threatened with $ 85,000 in damages. In the spring of 1933 the Paramount studio filmed the novel by Hermann Sudermann "The Best Song" under the new director Rouben Mamoulian.

The screenplay had turned the German romance novel of 1908 into a maudlin story: an innocent peasant girl, Lily, falls in love with a sculptor, and then falls into the hands of his patron, a lascivious baron. When the riding instructor on the baron's estate, falls in love and tows the girl into his hut, she accidentally sets the hut on fire. The premiere of "Song of Songs," as the movie was called, took place in the summer of 1933 in New York.

Around the time the filming began for the "Song of Songs" in faraway California, Paramount's studios, Hitler and his followers came to power in Germany. In any case, Marlene Dietrich did not want to go back to Nazi Germany, even though she would have been very welcome there. She chose Paris as a temporary European abode after completing the filming. She met emigrants, old Berlin friends, who inform her about the realities in Germany and immediately their relief work begins for those who have fled to Paris.

From her hotel suite in Versailles, she calls the Hotel Ansonia. It was a smaller, cheap hotel on a narrow side street near the Arc de Triomphe, where celebrities from Berlin's film glory, now unemployed emigrants, have lodged. This included the composers Friedrich Hollaender and Franz Wachsmann, the director Billy Wilder , the actor Peter Lorre, Max Colpet, the journalist Pem (Paul Markus) and others.

The librettist Max Colpet initially thought it was a joke when a male voice, the hotel guide of the Versailles hotel Trianon, told him and Franz Wachsmann that they should come to Versailles, Madame Dietrich was waiting for them. At first, Colpet did not react to the alleged phone call and finally said indifferently when the phone calls were repeated. Frau Dietrich would then like to send them a big car; they are destitute emigrants, as they would not have the necessary money.

To his astonishment, not least his embarrassment when, after some time, a 16-cylinder Cadillac with a chauffeur stopped in front of the small Ansonia to pick them up. "I'll never miss the moment we've met Marlene," says Colpet. The chauffeur opened the car. We stepped out and looked around in embarrassment. Wide, imposing steps led up to the entrance of the hotel. In front of it was a woman who looked like a lingering woman, the Blue Angel, in a fabulous chiffon dress, in to which the warm summer wind played. Next to Marlene stood her husband and the pretty little daughter."

The very minor monologue of a woman "Alone in a City" is reminiscent of the big city poetry of those years, for the Erich Kästner broadly set the tone. Longing for togetherness, and togetherness resonates! Collaboration with chanson author and librettist Max Colpet, who had begun in Paris in 1933, continued in later years, and both remained friends. Marlene Dietrich's relationship with the composer Peter Kreuder changed after 1945 when she had learned of his past in Nazi Germany. Kreuder has talked about her very poorly in his book "Only Puppets Have No Tears," Munich 1971. There were poisonous remarks about her. Marlene Dietrich acted very magnanimously with him by not mentioning the name Kreuder in her books.

At that time, in 1933, the production of the record with Wachsmann and Colpet in Paris was a form of financial support for the two emigrants. For the record to be sold in Germany, the copywriter and composer, both non Aryan in Nazi usage, were given different names. Wachmann was given the pseudonym Jose d'Alba, and Colpet was named Kurt Gerhardt. Nevertheless, it was known privately whom the text and the music were from. Marlene Dietrich's new album was a great success. With this and the following recordings, which were made from now on in Los Angeles and New York, Marlene Dietrich laid the foundation for her extensive and stylistically differentiated chanson repertoire. In the fifties this became her second career as a singer and launched her triumphant march through the world.

After tense workdays in the Paris record studios, where she supervised the French dubbing of "Song of Songs," Marlene Dietrich liked to go out with her friends and acquaintances. She preferred little ethnic restaurants such as the Russian Chez Kornilow or the Czech Chez Luis, whose specialty was quark dumplings. She often went to the kitchens of the restaurants and watched the food being prepared. One felt honored when Marlene peeked into the pots, as she understood a lot of cooking, or rather the art of cooking. And it was for the restaurant in question her presence was a welcome advertisement.

She already knew that she liked being in Paris, in the city with the broad avenues lined with magnificent trees, the elegant shops and boutiques that she loved as much as the many cafes with the colorful awnings. She came into close contact with Paris and the people of the venerable, yet so modern metropolis of France. She liked especially the actors, photographers, fashion designers, and chansonniers, many of whom have become her friends. Her exacting knowledge of the French language made it easier for her to settle in Paris, and so over the years, gradually arose the desire to settle down here forever.

The decisive factor for her was not least the fact that her husband Rudi Sieber lived in Paris, to whom she had obtained a position for him as representative with Paramount. Meetings in Paris were often an event that had meaning for all the family members. In September 1933, Marlene Dietrich returned to Hollywood to shoot her next film once again with Sternberg. The name was "The Great Czarina" and was intended as a "strict style exercise." The scenery and decor overgrew everything else so much that the film failed in its reviews. They spoke of 'downright idiotic mannerisms' and criticized the fact that the actors were pushed against the wall by grim icons, martyr statues, and somber architecture. For the film company, which was under fierce competition, such a failure was not without economic consequences. For the first time, cinemas' box office receipts could not cover the 900,000 dollars invested in the film.

There were signs that Paramount would no longer keep the self-willed, problematic director in the face of general economic difficulties. Despite this cinematic failure, Marlene Dietrich was at the zenith of her fame in this segment of her life. Her annual salary was $ 350,000; she lived in one of the usual exclusive bungalows in Beverly Hills, the "gold-powdered bowler colony," as Friedrich Hollaender jokingly called the celebrity's settlement. It was a coveted object of the photographers, where one gave interviews and parties. It had become something of an institution.

She lived no less luxuriously than other stars of her stature. She had her chauffeur, a housekeeper, and a nanny, and made sure that her daughter, who had been strictly shielded since the kidnapper affair, receive first class private lessons at home. In their household, she had fewer servants than other Divas. She did a great deal herself, remaining the Berlin housewife with a practical sense and an eye for reality.

Their generosity and helpfulness were much praised to friends and colleagues when they were in need. There are also many stories of how as she was born a Samaritan woman; she took care of ill employees of the film staff during filming. She drove to them, cooking her much-praised chicken soup for their fosterlings, tidied up the apartment and, if necessary, also scrubbed clothes.

Working for movies in Hollywood in the thirties was by no means as exhausting as one might suppose, given today's living and working conditions. You had lots of free time. Many Hollywood based actors, directors, writers and composers lived in Hollywood since the twenties, others arrived in 1933 and then at the outbreak of the war as refugees came from the occupied countries. There was a real German colony centered around Ernst Lübitsch, Berthold Viertel, Billy Wilder, the stage and lyrics poet Walter Reisch with their staff and families inviting and visiting each other. Driving friends to movie premieres in Grauman's Chinese Theater with it's exotic façade design, to theatrical performances in New York when a new play was broadcast on Broadway, making trips to the California Reserves, or driving out of the city to one of the many beaches of the Pacific Ocean, which were on their doorstep.

There were occasional trips to neighboring Pasadena with its famous Huntington Gallery, where Marlene Dietrich saw Gainsborough's "Blue Boy," in the English rococo style. In her Berlin years, this classic image of European art history once served her as a model for a costume party. She can be seen in a photograph as the perfect Blue Boys in the noble 1770 boy's costume, strikingly similar to the original.

Since then, she has enthralled the attendees in many parties and balls by the super elegant, always causing admiration with the surprising style of her clothing. The women were often envious of her, but the gentlemen applauded when they joined in and appeared in sailor's hats, navy blue blazer and wide white trousers, or surprised their guests in the afternoon with gold lamé suits, or later in the garden party they were surprised by short Bavarian lederhosen.

At the time, Marlene Dietrich wrote several articles for large magazines and periodicals. She explained to her readers that a so-called vamp, which she was not and did not want to be, was an unfortunate, miserable, loveless creature, which in the end had to destroy herself and was by no means an aspiring ideal. She also gave advice on cooking; how to make mushrooms or cucumber salad properly; if you should buy a mink coat; yes, if you have the money, I strongly advise too! Also; what meaning natural, healthy jealousy does for love. Advice and statements from her can be found in her later book 'ABC of my Life'. She had been saving them over the years, and in 1962, when she was urged to write her memoirs, she published these snippets in a book form to a New York publishing house.

Hollywood as a film mega-metropolis, tried to claim the German actress back in the early 1930s. The more her fame in America's grew, the more confident was the language of the press about her. The interview partners from the editorial offices of major American newspapers ensured that countless stories came into circulation. They found their way into the crevices of the 'feature' sheets, magazines, and tabloids, which in turn were proud to keep the nation up to date with the latest, if necessary, invented stories from the stars' private lives.

Marlene Dietrich was called "Hollywood's Number One Glamor Girl" in the thirties. Glamor: this was understood to mean the glittering splendor of wealth, beauty, and luxury that only the great names of the film world had to offer. The intriguing image of glitter was reproduced nonstop by the film company's publishing departments and was part of the business, indispensable to the neighboring fashion and cosmetics industries, which drew their millions in profits.

One of the leading American actors in "Blue Angel," who met Marlene Dietrich for the first time while working on this film, said to book author Charles Higham, who collected all the opinions about her: "She was generally sold as a glamor girl, while I found that she was an extremely domestic type, what the Germans call "cozy." She always brought some cake, home-baked, or pastry, which we all ate together for tea or coffee in the afternoons. She was more proud of her cooking skills than her acting skills."

"Although I had become a glamor star, I did not live in a Glamour world," Marlene commented. Dietrich as a "glamor girl" seemed to have an exclusively one-sided American way of looking at things. A well-known journalist, Ben Maddox, asked her in 1935 how she believed she had been changed by Hollywood: "In what ways do you feel that Hollywood has changed you?" She answered, "I think so not that I've changed, except of course that I've gotten older. And I have greater responsibility to carry. There is the feeling that a whole production is on your own shoulders. But Hollywood…? It does not do anything terrible to people. Certainly not those who are strong personalities and have a clear opinion of themselves."

She usually smiled at silly questions that the reporters often asked her, and when the subjects were overbearing, impertinent, and beyond the bounds of what was allowed, she could get pretty sharp. "It is said that you were dressed in an unfashionable fashion when you arrived in America. And then there's the trilby legend ..." To explain the trilby legend: Trilby is a harmless girl who has been transformed into a fantastic creature by the mage and demon hypnotist Svengali. After these two figures from the American literature, the director Josef von Sternberg was given the nickname "Svengali Jo" and Marlene Dietrich his "Trilby." In the memoirs of George Grosz, for example, both speak almost exclusively of these names.

Marlene Dietrich's answer to Ben Maddox's questions was again a meaningful smile: "This theory of having been dressed unfashionably on arrival in America and a simple-minded housewife type of actress is absurd. I came from Berlin, a cosmopolitan city. And I brought suitcases full of Parisian clothes with me. If you compare photos of me then and now, I look better today. But it's not a Hollywood polish. That has brought time. Look at your own photographs from earlier. They will be just as antiquated and funny. And as for the Sternberg Trilby legend, that amuses me. Anyone with reason can see that I have not been hypnotized. Unmistakably, I have something of myself behind this face. They could not put a brain into a woman's head if it was not there before. " "You mean, then, that Hollywood has not changed your lifestyle?" - "Not at all. My parents had money. I live the way I lived in Germany. Except that I have guards here (bodyguards) around me. "(Because of her daughter, who still had to be guarded.) The blackmailers could not be caught. Reporter Ben Maddox still wanted to know if she loved Hollywood. she replied, "Oh, yes, indeed." Irrespective of that, she returned to Paris almost every year, which she liked in a different and much better way.

Already in the spring of 1934, she was back on the Seine. On her return to the United States, she met writer Ernest Hemingway, who was to become one of her most enduring friends, on the passenger ship "lle de France." He nicknamed her Americans for Germans, affectionately "cabbage" or even "mamma"; she was devoted to him in respect and admiration as her beloved "dad."

The story of her acquaintance with Hemingway was strange. Hemingway volunteered on the ship Männlich-Galant as the fourteenth participant of a dinner party when her thirteenth guest, Marlen Dietrich, was invited and, superstitious as she claimed to be, refused to attend.

In 1935, the Paramount finally separated from her demanding director Sternberg. In the same year, Ernst Lubitsch, as his own producer, signed Marlene Dietrich and Gary Cooper for his classic film comedy "Desire" to film the story of a seductive, internationally sought-after jewel thief with these two stars. The script was created after a comedy by Hans Szekely and R.A. Stemmle, who was last employed in Berlin for the UFA and Werner Finck's "Catacomb." For the music, Lubitsch also committed a successful Berliner: Friedrich Hollaender, who now lived in Hollywood, where he was in high demand as a film composer.

The London "Spectator" said after the 1936 film that Marlene Dietrich was allowed to show that she was an actress and singer. "And what memories of a cheap Tingel-tangel (cheap dance bar) with a singer with a tilted cylinder hat that sings with this harsh voice!" She did not finish the film, "I Loved a Soldier," as there were quarrels with the director, who sought to interfere with her powers by dictating how she would appear as a cleaning woman in a scene, and how not. Such questions Marlene Dietrich did not like. At eight o'clock, she left the studio to the director, and the twisted fragment of the film was made history.

Her next two films, which came out in 1936 and 1937, 'The Garden of Allah' and 'Angel,' to the latter Friedrich Hollaender wrote the music, were considered well by contemporary critics and estimated as significant productions. The music had no lasting significance for

Marlene Dietrich's song repertoire, although there is a song in the film 'Angel'; however, Marlene Dietrich did not include it in her later concert programs.

Rarely heard in her repertoire as a singer was the song "Three Sweethearts Have I". She sings it in "Devil" in 1935, when Spaniard wraps herself in imaginative net like costumes.

Three sweethearts have I, I'm true I could have been true to you. I have three mistresses, I have faithfulness to all three, and I could be just as loyal to you.

The composers who wrote the songs for their films were, without exception, distinguished artistic personalities, such as Ralph Rainger (1901-1942), born in New York, a pupil of Arnold Schönberg, a pianist in Paul Whiteman's orchestra and a piano accompanist to Vaudeville singers. In addition to Friedrich Hollaender and Franz Wachsmann, who came from Berlin, he was one of Hollywood's most famous film musicians of the thirties. He wrote songs for more than 35 films, most of them with his librettist Leo Robin. Bing Crosby, America's favorite and star of many Hollywood music films, and has made quite a few of them famous.

One day Marlene met Bing Crosby in his dressing room in the movie studio listening to Richard Tauber's records. She was very interested in that because she had been one of the admirers of Richard Tauber since she was a girl in Berlin. Crosby told her that he studied the breathing technique and the peculiarities of Tauber's phrasing based on the recordings, which Marlene Dietrich immediately took for an American, and so "I loved Bing Crosby from this moment" on.

The singing actor Bing Crosby is not the only one she met from working together for the film. If the names Maurice Chevalier, Charlie Chaplin, or Sergei Eisenstein are mentioned, these are just a few of the considerable number that crossed Marlene Dietrich's path and one way or another through their acting skills and ultimately has influenced the art of the chanson tradition.

Several times Marlene Dietrich spent the years before the war in Europe - in Paris, Zurich, and Vienna. In 1937 she applied for naturalization in Los Angeles for the United States after giving up the Hitler regime, which had called her to return. Whether, indeed, offers have repeatedly come from fascist Germany cannot be proven. Marlene Dietrich herself has reported a direct interview with the German ambassador to the USA, who promised her the controlled press of the Third Reich, despite a unique film career "in the name of the Führer" and a "triumphal entry through the Brandenburg Gate" if she was prepared to return to Germany. It is also true that in request for US citizenship already made, it was treated with outright courtesy.

The "Middle German National News" already saw the Nazi dream come true when, in one of its editions in January 1938, it wrote in Goebbels-Schwulst: "We firmly believe that an actress like Marlene Dietrich, with her rich foreign experience, could be an invaluable asset for Germany's filmmaking. What an estimable task it might be for one of the best German directors to transform Vamp Dietrich into Frau Dietrich. Not a Gretchen with pigtails and thick red cheeks, but at least a woman who can shape her German nature out of her own resources."

Marlene Dietrich was not prepared, as one knows, to have her German character arranged on a brown canvas. (brown was the color of the Nazi uniforms). In her book, she writes: "The answer I gave to the Hitler regime when I was asked to return and become the reigning queen of the German film industry is well known." The final defection of the Nazi Culture politician of hers took place in 1939, when the photo went around the world showing her being sworn in as an American citizen. The "striker" also published the agency photo and put the following signature under it: "German-born film actress Marlen Dietrich has spent so many years with the Hollywood cinema-goers that she has now become an American citizen."

As a film actress Marlene Dietrich was at a low point in the years immediately preceding World War II. She was next to Joan Crawford, Greta Garbo, Mae West, and Hepburn as 'cash poison' for the cinemas and ranked on the star list of 1937 on 126th place. Paramount, depending on the market and sales business, released her from her contract to work elsewhere.

Existing projects were canceled. How did Marlene Dietrich react?... with equanimity. There was that feature of her nature, which she calls "laissez faire." Until now, they always wanted her to be 'legs'. Please, if you're going to have legs, then you get legs, was her attitude. She was that legs cult, one may believe her, at times very weary, but film was an industry and legs a very popular commodity. Now suddenly they wanted no legs and no Marlene Dietrich anymore. So she turned her back on the movie business for some time and left Hollywood to be together with her family in Paris.

In the summer of 1939, the Siebers spent an extended vacation on the French Mediterranean coast with the writer Erich Maria Remarque, Josef von Sternberg, who was a close friend of the family, and daughter Maria. One sees Marlene Dietrich at this time much together with Erich Maria Remarque. More often she is a guest in his house on Lake Maggiore with the collection of French Impressionists. In Paris, she also meets the poet James Joyce in a restaurant, who tells her that he saw her in the "Blue Angel," to which she replied: "Then you have seen the best of me!"

In June 1939, in Paris, she received a call from producer Joe Pasternak of the Universal Film Company, asking her if she would like to be a star with him in a western? This seemed entirely absurd for her, but Sternberg spoke to her, and since she gave something to his opinion, she said yes. Although the Directors of Universal were opposed to Dietrich's involvement, Pasternak, who knew Marlene from the "Blue Angel" from the Babelsberg studios, prevailed to get her the role. Her name was Frenchy, and she acted in "Destry Rides Again" (The Big Bluff) at a Wild West dance hall. At the time when filming started in California, German troops had invaded Poland.

The film became a resounding box office success. The world premiere at the Rivoli Theater in New York was a veritable storm of excitement. For the first time, after a long time, the voice of Marlene Dietrich was not only asked for her acting ability but for some action too. She asked not just for a 'coat rack,' to which she had told mocking the Anglo-Saxon humor. "Marlene Dietrich, Frenchy of the Wild West in a Tingel-Tangel as the "Blue Angel" … a hard-nosed, full war paint, deep whiskey voice, hits like "Little Joe the Wrangler and The Boys in the Back Room at their best," in the "New York Times.

Another paper praised her as the "heart and soul of this good, old-fashioned wild western." Marlene was in great shape, the compulsory break of one and a half years had helped her, and therefore she had not lost her voice. "See what the boys in the backroom want to have, she trills with her delightful alto voice, and we immediately go through the mark and leg. It is indeed amazing and overwhelming. "

Friedrich Hollander, composed the songs, which got as great as the turbulent action with cowboys beating the sheriff. Entrusting him with this task was the idea of Pasternak. "You've Got That Look that The Leaves Me Weak" and "The Boys in the Backroom" became total hits for the record companies and the music publishers. At the age of thirty-eight, Marlene Dietrich had a new, handsome success as a singing actress.

Her voice had also grown more rooted, exciting, and attractive. With the springy melody and ambiguous lyrics, the glory of "The Boys in the Back Room received the 'poison' they demanded. She took the cinema audiences with them. This was, after a long time, a true Marlene Dietrich hit. Marlene Dietrich also moves up from her 137th position as a cash poison at the end of 1939. From then on, she shot a few other films with Joe Pasternak. She calls her work for Universal, in terms of the war that had begun, the time of "Flight from Reality."

That was true as far as the subjects of the films were concerned. But there was another side that was sobering to look at as part of the money she earned. These films were spent on political and human ventures. It was to prove beneficial for many emigrants and Nazi opponents who had managed to escape and start emigration, and in many cases even as life-saving. In the movie city of Hollywood, everyday life initially continued as usual. They did their work, went to the premieres and spent the free weekends with their friends. Meanwhile, Rudi Sieber also stayed in Hollywood. He had succeeded in getting to America with their daughter Maria at the outbreak of war on the last British ship leaving France's coast. With that, the Dietrich-Sieber family was safe. Erich Maria Remarque, who arrived in America a few days after the war began, was also in Hollywood, where he lived with Marlene Dietrich in a bungalow on the Beverly Hills Hotel.

When the filming of the film "The House of Seven Sins" in the South Sea begins in the summer of 1940, Marlene Dietrich once again as a nightclub singer, the German troops were already marching in her beloved city of Paris. In the middle of August, the film has not finished; two German air fleets were beginning the "Battle of Britain" with terrorist attacks on the English civilian population. At the time when the films premiered in New York, the focus was on the Führer Headquarters with the draft of the directive in which it states: "The German Wehrmacht must be prepared to fight a war against and overthrow England & Soviet Russia in a rapid campaign (Operation Barbarossa)."

In California, the war and its horrors felt like almost nothing. The Roosevelt government practiced "benevolent neutrality" against the countries attacked by Germany, which consisted of weapons and equipment supplied by the United States. At that time, a select air committee was working in Hollywood, which had already been founded in 1933. Under the leadership of Ernst Lubitsch and Billy Wilder, it supported rescue operations for the politically endangered and persecuted, and organized practical relief measures for the arrived refugees. Marlene Dietrich was instrumental in this work from the beginning, helping wherever and whenever she could.

Naturally, others such as Heinrich and Thomas Mann, Max Reinhardt, Arnold Schoenberg, Franz Werfel, Eisler and Brecht, Carl Zuckmayer, Albert Einstein and Otto Klemperer were among the active German anti-fascists in the USA. Fritz Kortner, as well as Salka and

Berthold Viertel, whose house in Santa Monica near Hollywood became a center of political and artistic exchange of views. Meanwhile, the "Seven Sinners" was running with complete success.

The cinema crowd in big and small cities and countless US communities took a liking to the 'box poisons' and enjoyed this story with action in which beautiful singer Bijou, a lady of dubious repute, runs away from her beloved naval lieutenant not to ruin his career. There are again several exciting fights with a fabulous final brawl, in which the entire establishment is in ruins. The critics praised the movie, especially Miss Dietrich, who stretches almost too seductively on her hips, strumming her eyelashes, and conjuring up a cool, amused smile with her thick-painted lips, and at times letting go of the censored jokes to have missed laughing. Of course, she sings three sensual songs in the same husky smoky voice, notably "I've Been in Love Before" and "The Man's in the Navy" where she wears some dangerous clothes. Other critics liked the "tremendous comedy," the local color, and the fact that the movie had three vocal numbers. Who thought Marlene could sing?

A large New York daily newspaper prophesies the title "The Man's in the Navy" that it would become a hit. The "New York Herald Tribune" went even further claiming that vocal star Marlene Dietrich was better as a Wild West lady than in the "Blue Angel." The quoted remark, "Vocal numbers, just as Marlene could sing them," refers to the fact that her voice had deepened and darkened over the years. With the certainty gained in the reproduction of Lola's voice, Lieu songs: it was easier to deal with the word and melodic lines of a song.

A director who might have told her how to treat the individual songs did not have, and never needed to. She is her own director in all the nuances of her rhythmically resiliency, highly musical and delicate chant. When the critics came to the conclusion that they were songs, as only Marlene could sing them, they formulated the idea that Marlene Dietrich understood something of her industry and was not a dilettante, neither in singing nor in songwriting, and that someone had to be a professional. If she is confident in dealing with the boys, then she is also dealing with the text and sound material of her songs.

The "Dangerousness" always lies in the repetition of its choruses or individual lines. It can be stated more elegantly, their songs are tailor made dresses, which only get their value through the preciousness of the body that is in it. And between the staves always this eye opening voice, the half-opened eyelids, the half hints and hints that give more than the fulfilled illusions. You'll understand, darling, when I say:

"I've been in love before, it's true, Been learning to adore just you. Some old romance taught me how to kiss, To smile like that and sigh like this. I've been in love before, you see, So you mean all the more to me! A heart that's lived when it was true: I've been in love before, have not you? "

From the nightclub of the "Seven Sins," the new "Love" song quoted here began its triumphal march into the studios of radio and records. Universal, affiliated to the film company Music Corporation New York, copyrighted the new hit in 1940, and Robbins Music Corporation made it commercially available on the world market. On the records and the printed music, Marlene Dietrich's composer now appeared in the new, Americanized spelling as Frederick Hollander. With "I've Been in Love Before" and "The Man's in the Navy," she has won two more attractive songs for her performances during the war and for the repertoire of her tours, which she began in 1954. In the movies that follow "Seven Sinners," she sometimes has to sing again, but big hits they weren't.

In "The Flame of New Orleans" (1941), she acts as a fortunate adventurer, passing through the middle of the wedding ceremony giving her orator's vote to the richest man in New Orleans. It is the same woman who used to sing a song about the spring flora with an innocent look on her face. "Miss Dietrich, despite her fabulous appearance, is and remains more of an enigma than an actress," wrote the critic the "New York Times." In "Manpower" of 1941, she is given the umpteenth time the role of a run-down pop singer. The team Hollaender-Loeser had written two songs for the film, not very significant for the Dietrich repertoire. Both films did not reach the success of the previous ones. Otherwise, the directors who worked with her, such as Rene Clair, Georges Marshall, Raoul Walsh, William Dieterle, and Mitchell Leisen relied on the same surefire effects that established Marlene Dietrich's worldwide reputation: her charming, casual vocal performance, her extraordinary beautiful, slender legs, to their very nature, in short: on their certified sex appeal, which facilitated the work of the directors. They did not need to rehearse her because Sternberg, the creator of this fictional character, had already completed the work. There was hardly anything left to add, and if there was, Marlene Dietrich did it herself.

America was no longer neutral in the war. In December 1941, Germany declared war on the United States. The US had been in a state of war with Japan since the Japanese Air Force raided Pearl Harbor. The changed world situation forced Marlene Dietrich to think about how she should deal with this situation. She commented on her feelings as follows: "I felt a sense of responsibility for the war Hitler had caused. I wanted to help stop this war as soon as possible. That was my only wish. When Japan attacked America, I gave up what I had ... There were not many "celebrities" willing to share the inconvenience of the war with the soldiers. America had taken me in when I gave up Hitler Germany. You cannot only take - you have to give too. That's already in the Bible." War help initially included entertainment programs and tours within the country to collect money.

Marlene Dietrich sold "bonds," a type of war bond, in nightclubs, in factories and elsewhere, sometimes six to eight times a day, sometimes at night. Troop assistance on the fronts of the Second World War had not yet been organized. She was still able to take part in a number of films whose titles are merely to be mentioned here: "The Lady Is Willing" (1942), "The Spoilers" (1942), "Pittsburgh" (1942), "Follow the Boys" (1943)) and "Kismet" (1943). From a film critic's point of view, they are nothing special, as Marlene Dietrich knew, but she expected her family will need money while they are away, and so she assumed the roles.

The movie "Follow the Boys," mentioned before, is already a unique army entertainment movie, more like a celluloid show number program featuring big celebrities and music-hall stars like Sophie Tucker, Jeanette MacDonald, Orson Welles and Arthur Rubinstein at the piano. Marlene Dietrich made only one sequence for this variety music film. It was her Las Vegas Magic Number with Orson Welles who had to cut her apart.

Before Marlene Dietrich joined the United States Entertainment Organization in 1943 and joined the army, she spent time in Hollywood with a friend and actor Jean Gabin, who had come from occupied France via Spain to America. She helped him in his own words by "thick and thin, in love and admiration," provided for engagements, taught him English, studied the roles with him, cooked for him, set up a rural house on a plot of land with a garden and trees, so that he and his friends could feel at ease.

She portrays Gabin as a perfect gentleman, but utterly helpless in practical matters; he was like a "fish on dry land" and hung on her like an orphan. "I was willing to mother him day and night ... first, because I like to cook and have guests who eat for hours and enjoy it, second, because I only feel at home with French friends. Perhaps it was because I had lost my homeland in my childhood."

The homeland already lost by the First World War was called France, and the deep affection for this land was what Marlene Dietrich writes: "We were all uprooted and homeless. We were all in a foreign country, had to speak a foreign language, we had to get used to foreign customs and habits, to strange ideas. We felt lost, even though we were all famous movie people."

Marlene Dietrich lived in a rented small house in Westwood in 1942 with two beautiful Persian cats. In the house belonged the usual hobby room, which biographer Charles Higham portrays as a curiosity cabinet. An ice cream machine stood on the Ping-Pong table, next to it an ironing board, a broken candlestick, and a globe, and books were lying around on the floor. This was the right environment for the unruly Gabin. "Marlene sat for hours on the radio and listened to the radio broadcast, Mr. Anthony. Her favorite record, Rite of Spring, was constantly being played. She was a chain smoker and drank only a cup of black coffee for breakfast. "

During this time, she took great care of her daughter. Maria, now grown up, found more of a relationship to her mother's job. She wanted to be an actress. Marlene Dietrich supported these plans unconsciously and let her visit the drama school in Hollywood founded by Max Reinhardt. In order not to have her mother's name, she did not want that at any price, she initially called herself Maria Marlowe, later Marie Manton. As a beautiful, charming girl with intelligence and a pleasant voice, she had considerable successes in several pieces. Her mother was, of course, her best teacher, not just in terms of wardrobe and makeup. With Gabin, she often came to rehearsals and performances, praising and improving Maria's acting with pedagogical and psychological sensitivity as perhaps only she possessed.

In the spring of 1943, in the United States programs were organized to increase production in the growing war businesses. The event series with Marlene Dietrich was opened in the Shipbuilding Corporation of California. She got up at three in the morning to visit the workforce of the second night shift at four o'clock, and at noon twelve o'clock came again to a second appearance for the day shift. The program consisted of the songs of the Blue Angel and all the other hits that had been popular through their films in America.

At the time, she also supported Red Cross actions, as she has always been dedicated to this charity benefiting orphaned children, the blind and the disabled throughout her entire film career. In February 1944, she traveled to New York to negotiate the program for troop management in Europe on behalf of the United States Entertainment Organization. The first mission was proposed in North Africa.

In an old military plane, she started with a troop from New York in the direction of Greenland and then the Azores. Arriving in Casablanca and Algiers, Marlene worked with comedian Danny Thomas, an actor from Lebanon, who made it into the organization. The first performance with the small group, which included an accordionist, singer, and artist, took place at the Algiers Opera House. The soldiers were thrilled with enthusiasm when legendary Hollywood star Marlene Dietrich appeared on stage in front of them. The gig cracked like a bomb, and when did bomb explode nearby, and the lights went out, thousands of men shouted in unison: "Continue! Keep going! "They all switched on their flashlights and aimed the beam of light on the stage.

Marlene Dietrich sang her songs, after which there was an encore after encore. Finally, she reached for her singing saw, which caused another ovation. Her emissary recalled that there was a bomb alert during the night where he wanted to go to the basement of the hotel where they were staying, but Marlene thought that was superfluous, she just said, "If we meet them, we'll send them home!"

From North Africa, Marlene Dietrich flew on to the Italian front. She wrote she was ready to "participate until the end of the war." Mostly the group played directly behind the front. The small show had a fixed program with some variations. The stage was either a rapidly assembled board frame or a loading dock of the truck. With Jeeps, they were agile enough to give four to five performances in one day.

It was tiring, often dangerous, and required a high degree of discipline, perseverance, and cold-bloodedness, as few people from civilian life can muster. Inventiveness was a top priority. Danny Thomas used his steel helmet as a drum and sang songs that he had rewritten to more familiar tunes the soldiers knew, trying to be amusing and witty. The songs responded to the situation of the day, always trying to process the experiences of the American soldiers in the fight of the anti-Hitler coalition against Germany and Italy. "And we sang, laughed, slept, ate, and took cover. When you are at war, you first learn to duck. Otherwise, life is easy. Three things count: eat, sleep, take cover." As far as food was concerned, Marlene Dietrich was eager to take the meals with the crews, not the officers. They saw her patiently standing in line in a sweater at the food dispenser, talking to the soldiers, one or the other tried out of the cookware. She washed her laundry and stockings in a bucket as if she had never known it differently in her life. "She was a fabulous comrade," remembers a colonel who accompanied her to Italy and France for a while.

Others, including high-ranking military men, praised her soldiery virtues. Of course, they were allowed, in the admiration of a very fascinating female personality, to exaggerate a lot. She was, in the end, a famous and stunning woman. And as for Marlene Dietrich, in the face of reality, she had to prove that she could be more than the "heroine" in the cardboard backdrops of Hollywood movie studios.

In Italy, she developed severe pneumonia, which had to be cured in Lazar of Bari. After a short vacation, she spent in the US in June 1944, she returned in September with her show to the troops in France. Here the stages were mostly pushed together trucks or wooden scaffolding, which were illuminated in the evening by the headlights of the jeeps. When it rained, you spanned a makeshift tent above it. The army required that only 55 pounds of luggage be allowed to be taken along. While Marlene used to travel with 30 trunks and a dozen hatboxes before the war, she now had to confine herself to the essentials. The four dresses she carried were sequined, which was beneficial because they did not need to be ironed for the gigs. Her only big suitcase contained a stage robe, uniform pieces, a jacket, proper pants, boots, and a hat. There are also photos of her with a steel helmet. She had never complained about anything during the time on the frontline mission. She remembered people who were with her, and never forgot to take the flowers the soldiers gave her.

The songs she used to sing during her two years as a troop advisor were "The Boys in the Backroom" by Hollaender & Loesser, the Broadway tune "Annie Does not Live Here Any More," her beloved American songs. " Taking a Chance on Love "and" There I Go Again," Cole Porter's Musical Hit " You Do Something to Me,"" You Go to My Head " by Coots & Gillespie, and not to forget "Lili Marleen" in the English and French versions. The most in demand was "The Boys in the Backroom," and she opened her performance with it.

Of all the songs sung in her films until then, this was simply like no other song suitable for the fighting troups. For several reasons: The song was originally made in the USA and had become something of a national anthem of cinema fans long before America's entry into the war. It was also one of the beloved westerns with James Stewart and Marlen Dietrich everyone had seen in the cinema. It was Frenchy's song that suited the milieu and the landscape, it smelt of whiskey, the boys and lost love, and it had an optimistic, inspiring character. Who could have done more with it than Frenchy Dietrich, who had created it and presented it to the boys in uniform?

On the screen, of course, there were only shootings and only film deaths. In 1944, everyone had to expect that the next day you would be hit by a bullet, a bomb, a grenade, and Marlene Dietrich too. The stanza she remembered became ironic in her severe accent. When she dies, she says in the song, the boys should not spend their money on flowers or their framed picture, not on a pompous coffin of burning candles around them and not on a preacher's "for talking of my glory and my fame." No, none of that! They should remember their song, and that's why she wants to sing the boys one more time here and now: And when I die, do not spend my money on flowers or my picture in a frame - Just see what the boys in the backroom will have and tell them I sighed, and tell them I cried, and tell them I died of the same!"

This vital melody, for its own glory and that of the boys, is musically illustrative of the many good Hollaender hits that reveal this composer's ability for precision, well-fitting, unambiguous, unwavering, and immediately memorable formulation of thought. Ernst Krenek once described these characteristics as the prerequisites for a good hit which he advised that every composer should of seriousness consider.

There is still much to say about the Boys in the Backroom, which is worth considering. First, the song in the film is absolutely the same as a turbulent, comedic, parody, and action film. Yet if one takes a closer look at it, you will make another interesting discovery, namely, that in its melodic texture it is related to the Lola song from the Blue

Angel of 1930: "Children, tonight, that's what I'm looking for - a man, a real man!" Frenchy and Lola have the same entrepreneurial impulse and unleashed vitality, which must provoke cheerfulness. Besides, Hollaender uses a sound similar to the sequence as a prelude to the vocal part, and it is no coincidence that the opening lines of the choruses have the same number of notes and syllables.

Similar features can be found for the linguistic side of the two determined songs. Just as the UFA librettist Robert Liebmann put the genius of the "Blue Angel" milieu on a brilliant formula with his "Lola, Pianola," Frank Loesser, the composer, and librettist with whom Hollaender collaborates in America is also interested in phonetic precision. He only used short rhyming words like "sighed, cried, died," or "same, name, flame," to which Hollaender always accents a lot. In the last part of the song, Marlene Dietrich already commemorates that exhilarating coloratura dark voice that enabled her to realize the necessary amount of humor and thus to make a comment on the flickering film and in general her roles as a tingel-tangel, bar or pub singer, which were her destiny.

In later recordings, her comedic talent, with her fabulous capacity for self-irony, becomes even more noticeable when, parodying herself, she delights the audience with her own elegance and delicacy, because it was foolish on such films and eternally hopeful for a "Blue Angel.

Marlene Dietrich published a journal about her assignment to the army, the notes about the last winter of the war were quoted as follows: Short reunion in the south of France with Jean Gabin, who was a soldier in a tank division of the "Fusiliers marins", (French naval infantry) - Entry into the liberated Paris with the troops of the Allies. - Reunion with Ernest Hemingway, who had come to Europe as a correspondent and lived with his wife for a few days in the Paris in the Hotel Ritz: life threatening situations in the course of further combat operations. Encircled behind the Ardennes front in the last major German offensive. An American airborne division brings the rescue. Commanding General Gavin lands with his parachute right at her feet. She was proud of it. During this time, however, "many killed, many wounded and amputated, large casualties and many letters to families in the United States."

After another brief stay in Paris, they went on tour again, following orders in the rearward areas of the Western Allies' frontier, which was moving ever farther along the German border. While most of her beautiful colleagues were content to remember the soldiers through pin-up photos, Marlene Dietrich, a traveling comedian, followed the soldiers of the British and American armies on her way. She froze her hands and feet in an icy winter in the Ardennes, and spent the night in the dark and cold quarters, to be back on the truck platform the next day.

There were no hotels behind the line; what they called accommodation were tents, barracks, or ruins. Among the many hardships that such a "service" in warfare brought with it was not just the rain, the cold or the snow. There were also rats and lice, and everyone had to see how one coped.

Marlene Dietrich said her involvement in the war was the only real thing she had ever done, and nothing in her life had seemed so difficult and so rewarding to her. Yet she was already over forty when she volunteered for troop support. Her determination, her vitality, her innate sense of responsibility and duty, and not least her decidedly anti-fascist stance, helped her get through this period of probation. She learned a great deal of suffering, saw wounded and dying, and later, when she had long since taken off her uniform, she gave concerts in one of the great theaters in London and Paris. She sang in her songs; "Tell me where the flowers are?" and "where did they stay?" the pain for the fallen, mutilated, buried, and murdered men of the cursed war.

As part of its propaganda campaign, the American Office of Strategic Services decided during the war to circulate several records with her songs. On it, both perennials in German and English were to be heard as well as the soldier's favorite song, "Lili Marleen." In the autumn of 1943 Marlene Dietrich included it in the repertoire. This song by the lyricist Hans Leip, which in English was now called "Lili of the Lamplight," was the opposite of the "Boys in the Backroom." Marlene Dietrich sang it as a soldier, to a certain extent, even if she was only "attached" to the army, to soldiers whose feelings she felt with her unique ability to empathize. Carl Zuckmayer once used the word "glorious" cinematography to express in the tone of contrived romanticism. The fact that she put the song first in her repertoire was and remained a political fact and a demonstration against Hitler's Germany."

There is an important story about her and the song, where she interrupted herself once during a broadcast by British radio and continued in German: "Guys, do not sacrifice yourself. The war is shit! Hitler is an idiot! "When she began to sing in German, quite impulsively," Lili Marleen," she was interrupted by the moderator, saying that this was an English broadcast. Miss Dietrich said nothing for a moment and then switched to the English version of Tommie Connor:

"Underneath the lantern by the barrack gate, darling, I remember the way you used to wait. 'Twas what that you whispered tenderly that you lov'd me, you'd always be my Lili of the Lamplight, my own Lili Marlene. My own Lili Marlene."

Had she performed in front of units of the French troops, she sang the French version of the "Lili Marleen," as it had been translated by Henry Lemarchand:

"Devant la caserne quand le jour s'enfuit, la vieille lanterne soudain s'allume et luit. C'est dans ce coin là que le soir On s'attendait rempli d'espoir tous deux, Lily Marlene - tou deux, Lily Marlene."

Marlene Dietrich raises the stanzas from the dust of the marching boots into a clean, poetic sphere where the feeling can be accepted through the absolute unsentimental, masculine manner of feeling in which she recites the "Lili Marleen." Once in the vocal-rich, tender French language, her "Lili Marleen" transforms into a real chanson. That is why the Belgian film historian Johan Daisne, in his essay on the history of the song, comes to the unusual statement that the "Lili Marleen" by Hans Leip is just as poetic for him as the best songs by Charles Trenet. This is high esteem considering Charles Trenet was the star of French chanson heaven in the 1940s. As the saying goes by American novelist John Steinbeck: "The most beautiful love song of all time. Too bad that it was written in German." How did it come about?

Of all the Marlene Dietrich songs, it is, one must first say, the song with the longest time of creation. The Hamburg Hans Leip wrote it as a soldier on a spring day in the year 1915 in Berlin, when he stood guard on the barracks. The song had only three stanzas, its own melody, and was pictured in his manuscript. In 1936, for the first time, a Munich composer set a professional soundtrack to it, Rudolf Zink, without much success. Of three stanzas, the song grew to five verses in 1935, when Leip put together his band "Die Hafenorgel" and recorded a poem in it. It must be said that the known melody comes from the Berlin composer Norbert Schultze, a particularly active partisan of the National Socialists, u. a. "Bombs on England Land," "Tanks Roll in Africa," and provided about twenty more "final victory" bombers for the fascist system marching into bankruptcy.

With the defeat at Stalingrad, was "Lili Marleen" because of the metaphysical final stanza, which was considered a destructive force,

"…From the quiet room, out of the ground reason lifts me as in a dream in your love mouth. When the late mists turn, I'll stand by the lantern like Lili Marleen once did."

Banned by Goebb it was officially no longer sent and sung. It was no longer in the prescribed "final victory" mood, and the melody was known to every schoolchild, for they already had political parodies like the following:

"Listen, you German Michel, / you will conquer yourselves to death! / The hammer and the sickle, / they will remain red forever! / You will never see Moscow / rather perished by it / as Napoleon once did!"

A favorite among the old timer records sought and collected in individual countries still today are recordings sung by the dark, heartfelt voice by Marlene Dietrich, as Belgian film historian Johan Daisne writes. In the sixties and seventies in her international performances,

Marlene Dietrich always gave this comment to the title: "And now a song that is very close to my heart. I sang it during the war. I sang for three long years: in Africa, Sicily, Italy, Alaska, Greenland and Iceland, England, France, Belgium and Holland, Germany and Czechoslovakia."

The remark "Czechoslovakia" refers to a meeting with the Soviet Army in May 1945 in Prague. Marlene sang her songs from a Soviet tank and received unusual applause in front of this auditorium. It was a sympathy rally from both sides. When she gave concerts in Moscow and Leningrad in 1964, she repeatedly talked about the meeting. She received the Congress Medal of Freedom from the US government after the war for her active service in troop management. The French government awarded her the Order of the Knights of the Legion of Honor and Officer of the Legion of Honor.

More valuable and essential to her was that she had discovered her ability to work alone on these war tours. She did not need any fancy studio equipment with all the trimmings, as was customary in film and theater, just a good pianist lighting technician for her solo appearances. She was only responsible for herself and her audience.

Alone, with only her voice, she could carry a show. This was a new experience the war had taught her and provided a far reaching importance for her future life.

On 8 May 1945, the war in Europe came to an end and in August liberation for imperialist Japan. Marlene was on German soil with the allied troops, so she visited her sister, who lived near Bergen-Belsen, and saw her mother in Berlin.

Over this time, there is a memory of Hubert von Meyerinck, who counted Marlene Dietrich among his "famous friends." He writes about his first reunion with her after the war: "We had not seen each other for many years, Marlene, when a letter fluttered into my dressing room one evening; I was playing Mackie in 'The Threepenny Opera.' "Hupsi, please come to my mother's apartment - I'm here - but do not tell anyone. Your Marlene." At the time, there was still no fraternization order. In a kind of dew, I finished the last act. And then I went by bike to you, all Berlin was cycling at that time. Your mother, Frau von Losch, opened it for me. I waited a while in the little furnished room where your mother lived, for she too had lost everything and my heart was pounding. So much had happened since we last took leave of Paris. So much horror, so much fire, and crime - how would you greet me this time? And then it was like always. Only you wore uniform this time. You traveled with the American army and sang your songs to the soldiers. You also sang "Lili Marleen"

... Your hair was blond and silky as it used to be, and your legs, those famous legs, under the short uniform skirt, slender as ever. But your face had become tired. The next day I brought you quickly to some colleagues. Heinz Rühmann and Hilde Körber, Walter Frank and Alexa von Porembsky, and it was you who gave Rühmann the tip for the piece "Harvey," the part with which he later had such a great success.

Then I saw you again shortly afterward. Your mother died soon after your visit, and you came from Paris to her funeral. You stood at the grave, slim, black, and still. It was raining, and there were ruins around us."

On her return to the United States, Marlene Dietrich had bitter experiences, like all the demobilized American soldiers who suddenly stood on the street, felt little of the fatherland's gratitude, and found themselves rather superfluous. She describes her arrival in New York as follows: "We were dropped off at La Guardia Airport. Of course, it was raining. Nobody was there to help us. We carried our stuff ourselves, were inspected from head to toe, and all our beloved warriors had to give up thinking.

There we stood, without a penny in our pocket, in front of the taxi-stop, and did not know where to go. If you have no money, you're completely lost, especially in America. It did not help, as we said, we just came from the war; nothing to do. "We are busy. So get on with it!"

Critically, she recounts in her memoirs: "None of the many promises were made ... We returned when it was all over, and we were greeted with nothing but stupid comments. The men were not allowed to enter a restaurant without ties, regardless of the medals on their paratrooper uniforms ... Those gentlemen behind their big fat steaks, who had never experienced war, never heard a bomb, were firmly established; we were the outsiders, and I have to say that we liked it. We all wished them to hell. "

The disappointing experiences of the first months after the war ended in the US sharpened her critical eye for this country and its blatant contrasts. She writes that in her political views she is quite realistic that America is not built on honesty and that one cannot judge other countries if life in her own country is based on fraud and robbery, on war against the weak, on the annihilation of the Native Americans, which gave them a dollar for the peninsula known today as Manhattan.

The experience of the war and the experiences with the country in which she lived, whose citizen she had become, had undoubtedly influenced her further life, her political views and the message of her concert programs that brought people together. Marlene Dietrich progressed in those years in unusual ways to engage in worldwide catastrophes for reason and humanity. Now the war was over. She had to see where and how she furthered her career as an actress and who her connections would be.

Erich Wolfgang Korngold – film music

Erich Wolfgang Korngold (May 29, 1897, in Brno - November 29, 1957, in Los Angeles) was an Austrian composer, conductor, and pianist. He became one of the most respected film composers in Hollywood even though he was a classically trained composer with young ambitions destined for the concert hall. During Korngold's time in Hollywood, he was very much in demand for writing the music for feature-length films. He received two Oscars for his work on the movies Robin Hood and The King of the Vagabonds. Korngold was one of the first international composers to gain recognition in Hollywood.

Initially, he gained wider fame through the opera 'The Dead City' from 1920 where he saw himself as a representative of modern classical music. When he was 11 in his native Austria, he wrote ballet music which was highly regarded by the critics. He was hailed as a Wunderkind and was prompted to pursue his musical talents on his instrument, writing original works, as well as conducting their premiere.

The young Erich Wolfgang was considered a child prodigy in Vienna. At the age of eleven, he caused a sensation by composing the pantomime ballet 'The Snowman.' The original piano work was orchestrated by Alexander von Zemlinsky and premiered in 1910 to the choreography of Carl Godlewski under the direction of Franz Schalk at the Vienna Court Opera. After that success Korngold was encouraged and promoted by the Viennese high aristocracy. At the age of thirteen, he wrote several piano sonatas soon followed by a drama Overture and a

Sinfonietta. His early works were often performed by prominent twentieth-century musicians, such as Bruno Walter, Artur Schnabel, Arthur Nikisch, Wilhelm Furtwängler, Felix Weingartner and Richard Strauss.

Other early works were his Piano Sonata which he wrote when he was 13 and two one-act operas. The second opera "The Ring of Polycrates" was premiered in Munich under the star conductor Bruno Walter. It wasn't until the premiere of the opera "the Dead City" at age 23 did he received international acclaim as a composer.

Through his music, he also became better known as a conductor. He came to the United States in 1934 to compose film music as this was becoming a not uncommon career direction for composers of this time; Igor Stravinsky, Aaron Copland, Sergei Prokofiev, and Leonard Bernstein, to name a few. In 1938, because of his Jewish background and growing National Socialism, he finally decided to stay with his family in the USA.

Erich Korngold was the son of the music critic Julius Korngold and the nephew of the theater actor and writer Eduard Kornau (actually Eduard Korngold). His first composition teacher was Robert Fuchs. Later he became a pupil of Alexander von Zemlinsky and Hermann Graedener. The famous composer and conductor Gustav Mahler, heard Korngold play a piece of his and called him a 'musical genius.' Gustav Mahler then told Korngold's father it would be a waste of time for him to study at a conservatory as he was far too advanced for that. It was through Gustav Mahler that the young Korngold became a pupil of Zemlinsky.

Korngold's opera compositions 'The Ring of Polycrates' and 'Violanta' (both 1916), 'The Dead City' (1920), 'The Miracle of the Helians' (1927) had great success in their time and made him, along with Richard Strauss, the most performed opera composer in Austria and Germany. His most significant success, at that time, was the opera 'The Dead City.' A recently staging by Johannes Erath has been revived in the Graz Opera in 2015. In 1926 he received the Art Prize of the City of Vienna.

In 1924 Korngold married Luise (Luzi) Sonnenthal (1900-1962), the granddaughter of Adolf von Sonnenthal, with whom he had two sons.

Korngold felt like a representative of the modern age. His G major Violin Sonata op. 6 was played on March 9, 1919, in Schönberg's Association for Private Musical Performances. However, he never left the 'old' tonality. In the 1920s, he took more and more the views of his father, who was an outspoken opponent of musical modernity. So he composed in 1931 the 'Four Little Caricatures for Children' op. 19, in which he caricatured the styles of Arnold Schönberg, Igor Stravinsky, Béla Bartók and Paul Hindemith.

Korngold was not only an opera composer but also liked to write in the operetta style. He worked from Leo Falls estate on the operetta 'Roses from Florida' and brought it successfully to the stage. The premiere was on February 22, 1929, at the Theater an der Wien (Vienna). Based on another operetta 'The Queen's Lace Handkerchief' by Johann Strauss (Son), he created the stage work (The Song of Love) in 1931 in the Berlin Metropol Theater. By reworking the instrumentation and extending the harmony Korngold succeeded in playing to the style of the 1920s.

During the time of Austro-fascism in 1934 Korngold followed the invitation of Max Reinhardt to Hollywood. Korngold was to arrange film music for Reinhardt's film 'A Midsummer Night's Dream.' He was one of the first to receive a contract to write film music without ever having any prior experience writing for film. Korngold had already worked with Reinhardt in Europe on operettas like 'The Fledermaus' and 'La Belle Hélène.'

Korngold set new standards in the still early history of film music by enlarging the orchestra from dance band size to a full symphony orchestra. He partially intervened to direct the language of the actors to fit the rhythm of the music. Korngold also adapted the music of Mendelssohn to Reinhardt's drama, recasting Mendelssohn's broad passages and partly using motifs from Mendelssohn's other works. The reviews on the film led Reinhardt to make no further films; however, Korngold's music was unanimously praised.

In the next few years, he spent the winters in California as a film composer for Warner Brothers. Korngold's engagement in Hollywood meant prestige. He was also given more freedom than other film composers as he was mostly free to choose his projects and of course, received a generous salary. For the 1936 resulting film 'Anthony Adverse' he was nominated for an Oscar. In the following year, Korngold received an Oscar in 1938 for 'The Adventures of Robin Hood'. These and his other works were influential for the entire industry, including the music of John Williams on Star Wars. In total, he wrote the music for 19 films between 1935 and 1946, many for adventure genres such as 'The Lord of the Seven Seas' (1940) and 'The Sea Wolf' (1941).

At the time of the annexation of Austria to Nazi Germany Korngold was busy in Hollywood with the work on Robin Hood. His contacts with Warner Brothers enabled him to bring his family and parents to the United States.

The film historian Ruth Behimer wrote about his music for film: "Korngold's score was a splendid added dimension. His style for the Flynn swashbucklers resembled that of the creators of late nineteenth-century and early twentieth-century German symphonic tone poems. It incorporated chromatic harmonies, lush instrumental effects, passionate climaxes—all performed in a generally romantic manner. Korngold's original and distinctive style was influenced by the Wagnerian 'leitmotif', the orchestral virtuosity of Richard Strauss, the delicacy and broad melodic sweep of Puccini, and the long-line development of Gustav Mahler."

The composer & conductor André Previn also spoke about the composer: "Korngold was a master film composer. His wonderful melodies, orchestrated in the most gorgeous Richard Strauss-oriented manner, are a joy to hear, even when the films are forgettable. Robin Hood, The Sea Hawk, and Elizabeth and Essex all display Korngold's musical extraverts, and for some reason, his unmistakable Viennese kind of sentiment helped Errol Flynn be a convincing English hero."

In 1946, he finished most of the work on film music and turned back to classical orchestral music. (1946 the cello concerto op. 37, and the violin concerto D major 1947). His violin concerto is recognized as part of today's violin soloist's repertoire. Between 1949 and 1951 he stayed in Austria, where he was well received by the audience but not by the music critics. During this period, the Symphonic Serenade in B flat major op. 39 was premiered by the Vienna Philharmonic under Wilhelm Furtwängler, as well as the 'The Silent Serenade' op. 36, both in Vienna. During the second trip to Europe in 1954/55, the premiere of his only symphony in F sharp major op. 40 by the Vienna Symphony Orchestra took place in October 1954 as part of a radio concert with the Society of Music Friends. The review of the performance said it was "poorly rehearsed and performed." Five years later the conductor, Dimitri Mitropoulos wrote, "All my life I have searched for the perfect modern work. In this symphony, I have found it. I shall perform it the next season." But Mitropoulos's died before that could happen.

The attempt to return to absolute music after 1946 remained largely unsuccessful for Korngold. His late work was accompanied by the contemporary reception in the US and Europe with sharp criticism and often disregard. Korngold's music was increasingly forgotten. He died on November 29, 1957, after a heart attack and was buried at Hollywood Forever Cemetery in Los Angeles. His wife Luzi followed him in 1962. The simple grave plate adorns the notes from his famous opera The Dead City.

After a publisher reprinted his works in the USA in 1972, Korngold's compositions experienced a renaissance internationally. About Hollywood and opera music Eric Korngold once said "Puccini's Tosca is the best film score ever written."

On Broadway

Eight times a week, every day except Mondays, just before 8pm, Wednesdays and Saturdays in the early afternoon, the mood around New York's Times Square is almost like Christmas. People rush in a festive mood with expectant faces in one of the many theaters. (about 15 million people last year)

Although hardly any of the stages has a public wardrobe and you have to stow your coat under your seat in winter or in the rain, you've got yourself dressed up. Before or after the performance, a dinner is planned in one of the many theater restaurants; perhaps even at Sardi's on 44th Street. Buses have brought visitors from New Jersey, Connecticut or Long Island through the Hudson Tunnel and across the East River bridges into the heart of Manhattan.

On Duffy Square, one of the traffic islands in Times Square, the queues at the TKTS pavilion dissolve slowly just before Showtime. Here you can get tickets for one of the not sold out performances for half the price. In the lobby of the Palace Theaters opposite, where Judy Garland once celebrated her great triumphs, a lady from Key Biscane, Florida, has just arrived for the musical "Beauty and the Beast." Program books, posters, T-shirts, drinking vessels and other souvenirs with the logo of the show are now available everywhere. The foyers are the same as at a Christmas bazaar. There's 'No Business Like Show Business.'

From his stone pedestal on Duffy Square, the old comedian, George M. Cohan, stands in bronze now over a century past: "Give My Regards

To Broadway!" Because only here, in the stage houses of Broadway and its side streets 40th to 54th and because of its floodlights so-called Great White Way, has made Irving Berlin the idiom in "Annie Get Your Gun".

Only on New York's Broadway, is it decided today whether a show will be a global success or not. Since Andrew Lloyd Webber's sensational American opening in 1982 with the musical "Cats" based on poems by T. S. Eliot, which no one believed, was still one of the most successful shows of all time. Lloyd Webber's "Really Useful Groups" and the London show mogul Cameron Mackintosh with his French authors Alain Boublil and Claude Michel Schoenberg ("Les Miserables", "Miss Saigon") dominate part of the terrain so confidently that the term "Britain The "invasion" has become a household word in theater circles.

In addition, there is the Off-Broadway, which produces small musical comedies and music dramas that are easily playable all year thanks to their smaller budgets. In Canada's Toronto, with the La Jolla Playhouse in San Diego, California, and the Goodspeed Opera House in Connecticut, new, creative musical centers have emerged on the American continent. Also in Oslo (»Chess«), Vienna (»Freudiana«, »Elisabeth«) Amsterdam (»Cyrano«) or in Alsdorf near Aachen (»Gaudi«), musicals have emerged that withstand international standards - but hits only in their own country.

None of these productions, including Toronto and San Diego, will be globally valid unless they have passed the Broadway test. Whoever writes theater in America thinks in the categories of New York. No critic of a major New York daily newspaper would keep his dignity discussing a play being given in Brooklyn, on the other side of the East River. Only if the same piece is played on Broadway, it deserves attention. No one knows exactly what the difference is in theatricals premiere on Broadway and the premiere of a new play in the provinces. That only the premiere audience of Manhattan can judge the qualities of a theatrical production expertly is a cliché, but certainly not entirely unfounded.

"A law applies to all the different productions in the flimsy Manhattan Theater City, "said the late critic Frederick Mellinger, "they have to be technically wholly mastered. The taste in New York can be argued equally everywhere. But nowhere you're so sensitive to amateurish dilettantism as on Broadway. " Perhaps this is because, as a rule, everyone involved in a show, from the managers, directors, actors, singers, and musicians to the shining, stagehands and usher in New York lives in the spirit this city, popularly known as the Big Apple, has been breathing Broadway from childhood.

What does not come across, really, has no chance. The tiniest error of detail can be deadly. The show business of this city has the highest standards and has the oldest tradition. Manhattan, the centerpiece of the city's five districts, is divided into rectangles from the 14th street onwards; it's hard to get lost. Broadway is the enfant terrible. It runs across the city from southeast to northwest, 21 miles long, from Battery Park to the Bronx. Originally, it was a warpath of the Algonquin Indians, to whom the Dutch had bought the whole island of Manhattan for a few hands full of glass beads some 400 years ago.

Following its path, the giant city has widened from south to north, leaving relics of show business on every street corner: theaters and dance halls, cafes and gambling dens, bars and brothels - at City Hall, Union Square, Herald Square, and finally Times Square, "Every class of society, every nationality, every imaginable species is represented here," wrote the chronicler James McCabe in his book Lights and Shadows of New York in 1879: "Here high and low, poor and rich are rushing at a speed which is peculiar to New York and very confusing to a stranger. On the street there is a real republic mess of elegant gentlemen in fine wool cloths, jeweled ladies in silk, and beggars in miserable rags. From early morning until midnight, the stream does not break." Even this quote, formulated more than a century ago, could explain why the musical is as it is.

From ancient times and until today, New York has been a melting pot of all skin colors, denominations, and conventions. What is unique about this is that the ethnic minorities do not really merge but maintain their particularities in closest proximity: Chinatown, Little Italy, the

Brighton Beach of the Russians, the Brooklyn of the Jews, the Spanish Harlem and the Harlem of the African-Americans. Already the next street, the 48th, is again the territory of Asians and Italians. The road ahead, the 46th, operates under the number "Little Brazil."

Each of these nationalities brought their cultural and entertainment traditions to the city's vibrant theater, which now blended into something entirely new - like New Orleans' African drum rhythms, protestant chorales, and European jazz marching music. Thus, the swing of the theatrical orchestras came from jazz, and that is from the blacks from the southern states, which immigrated in bright flocks to the former white Harlem at the beginning of the century. Musical comedy owes its wit to English settlers, religious refugees from the British crown, the eastern European Jews, and again the blacks, which laughed with irony and ambiguity literally for their lives.

The Broadway musical is, on the whole, a conglomeration of ethnic traditions and ethnic humor, with the city's various minorities always powerful enough to eliminate miscarriages and inconsistencies immediately. Not so much the strict critics in the mass media are the supreme supervisory body for the entertainment artists, but rather the public. In the commercial theater system, the success of a piece is decided exclusively at the box office and musical that has passed this test can rightly hope for worldwide success. That's why Broadway is such a focus for art. Plays such as Rodgers and Hammerstein's "The King and I" playing in Siam, or "The Sound of Music" about the Trapp family in the Alps, Jerry Bocks and Sheldon Harnick's "Fiddler On The Roof" deeply rooted in Eastern Jewry, Stephen Sondheim's "Pacific Overtures" (Japan in the 19th century), John Kanders and Fred Ebbs "Cabaret" (the thirties in Berlin) correspond to emotional and cultural archetypes that people consciously or unconsciously remember. That's the secret of why American popular culture, including the musical, could be so wholeheartedly accepted worldwide: parts of its national traditions are culturally deposited and commercially tried, or at least not in conflict with its values.

Wherever such a thing stirs, as in the protectionist France of the Minister of Culture Jack Lang in 1994, a spokesman for Euro Disneyland can explain in a snazzy, but not entirely unjustified way: "We try to sell nothing but fun, pure entertainment." This, however perfect, "Broadway Celebrates": Throughout the summer of 1993, the New York entertainment theater around Times Square, as we know it today, was celebrating itself. Theaters, in addition to the repertoire routine, had individual performances. Tap dances: danced in the streets, theater stars were seen and heard, the industry papers came out with extra editions. The special edition of the Show-Business-Vibe "Variety" quickly became a sought-after collector's item, as did the special edition of the "New Yorker" with the pearls of his theater criticism from a whole century. For on May 22, 1893, the first stage palace in the area was opened on 42nd Street with the American Theater - just a stone's throw away from Times Square, Manhattan's throbbing heart.

Until then, New York's entertainment district had stretched up Broadway from Herald Square to only 39th Street, with the Casino Theater as the northern point. In the south, this was initially limited to gas lanterns, later electrically illuminated nightlife by Tin Pan Alley, spans to the 28th street with its music publishers. The Metropolitan Opera with its yellow brick building, the mighty publishing houses of the "Herald" and the "Tribune" as well as the monumental department store Macy's dominated the architecture. "In a straight line to Times Square," says Nick Cohn in his book, "The Heart of the World," "Theaters and hotels, dark red-furnished cafes, and brightly red-framed bars lined up uninterruptedly to each other, and overall there was an incessant glare on those lights, brighter than any sun."

"The names alone," Cohn went on, "sound like a psalmody: Frohman's Empire and Brown's Chop House, Albany, Continental and Knickerbocker, Weber and Field's Music Hall, Daly's and Garrick's, Palmer's and Miner's, the skyscraper electric billboards for Budweiser and Edison Phono, the Kid McCoy Saloon, the original Real McCoy, and the most screaming, fanciest of all, The Fiery Chariot Race in New

York, a picture of twenty thousand light bulbs so artistically arranged, that it looked like these pre-neon-era horse-drawn carriages were actually going around in a circle, as if the horses were really galloping, kicking up real sand and dust. "

When theater manager and speculator Henry T. French, the son, and associate of a publisher of stage works, began building his American Theater on 42nd Street in the early 1890s, there were no businesses in the neighborhood, neither subway connection nor car traffic and no street lighting. Small pubs and bars at best illuminated the darkness in this almost provincial residential district. French went from the beginning to the full-blown. In the half-block between 41st and 42nd Streets on the Eighth Avenue, he set up an amusement cathedral for 2100 visitors. A golden dome spanned the great theater hall. For the first time, visitors, electrically lifted, drove in elevators to their seats in the balconies.

There were Variete and Tingel-tangel: American Vaudeville. The diversity of live entertainment in the Giant City at the turn of the century and in the first two decades before the dawn of the cinema era is almost unimaginable in the age of television. Literally on every street corner, in the late nineteenth century, there were concert saloons, dumps and slaps, honky tonks, and other sites of rude, folk amusement with acrobatics and equilibrists, sword swallowers, jokers, sorcerers, pianists, and bartered prima donnas. But also some later prominent variety talent got their first chance here.

Minstrel shows with profane jokes and with the Commedia dell'arte, delighted Americans throughout the nineteenth century. In 1919, the comedian Al Jolson sobbed the Minstrel song Swanee on the revue stage of the New York Winter Garden Theater. The young composer George Gershwin had inspired the Stephen Foster hit Old Folk's At Home aka Swanee River from Opa's eighties; it became his first hit. Al Jolson helped as the jazz singer 1928, again in Minstrel disguise. Walking stages, which presented a mixture of Minstrel jokes, dressage, operetta and mumbo jumbo in short sketches, began to move through the States from 1880 onwards. In 1880 there were about 50, around 1900 more than 500.

Vaudeville theaters were built especially for them in all major American cities with the biggest of course in New York. Opened in 1913 and run by show-business entrepreneurs Benjamin F. Keith and Edward Franklin Albee until 1932, the Palace Theater on 47th Street and Broadway became the symbol of a whole epoch, surpassing the old American Theater of Henry French by far in its splendor and glory. Around 1920, Keith and Albee controlled about 400 theaters across the country and influenced the entire American entertainment industry.

Only one block from Times Square, between 43rd and 44th Streets on Sixth Avenue, the owners of New York's Luna Park, Frederic Thompson and Elmer S. Dundy, had at one time a cost of what was then an astronomical one-quarter million dollars to build the Hippodrome Theater. On the 115 foot-deep stage with its two circus rings and a pool for water games, so-called extravaganzas were performed here for twenty glittering years: elaborate melodramas with marching music and intermezzi circus attractions. Staged aerial battles and car races, sandstorms, and earthquakes showing eagles, cowboys, Indians, and fabulous horse riding that occasionally ended in the pool.

Restricted by the two streams Hudson and East River in its horizontal spread, Manhattan, in the guise of skyscrapers with precious copper roofs, grew into a city, boring not one, but three, competing subway systems in the massive granite of it's foundation. Just as quickly, the metropolis's nouveau rich society rose above the plebeian distractions of men at the cranes and deep drills in their vaudeville. From London, Paris, Berlin and Vienna European operettas dominated the end of the 19th century.

In the 19th century, the gambling plans of New York's fashion-conscious music theaters - along with a few operas for the cultural elite, Jacques Offenbach's "Paris Life" made Montmartre a Dernier a name in the eighties. Ballrooms were Parisian where fashion created a French style and Can Can celebrated its first transatlantic triumph. Franz

Lehar's "Merry Widow", the "Waltz Dream" by Oscar Straus, and Leo Falls "The Dollar Princess," struck Broadway between 1907 and 1909 in three-four time intervals. Above all the English imports "H.M.S. Pinafore" and "The Mikado" by Gilbert and Arthur Sullivan were played around the turn of the century.

Under their influence, Gustav Kerker's "The Belle of New York" (1898) and Sigmund Romberg's "The New Moon" (1928), to which the librettist Oscar Hammerstein II wrote the lyrics, were among the composers to serve stages with operettas made in USA. Dungeon, Romberg and their colleagues Ludwig Englander, Karl Hoschna, Gustav Lueders, Rudolf Friml, and with the 25 much-played stage works of the extremely successful Victor Herbert, all came from Europe and composed so much for the pleasure of wealthy Americans.

When eighty-year-old multimillionaire Andrew Carnegie was asked how he thought of heaven, he said, "Sit quiet, do nothing, and listen to Victor Herbert's music all day." The comedy writer, composer, actor and later theater director George M. Cohan, was from an old comedian family from Providence, Rhode Island. On January 25, 1901, with the patriotic vaudeville sketch "The Governor's Son" in New York's Savoy Theater had to be closed after 32 performances. He sang "Give My Regards To Broadway," in 1904 in his third show, "Little Johnny Jones," on Broadway returned with good reception.

Flagging and little success, the comedian appeared in the role as an American jockey on the stage, which at a derby in England, won with the horse named King George. It had a simple story and then he sang the song "Yankee Doodle Dandy" to become a smash hit applauded by all of New York. Because of the birth of the Musical Comedy and Cohan's song of victory from "Yankee Doodle" George Cohan, rightly so, has a bronze statue of himself in Duffy Square on Broadway.

The European Victor Herbert and the American Cohan were so dissimilar in origin, tradition, and conviction that they could not represent Broadway at the beginning of the twentieth century, but rather competing against each other. But they defined the character of American music theater between 1900 and 1910 as opposing poles so clearly that Jack Burton could overwrite a chapter of his Blue Book of Tin Pan Alley with the titles of the most famous pieces by these two playwrights: Mlle. Modiste against Little Johnny Jones. " With the motto "Speed, Movement ... and as much as possible!" George M. Cohan made the vaudeville tradition of America flag wavering, dancing and singing patriotic poems popular within a decade. His call to grant country-born authors, composers, and performers the same theater-like opportunity as European composers and English mimes opened the stage door for America's comic talents of the Tingel-Tangel and the commercial pop song.

In the summer of 1906, a young wealthy revue producer, named Florence Ziegfeld, embarked for Paris to visit the Folies Bergère. A year later he opened his first "Ziegfeld Follies" on the roof garden of the New York Theater, in the Jardin du Paris, where he beat the pomp of the previous show with each production until 1931. Ziegfeld took over the opulence and the fashionable elegance from Paris. He made stars like Nora Bayes, Sophie Tucker, Fanny Brice, Mae Murray, Ruth Etting, and glorified his Chorus Girls, the most attractive far and wide.

Irving Berlin gave him a 1919 hit song for the "Follies" with the headline by "A Pretty Girl is Like a Melody. " Irving Berlin was the composer who had sold one million pages of sheet music in 1911 and a good 30 other rags - almost all of them hits. And that was the novelty of Florenz Ziegfeld: in addition to well-known operetta music, he hired all these young hit-makers of Tin Pan Alley as song composer for his "Follies": Louis A. Hirsch, Gus Edwards, Jerome Kern, Irving Berlin.

The Ricky-Ticky sound of ragtime.

"It was noisy, untamed music that was heard everywhere," noted the operetta chronicler Bernard Grun, "exciting as the Marseillaise, stirring as the Radetzky March, American as the Dixie song." (1917) As the Original Dixieland Jazzband jazzed ragtime in the New Orleans style for the first time, the swing in the orchestra trenches of the revue theaters became even sharper, true to the motto of George M. Cohan: "speed, movement ... and possibly much of it."

This was the ground on which between 1910 and 1920 the new musical of entertainment form sprouts: the birth of musical comedy from the spirit of ragtime, revue, vaudeville, and jazz. The shows were still out of order, songs and skits were unmotivated and only superficially linked side by side. It was now the hour of the book authors, the librettists.

Telling stories became necessary, and action was required. To date, it is unclear which of the many results of the long literary and dramaturgical learning process of New York comedy writers the label 'musical' really deserves. Accurate dating would always be given arbitrarily, and the abundance of shows was hesitant as the progress of their integration occurred for more than a decade.

One of the most important birthplaces of this art was the Princess Theater with squares on 39th Street, which offered intimate musical characters between 1915 and 1918. The first successful of these pieces, "Very Good, Eddie" (341 performances in 1915) described, psychologically already surprisingly chiseled, the errors, twists, and turns of two couples on their wedding voyage on a cruise ship. For this purpose, a farce from the year 1911 by Philip Bartholomae "Over Night" was musically pepped up with the help of the lyrics of Guy Bolton and the composer Jerome Kern: which became the model for the production process of many musicals until today.

As the hugely clever songwriter P. Wodehouse for "Oh Boy!" (463 performances, 1917) complemented the creative team of the Princess Theater shows, the shirt-sleeved Americanism of George M. Cohan's comedies in the New York theater scene was given a more European-literary counterbalance. Bolton's polished dialogues, Wodehouse's cockney-tinged wit, Kern's musical dignity, and elegance made an anonymous New York theater critic write: "This is the trio of musical fame: Bolton and Wodehouse and Kern; Better than anyone else you can name: Bolton and Wodehouse and Kern. Nobody knows what on earth they've been bitten by all I can say is I mean to get lit an' buy orchestra seats for the next one that's written by Bolton and Wodehouse and Kern."

In those years more and more at the heart of the songs were the libretti. Wherever sung, the plot became an emotional knot that bound joy and exuberance or frustration, melancholy and grief. The lyrics required linguistic awareness. They learned about the dialects, ethnic idioms, vernaculars in the countryside and the big city, but also about high poetry. Irving Berlin likened a pop song to a well-written three-act drama that runs in just three minutes. The librettists forced the lyricists into lyrical condensation, and it was not uncommon to find verses that went far beyond the scenes for which they were written. "I'll get along as long as a song is strung in my soul" it's said in a song by Vincent Youmans (music), Billy Rose and Edward Eliscu (text) from 1929, or even: "I only know there ain't no love at all without a song," postulated Theodor W. Adorno in the eyes of his friend Kurt Weill, "to invent their own melodies in the image of the moment. Only this, most perishable, "is permanent."

According to Irving Berlin, this job required "to formulate familiar concepts and findings in such a way that they sound like new. People believe in each song to know the next line in advance. Our art is not to give them what they expect, but to surprise them."

The composer and copywriter of well over a thousand popular songs knew what he was talking about. Pop songs play an important role in our emotional sphere. They accompany love experiences, help with the management of conflicts, release imagination and from depression. Often they act as keys to open locked regions of our memory. By the twenties at the latest, the art of songwriting on Broadway became a high culture. More and more songs blew up their scenic ties, became standards, in the best cases perennials.

Lorenz Hart, a descendant of the German poet Heinrich Heine, sat down with the composer Richard Rodgers the standards: "We'll have Manhattan The Bronx and Staten Island too ..." Lyricists such as Ira Gershwin (The Man I Love), Cole Porter (Night and Day), Dorothy Fields (Can not Give You Anything But Love), Oscar Hammerstein II (Ol' Man River), E.Y. Harburg (Over The Rainbow), Alan Jay Lerner (Could Have Danced All Night), Johnny Mercer (Come Rain Or Come Shine) and Stephen Sondheim (The Send In The Clowns) produced word games for Broadway and Hollywood that stamped the normal phrasebook full.

From then on, they were measured by the ingenious internal rhymes of Cole Porter's "Anything Goes": 'You're the Nile, you're the Tower of Pisa, You're the smile of the Mona Lisa. I'm a worthless check, a total wreck, a flop, But if, baby, I'm the bottom, you're the top!' Since the Roaring Twenties, Broadway has produced songs with verses of this kind that are comparable to the best expressions of the German art song of the Romantic era, the French chanson, and the Italian Canzone.

At the end of the 20th century, they are experiencing a new heyday under the name Cabaret in New York. The thirty hotel bars, supper clubs and cabaret rooms offer high-class song interpretations of the classic repertoire of Arlen, Berlin, Gershwin, Porter and Weill, alongside new text creations night after night in the mid-nineties in Manhattan: the Cafe Carlyle on Madison Avenue, the Russian Tea Room next to Carnegie Hall, the Rainbow & Stars on the 65th floor of Rockefeller Center and so on. "Cabaret," says Arthur Pomposello, manager of the Oak Room at the Algonquin Hotel, "is something other than anti-government poetry in German council cellars."

It's the center next to Broadway, with the iconic literary hotel Algonquin on 44th Street, that's the lively scene of American song culture. Judging by the perfection of this Asphalt poesie libretti the musical comedies in their twenties still left much to be desired.

The songs were not always logical from the plot. With intermezzi, interludes, as they are from the operetta were very rare. Leonard

Bernstein knew the widespread divergence of music and plot in the scores. They were left alive and played games, recitatives, taking the example of George's and Ira Gershwin's "Oh Kay!" of 1926 was amusing in one of his TV shows: "With the lovely little tune 'Someone To Watch Over Me' I now have the faintest suspicion that it was written before the text had existed at all. It does not quite fit the situation in which it has a young girl singing it."

Bernstein continues "The situation is as follows: A girl falls in love with him. He has already promised marriage to another. The girl sits on the sofa and gives the keyword: "Oh, I know that I shall meet him again someday. "And then she suddenly begins the introduction of the song by singing:" A certain lad had in mind ... had in mind! After playing three scenes with him! Nonetheless, she continues, "Looking everywhere, have not found him yet!" ... have not found him yet! What did the first act actually do?" Plausibility was not yet indispensable.

Finished songs were added if the director thought he needed another hit and also canceled if they did not 'hit' at the audience during rehearsals in the provinces. For example, the song "The Man I Love", which some chroniclers regard as Gershwin's best creation, was removed from two shows before the premiere, because it slowed down the plot tempo: "Lady Be Good" (1924) and "Strike Up The Band" (1927). Conversely, according to this production concept, it is still possible today to tailor new musicals from Gershwin's perennials, loosely based on his classical music comedies - such as with the successful pieces "My One And Only" in 1983 after "Funny Face", and "Crazy For You" 1992, from "Girl Crazy", 1930.

In Woody Allen's "Bullets Over Broadway" (1994), the emergence of a Broadway show in the 1920s is depicted as a sidesplitting comedy. Relatively early in this theatrical hit comes a phrase that the viewer, unfamiliar with New York's theatrical system, cannot yet understand at this point: "By the time we get to Boston, it's as fat as my sister-in-law's ass." An actor who eats so many sausages and pies that he is getting fatter can be visualized. But why is the ensemble in Boston? It is the capital of the US state of Massachusetts north of New York and is - as Washington, Philadelphia or Newark (New Jersey) - for the New York Theater a so-called tryout town.

Here, musicals and shows are tried before their premiere on Broadway in front of an audience. "Lost in Boston" is, therefore, the winged record label for several CDs, on which Varese Sarabande offers first-class interpretations of fine songs by famous composers on the way to the Great White Way but have fallen by the wayside. The classic tryout cities with their nearly one-hundred-year theatrical tradition have now joined other rehearsal and production centers jet age global network.

Closely linked to Broadway since the great days of ingenious comedy writer and comedian Noël Coward in the thirties, London's West End developed with the music of Joan Littlewood, Lionel Bart, Anthony Newley, and Leslie Bricusse in the Fifties and Sixties to the musical metropolis of the Old World. Andrew Lloyd Webber's Musicals, which premiered partly in London and partly in New York, have strengthened the West End-Broadway connection since the 1980s so firmly that US producers are already rehearsing their New York-themed pieces in London for cost reasons.

Toronto and San Diego are becoming increasingly attractive. Three-quarters of a century ago, when most modern chroniclers, Rodgers and Hammerstein's "Oklahoma!", had finally tested their tires, the distances were even more manageable, and the scenery was not yet high-tech.

When the curtain rose for the first time in March 1943 for a premiere in New Haven, Connecticut, there appeared a middle-aged farm-maiden perched on stage making butter. Behind the scenes, a tenor-voiced sounding like a ballad folk song. Should this be the opening of a musical? Only in the middle of the first act did the choir and ballet appear. Foreseeing a flop, New York star critic Walter Winchell had merely sent his secretary to New Haven. Before she boarded the train for the return journey, she cabled her boss: "No legs, no jokes, no chance."

The song, with over 2000 performances, became the biggest hit on Broadway and finally established the musical in the understanding of the public as independent theater form…a milestone undoubtedly. As the first product of the epoch-making collaboration of composer Richard Rodgers and the book and songwriter Oscar Hammerstein Il, whose works influenced Broadway for two decades, and also for its success, the exclamation point behind "Oklahoma!" was justified. However, for its coronation contributing to the development of the genre "Oklahoma!" is probably overestimated.

The latest reissue of the classic "Show Boat" by Jerome Kern (music) and Oscar Hammerstein Il (book and song texts) from the year 1927 in a display of the premiere show of "Lady Be Good" in 1924 on Broadway (Liberty Theater), the staging of Harold Prince at the New York Gershwin Theater in 1994 forced a rethink. "A dramatic event in the history of American musical theater," Frank Rich called this flawless production in The New York Times.

The sensational reworking of the original American material from the "Ol 'Man River Mississippi" as a symbol of majestic equality in the birth and decay of the generations has de-dusted the piece and finally put it into its proper historical perspective. Especially the orchestration, the romantic duets "Make Believe" and "You Are Love" and the dramatic mastery always had "Show Boat" as the closest American operetta. Harold Prince, as a director and/ producer of more than 50 musicals, operas and dramas, the most creative head of US music theater in the last half of a century, presented "Show Boat" not just-as-any but as "the first large, contemporary, modern musical ever".

Prince: "For the first time, it combined the happy-go-lucky naivety of traditional Broadway musical comedy with serious themes. The score ranged from the easy-going 32-bar pop song to the echoes of grand opera. It's without question Jerome Kern's Porgy and Bess." Sensitive critics were aware of the significance of the work immediately after its premiere on December 27, 1927, in New York's Ziegfeld Theater, although that season was the most prolific in New York stage history.

In Christmas week alone, no fewer than 18 new shows celebrated their premiere. Brooks Atkinson of the New York Times saw "Show Boat" only a few days later and then described it as "one of those epoch-making works about which old men still chatter in 25 years when the scenes long ago have been carted to the trash."

The story of the musical is the step-wise integration of its elements. A quarter of a century passed before the conglomerate forming Musical Comedy, an American musical comedy with an unmistakable profile. Almost another century passed before the musical play (also Book Musical) with its mammoth seasons had become popular in the public eye. According to common chronicler opinion, this status was achieved in 1943 with "Oklahoma!" But from the first beginnings in the twilight of the turn of the century, a European-influenced and a genuinely American entertainment concept on Broadway was in conflict.

The "European" line began with the operettas of Victor Herbert and led to Andrew Lloyd, without any major differences, through Jerome Kern ("Show Boat"), Rodgers and Hammerstein II ("Oklahoma!"), Lerner and Loewe ("My Fair Lady") Webber and Claude Michel Schoenberg. Romantic melodies were a weakness for (from New York) exotic subjects with love as the main theme and one of the benchmarks of European operetta and opera sounding instrumentation. Today it is a story of the gradual integration of the appropriate tune with the right character.

The "American" line is in clear opposition to the operetta with George M. Cohan ("Little Johnny Jones"), who considered movement, swing, tempo and an aggressive impetus was more important than romance and orchestration. It leads through George Gershwin ("Lady Be Good"), Rodgers and Hart ("Pal Joey"), Irving Berlin ("Annie Get Your Gun"), Cole Porter ("Kiss Me, Kate"), Frank Loesser ("Guys and Dolls), Leonard Bernstein (West Side Story), Kander and Ebb (Cabaret) and Jerry Herman (Hello, Dolly!) to Cy Coleman (City of Angels), William Finn (Falsettos), Jonathan Larsen (Rent) and especially Stephen Sondheim. Specifically American, often big-city subjects, a satirical-socially critical attitude, swift, succinct melodies, jazz, rock or experimental sounds usually characterize works of this kind.

Of all these composers, Europeans as well as Americans, the Briton Sir Andrew Lloyd Webber, artistically controversial, has his musicals "Joseph", "Jesus Christ Superstar", "Evita", "Cats", "Starlight Express", "The Phantom of the Opera, Song and Dance, Aspects of Love, Sunset Boulevard, Jeeves and Whistle Down the Wind. With his "Really Useful Group" he managed since the early eighties to organize the international musical events of the upper financing level almost monopolistically.

At the age of eight, he studied violin and French horn at the Royal College of Music in London and at 13 he won a scholarship to attend Westminster School. He owes his father William Lloyd, composer, and director of the London College of Music, a deeper understanding of classical music. When Andrew, already famous, played the main 'Memories' song to him before the "Cats" production, asking whether that might sound too much like Puccini, Daddy said, "No, it sounds like a million dollars."

The preference for the operas of the 18th and 19th centuries, for composers such as Puccini, Salieri, Rossini, and Meyerbeer, shaped his childhood and remained in his musical imagination. But he eventually grew up in the age of rockers, scooters, Beatles and hippies. That's why opera and pop were probably close to him.

On the occasion of the American premiere of the "Phantom of the Opera" in January 1988, the composer and pianist William Bolcom ("Songs of Innocence and Experience") tried to understand the Lloyd-Webber phenomenon for the New York Times: "We are dealing here with mass entertainment. With that in mind, Lloyd Webber shows more artistry on this show that he might like to blame. There is a certain amount of cunning in the details: the whole-tone scales for the opera of the phantom, the gap-like insets, the way in which scenes are musically structured. There was always a deep gap between opera and pop. And this kind of theater tries to bring both together. It's a style of transition, the encounter of two kinds of music."

"Lloyd Webber's musicals did not mark any style of transition but claimed the author of the successful German-language play Elisabeth," Michael Kunze. Rather, they are a completely new product: "Operas of the rock genre with great emotions, dark powers and fads of fashion." The classic musical like Frank Sinatra and Benny Goodman belonged to the swing era. The musical by Elvis Presley, Little Richard, and Led Zeppelin, invented by Andrew Lloyd Webber and based on pop and rock charts, correspond to the bombastic spectacle of rock music.

Kunze: "With the Broadway musical, this new musical is only remotely related." Objection, Your Honor! To characterize the genre, I proposed a definition in 1965 that still applies today: "The musical is a music theater that has become popular in New York, usually a two-act model of popular theater, the elements of drama, operetta, revue, variety, and - in exceptional cases - the opera connects. It is often based on literary models and uses the media of American pop song, dance and entertainment music, and jazz. Show scenes, songs, and ballets are integrated into the plot."

If you realize that today's dance and entertainment music is rock, rap, reggae, house, hip-hop or disco, and the term opera is mentioned explicitly, then this definition also applies to Andrew Lloyd Webber's stage plays. They are fully in the tradition of the Broadway musical. Even spectacles like the falling chandelier in the "Phantom" or the veritable helicopter on the stage of "Miss Saigon" are "show scenes." Although authors such as Jerry Herman, Alan Menken, Kander & Ebb, and others have delivered more successful performances over the last two decades, Stephen Sondheim is Andrew Lloyd Webber's real antipode in the orbit of the musical at the end of the century; an American with a universal flair, creative, uncompromising, idiosyncratic, cranky with a touch of genius.

Pupil of librettist Oscar Hammerstein Il, songwriter for Leonard Bernstein's West Side Story, Sondheim has been writing music and poetry for his shows since his musical satire "A Funny Thing Happened on the Way to the Forum" (1962). With each piece, Sondheim has opened up new territory, both subjectively and formally, Doors open to unknown, sometimes abysmal, decadent or morbid soul landscapes.

"Company" (1970): Relationship crates and mid-life crises of bored city couples between hashish and hard drinks. "Poster of the premiere series of" "Follies" (1971): a meeting of two withered stage stars in their theater in the evening before it is demolished, "Sunday in the Park with George" (1984): the painter and his model in front of Georges Seurat's famous painting of Sunday afternoon on the island of La Grande Jatte. "Assassins" (1991): the American presidential killers and their motives. "Passion" (1994): the shameless passion of a dying man for a young officer.

Again and again, formal adventures, tonal and dramaturgical experiments with elements of Kakubi Theater and Far Eastern sounds in "Pacific Overtures", operatic sound eruptions in "Sweeny Todd", minimalist sound shades in "Sunday in the Park with George", It's rare that the composer, who abhors repetition, has produced memorable songs like "Send In The Clowns" or "Being Alive", but the number of performers challenged by this difficulty is in the legion.

Beatles Fever

It was a crazy day, this June 23rd, 1966. A Thursday with perfect weather with a cloudless blue sky. At ten in the morning, the sun is burning so hotly on the streets that fried eggs can be cooked on the asphalt. On such days, Munich sits crowded in the outdoor public pools or beer gardens. One does as little as possible on these days.

Everything is a bit different on this Thursday. Since April the city has been preparing for it - in the editorial offices, at the airport, in the police headquarters, in the schools.

Now the time has come: the day the Beatles come to Munich. The students skip classes. Already at eleven o'clock, they gather at Riem airport in Munich, taking their place in front of the barrier gates at the northwest exit of the area. Alone 600 fans jostle near the entrance guarded by a hundred of the Munich police. Crowded they all stand on the access roads: girls in colorful mini skirts, boys in tight jeans, their hair just shoulder length with self-painted posters and big photos in hand. At 12:40 pm the BEA plane is to land from London, but the flight is late. Minutes become hours and stretch endlessly on. From the police loudspeakers swirls music, the music of the Beatles. This should calm the fans, as riots should be prevented.

In between announcements: "Another five minutes." But there are more. More than six, seven minutes, ten, fifteen, sixteen - finally, at 12:56 pm the comet IV lands. It is a regularly scheduled flight, no private plane, no particular plane. On board are the group, the managers, caregivers, business travelers and Beatles fans, who spent almost two hours flying time to see their idols up close. 100 journalists, photographers, cinematographers of the television and the newsreel are allowed to take the airport bus onto the runway and witness the arrival first hand.

Even before the plane comes to a halt, it is relocated. The ground staff can hardly roll the gangway to the machine. The door in the fuselage swings open and two customs officers fight their way up the stairs, giving each other as much tedium and routine as possible. On the plane, they check the passports; ask for goods to be cleared. Outside, a white Mercedes appears at this moment with a loud honking: it is the car for the Beatles.

And then finally they come: first Paul McCartney, grinning in a black suit. He waves to give a signal to the fans. Yelling, shaking, the posters and photos are held up. In vain, they attempt to climb over the barriers. Then John Lennon in a bright sports jacket, followed by George Harrison in a wine-red corduroy jacket, a crumpled corduroy hat on his head. A square pair of sunglasses almost covers his whole face and finally Ringo Starr with a Tyrolean hat. They are there. It's practically a dream. But the sun is shining and it's daytime.

The four of them jump down the stairs, into the Mercedes, which leaves immediately. First a police patrol, then the Mercedes with the Beatles, another police patrol, then the five white Mercedes for the caretakers and managers of the group. Finally, again, two radio and tv trucks followed by more police. The sirens are switched on, the blue light can hardly be seen in the bright midday sun.

So it all goes to the northwest exit, at a fast pace through the gate, not waiting for the screaming and waving fans. A girl walks beside the car, wants an autograph, but a policeman catches her by the arm and pulls her back behind the barrier. The driver stops briefly and immediately, five boys jump on the trunk. Short and suddenly full throttle again, and they fall down like stacked potatoes.

It's 1:10 pm. The column turns into Riemer Land Street. The traffic lights are switched to green; also, policemen regulate the traffic at the critical intersections. Motorists follow the group, drive next to the Beatles car, and can get autographs from the open car window. The journey into the city takes 30 minutes to the Hotel Bayerischer Hof Hotel. There are many more people along the route. Not all are as young as you imagine since curiosity knows no age limit. Being there is everything on this day.

At 1.45 pm the first radio patrol car turns into the Pranner Street, disappears into the underground car park of the hotel. The supplier garage door is opened as this is the only way the Beatles can get into the hotel. In front of the main entrance are waiting over 3000 fans and the street is totally blocked. Four different suites are reserved for the Beatles, and all on one floor. Waiters know precisely which. They sleep in two double rooms. The beds are moved apart. First, they order tea with sugar nine times. For two days the Beatles will stay in Munich. This Thursday, apart from a press conference at 4 pm, there is nothing left on the official schedule.

Press manager Tony Barrows has planned for 500 journalists, photographers, and cameramen who have also received an invitation for the hotel nightclub. This invitation is also their passport to other events. No one is allowed to go to the hotel without them. It is all controlled as if one wanted to protect an essential head of government from a bomb attack. Ten minutes for photos, then ten minutes for questions, then the same time for radio interviews and finally television, also only ten minutes. Tony Barrows explains all this with the air of a royal ceremonial master, standing in front of a raised platform with the table where the Beatles will sit.

But they arrive twenty minutes late. "The elevator got stuck," they explain when they finally come. Faint applause accompanies the manager on the way to the table. And there they are: Ringo in a suit with centimeter-wide red stripes, John wears a crumpled jacket, Paul has stayed in dark colors, and George shows himself in a maroon velvet jacket. Manager Brian Epstein, on the other hand, looks English & stiff in a white shirt and a tie in blue.

The press conference begins almost listlessly after the photographers have cleared the area in front of the table. The Beatles spent the night before departure in the recording studio, and the heat seems to paralyze them even more. They seem like private people, sitting behind the table, in front of a protective wall of microphones. They are not reachable, but staying together by themselves.

The answers are polite, John Lennon is witty and clever, but the concise answers are irrelevant and not binding. The Beatles do not even scratch the surface, they joke with themselves and the reporters. They appear distant, bored-arrogant, but not refusing. They are stars, and in ten minutes you cannot get to know them or understand them. Admiring ten minutes; that's all the reporters can do this afternoon. A press conference like so many with the Beatles: Brian Epstein thanks you for your interest, and his protégés disappear.

For the next 24 hours, the Beatles stay by themselves, invisible to the public. If the fans were not standing in front of the hotel, regularly calling for their idols and scream nobody would notice anything of the Beatles. As the fans shout in vain, it seems to be a dream. In the corridors of the Bayerischer Hof between the sink, clothes rack and beer bottles: finger exercises before the performance in the venue Circus Krone. Police keep watch. Should a fan really succeed in getting into the hotel, he will not get into one of the group rooms. There is no trick to disguise you as a room waiter. Room waiters and police know each other. Cheating is impossible.

No one knows what the Beatles are doing in their rooms, whether they are reading, playing, or sleeping. In the evening, the Beatles appear at the hotel's swimming pool. Paul McCartney has a letter while his friends prefer to sit on the edge of the pool and cool from the inside with whiskey and coke. Again, they are among themselves.

Paper balls, girl's shoes, and teddy bears

The day on June 24th starts at 1 pm; late for the Beatles. They have breakfast in their rooms, and then prepare for the two concerts in the evening in Munich's Circus Krone. Police officers are at their posts. Already the first fans appear. The police are reinforced; after all, 250 officials regulate the traffic and ensure order. Also, there are water cannons, loudspeaker that entertain the waiting fans with music, and a police camera caravan that films the scene, as a lesson for future cases.

Another problem the police have to deal with: Fake maps have surfaced. They are sold at very high prices. The four map publishers are arrested the evening before the concert. Some of the concert tickets are found with them, but no one knows exactly how many were actually sold. Every visitor must be carefully counted. At 4.30 pm, the doors will be opened.

Immediately a pushing and jostling begin as if it were about getting the last rescue boat on a sinking ship. Dark clouds rise in the sky, lightning flashes across Munich, the wind stirs up dust as a storm arrives. But the fans do not leave. Only when it pours out of buckets, will the curious get there's. Almost without any problems, ticket-holders can now enter the rotunda.

No one is happier about this thunderstorm than the police command center. Almost all issues are abruptly eliminated, and luckily, as the police say, the rain does not stop. That holds at least most of the curious at home. It becomes turbulent shortly after 6 pm. The concert has already started.

The first group to perform is "Cliff Bennet & The Rebel Rousers." Then the "Rattles" appear. "Mood", The Hamburg group is almost as popular in Germany as the Beatles. The voltage increases. But the Beatles have not arrived. Only now does their car drive through the back door. When the gates cannot be closed fast enough, more than a hundred fans try to storm the building. Apparently, the police are ready to act.

The stage now features "Peter & Gordon". Peter is the brother of Jane Asher, the girlfriend of Paul McCartney. The two sing gentle ballads, just before the storm for some quiet moments. Then the time has come - finally. The announcement goes out with the screams of the fans.

In dark green suits, they jump on the stage: John, Paul, George, and Ringo. The guitars are connected to the amplifiers, the hands move, the Beatles' lips open - they sing, but one hardly hears anything. The devil is going down for 25 minutes. The fans stand on the seats, stretch their arms, shake their heads. 3000, who act crazy, hypnotized staring at the stage, screaming, crying, cheering again and again. Paper balls, addresses, girls' shoes, teddy bears fly in large numbers on to the stage.

It hardly gets any softer between the songs as the enthusiasm is always full force. Those who are not lucky enough to sit in the front row do not understand a word and do not know which hits the Beatles are playing. At that time, the Beatles' equipment was 800 watts strong - critics said that it was big enough to turn the "running noise of an ant into the thunder of a frightened elephant herd" (Süddeutsche Zeitung, June 25th, 1966). And yet the fans override any sound that comes from the amplifiers. Against the electronics of today's groups, the amp was nothing more than a portable radio in relation to a stereo system. Much has changed since then, but then it was the absolute biggest available. No other group in the world played as loud as the Beatles….but not loud enough.

The Beatles played eleven songs on this tour, including Yesterday, She's A Woman, Paperback Writer and I Wanna Be Your Man. But you can only guess that by the fragment of sounds. After each song, the Beatles bow - the only sure sign that a new song begins. With this bow, they thank you for the applause - but provoke only a stronger shriek. And suddenly everything is over, like a haunting. With the last guitar sound, the Beatles disappear, even before the fans get the idea. When they catch themselves, asking for encores, the four are already sitting in the dressing rooms enjoying their dinner before the second show.

Roadies are starting to clear the site. Fans are already waiting in front of the doors to watch the Beatles at 2 o'clock. Tumult in Hamburg June 25th starts very early for the Beatles. Already at 8:25 am the train leaves the station. It is the same train in which a year earlier the English Queen Elizabeth II traveled on her state visit to the United States and Germany.

As a precaution, the platforms are closed off, as well as the entrance. But only a few fans have come. There's not much to see. The Beatles run to the train at the very last moment, disappearing into the compartment behind windows with drawn curtains. Without stopping, it goes to Essen. Again two concerts are on the program. A total of 16,000 fans come to the Concert Hall. Special trains are used again. They come from Frankfurt, Cologne, Dusseldorf, Solingen, Dortmund, Aachen, Osnabrück, Siegen, Minden, and Giessen. Again, thousands of fans stand in front of the hall, waiting in vain for a ticket, offering up to 300 marks for a seat.

Immediately after the concerts in Essen, the Beatles continued to travel by special train to Hamburg during the night. At 5.25 am on June 26th, the train enters Ahrensburg. 200 fans are already waiting at this early hour. Again they go in a convoy to the hotel, to the castle hotel Tremsbüttel. For the Beatles to sleep, a hundred police are in the area with water cannons. Thousands of people wait in the afternoon in front of the hall for the first appearance of the Beatles, hoping in vain to be able to see their four idols.

As darkness falls, more and more young people gather in front of the hall, in the park. The view outside resembles the scenes of Munich and Essen: screaming, waving posters and pictures, clapping and whistling. The police tried in vain to get the fans to leave. Water cannons are used, mounted police on horseback are there to put fear in the fans. As a fan goes with a knife on one of the horses, police pull rubber truncheons out. Only then do the fans retreat in a large group and in the direction of the city center.

Trash barrels are set on fire, trams forced to stop, shop windows smashed. 600 police officers are on duty. Eight policemen are injured, two are being hospitalized, 117 are being arrested, and eleven have been sentenced to fines or arrest for ten days to four weeks. Meanwhile, the Beatles celebrate at their hotel until just before four in the morning. Then, after a few hours' sleep, they continue to Tokyo, where they perform on June 30th.

At the time, the fans did not suspect and know that these six concerts in Germany were the only way to see the Beatles together. At the end of the year, they announce that they no longer want to perform. Ten years pass and the reputation of the Beatles has not suffered. On the contrary they became legends, even though each one tried with new records to escape the shadow of the Beatles for good. They have not all succeeded so well.

The sales were getting more significant, the masses more and more hysterical: The Beatles broke all records. They were the first to play in a stadium, the Shea Stadium in the United States, with 56,000 seats. What they sang was heard only in the first rows. The biggest in the sky but who were these four young men who roamed the world like Pied-Pipers of the twentieth century, bringing the youth to their feet in every country?

Today, the reports about the Beatles' only tour in Germany sound overly exaggerated, like fairy tales or sensationalism, similar scenes are unthinkable. But what happened in Germany was harmless against the mass hysteria of concerts in England, Australia, Japan, and America. If there were only hundreds or thousands in Germany who kept the police on the run, it was hundreds of thousands in other countries. The Beatles fever had packed concerts everywhere. The symptoms were the same everywhere. A musical event had become a social phenomenon: the lifestyles of a whole generation had changed.

Of course, the Beatles were not the saints they were then sold to be. Details about them came to the public later, mainly after the death of their manager Brian Epstein on August 27th, 1967, at a time when the Beatles were no longer performing, only working on their solo records outside the group. As long as Brian Epstein lived, the Beatles were screened. He censored news and photos. He was present at every interview to be able to interrupt at any time if the questions were too private. He allowed travel with friends, only photographers on tour. Brian Epstein had everything under control.

The Beatles should be four straightforward, happy boys. And who in those years believed everything the Beatles actually had to be considered harmless and appropriate. Everything was fun and happiness, with no misunderstandings disturbing the harmony. Within the group, there seemed to be no tensions, no arguments. They seemed to live like monks, without alcohol, and their relationship with girls seemed to be purely platonic. As far as we know the Beatles took advantage of their image of poor boys from the slums of Liverpool.

In June 1975; a photo from the time of the Hamburg "Star Club" was published, showing the Beatles with tubes of the stimulant Preludin. All bands seemed to swallow this drug at that time; otherwise, the long Hamburg nights were hard to endure. Eight hours on stage, singing in cigarette smoke and doing a show took its toll. But Brian Epstein did not want it to be talked about; it could hurt the image of the Beatles. So they formed their own exclusive circle, into which nobody came or left. But everyone was keen to be one of them.

Everyone wanted to be there to belong to them. So if you believed every story, all news was devoured. So did you grow your hair long, not wear your shoes, you dressed like them and saw the group as it officially presented itself: happy and disobedient? Then, the coverage of pop stars was one and the same, fans only hear about their idols as manufactured.

Mistakes and weaknesses are only mentioned if attached to the manager for the image of the group; cheerful to the bitter end. Only now known: with stimulants Pete, John, Paul, and George managed to play for seven hours every night in Hamburg's "Kaiserkeller." But even the fans are not willing to admit that they are basically no different from other people. They construct a monument to their stars, which only rarely, indeed not at all, corresponds to reality.

The star cult can sometimes take on ridiculous forms. For years, John Lennon was struck by the short-sighted nature of his life. Only from the end of 1965, he admitted it openly, he wore glasses. From that moment on, however, his glasses became an attribute of the intellectual John Lennon, who not only wrote witty lyrics but also painted and wrote books. A pair of glasses fits perfectly into the created picture.

John Lennon's wife Cynthia and his son Julian are not perfect for the image. The two were not taboo, John Lennon did not hide their existence directly - but it was not talked about. Again, it was Brian Epstein who did not want that. He believed that the Beatles female fans would react sourly when openly talking about John Lennon's family.

Today, this cult goes so far that stars conceal their real date of birth, make themselves younger, are officially 30 years old for years. Hardly a new group dares to declare that their members are already over 20 or even 25 years old as that could harm the success. And the fans are more or less involved in these games. You're just not ready to see the star as what they all are: people, full of flaws and weaknesses, no better than anyone else in our own circle of friends or acquaintances.

There is only one thing that distinguishes a star from us: their talent for composing songs, writing lyrics, playing the guitar or singing, and maybe some luck too. They earn their money and generate admiration, that's their job, but their talent is far from a reason to worship as a deity or demi-god. We welcome stars into our lives to remove the artificial or objectiveness of the every-day. At a time when smartphones and artificial intelligence are no longer science fiction and illusions, extreme notoriety can crumble the facade of an artificial fairy tale quality of stardom. Alone the word star expresses everything: far away, impossible to reach, only visible at night which is sweetened by sleep and dreams.

And the Beatles were stars, the biggest and most beautiful in the sky, so unreachable far away, so unapproachable, so iridescent and yet indefinite. Into them, all dreams and ideals could be projected onto it. And John Lennon was the leader of this "wonderful" group. Fans and finances when it became known in June 1963 that the Liverpool 'mushroom heads' wanted to release a new record, 500,000 of them were pre-ordered. It appeared at the end of August 1963 and immediately became number one on the English hit parade. It was: 'She Loves You,' the record that made the Yeah, Yeah, Yeah the Beatles famous all over the world. These three words became the battle cry of a whole generation in Europe and America.

But the Beatles were not more than just a new and exciting music group. Four hits were not enough to make four musicians world stars and to make them a sensation. That changed abruptly on October 13th, 1963. On that day, the Beatles appeared in the London" Palladium." Shows in the "Palladium" were regularly broadcasted by television. But everything was different that day. Thousands of fans, mostly girls, besieged the Palladium on Argyll Street in London, and five-and-a-half Englishmen saw policemen in vain trying to keep order in the traffic chaos of girls fainting.

The prominent daily newspapers reported the event on their front pages the next day. The Beatles had become a sensation. Nobody wanted to know which songs they played, and were musically good or bad. All this had become insignificant…. and so remained for the next three years.

Wherever the Beatles appeared, there was the same mass hysteria, girls fell in love, fainting, and police were entirely in action. The buzzword of "Beatlemania," of Beatle's fever, arose, a mass hysteria, not experienced in the world till now. The Beatles made it seem effortless almost anywhere in the world. When they flew to Sweden on October 24th, 1963, it came to chaos at London Heathrow Airport. The fans gathered in the visitors' balcony, in the departure hall, flooded the parking lots and access roads. When John, Paul, and George landed in Melbourne on June 13th, 1964, 250,000 fans blocked the access roads to the airport.

In the future, the Beatles' travel plans and departure times were among the best-kept secrets, and concerts had to be planned on a need-to-know basis. Nevertheless, the fans kept coming to know when and where their idols flew. On November 4th, 1963, the Beatles were the star guests at the Royal Variety Show in London's "Prince of Wales Theater." The audience included Princess Anne, the Queen Mother, Princess Margaret, and Lord Snowdon.

Although the audience wanted to respond to all Beatles performances, they did not dare with them in the presence of the Queen. So on that night John Lennon's famously said "Those in the cheap seats should join in, those in the expensive places can rattle their jewels." The Liverpool boys had broken the ice of etiquette. But no trace of success passed them by.

In November 1963 they had to cancel a concert in Portsmouth, as Paul McCartney was suffering from nervous stomach trouble. Soon followed a three-week appearance in Paris, in the "Olympia." At that time the most famous stars of the show business appeared in this theater. A concert at Olympia was a tough test. But the Beatles took that too with flying colors. As soon as they returned from Paris, they flew to America for the first time two days later, on February 7th, 1964. A contract was signed in December 1963 with a major American record label to eliminate most financial risk from the outset of the America tour. Negotiations for performances only began after the first Beatles recorded 'Want To Hold Your Hand'. January 1964 it was on the US hit parade.

When the Beatles landed in New York on February 7th, 3000 fans were waiting at the airport: The Beatles fever had also hit America. The final breakthrough came with their first appearance on the Ed Sullivan show on 9. February. They sang five songs: 'All My Loving', 'Till There Was You', 'I Saw Her Standing There' and 'I Want To Hold Your Hand'. Two days later, they appeared in New York's Carnegie Hall. The tickets for the concert were sold out within 24 hours. When then, the world's best-known magazine, Life, made a photo session with the Beatles for a story, the Beatles had made it: the dream of great success in America had become a reality.

From August 19th to September 18th, 1964, the Beatles performed 26 concerts in the USA. A year later, however, every hall in New York was too small for a concert. The organizer Sid Bernstein rented the Shea Stadium for August 15th, 1965, and Brian Epstein was assured his fee for nearly $10 million. It was not even 24 hours before the 56,000 tickets were sold. The Beatles were the first group in the world who dared to perform in a stadium. Even today, the triumph in the American hit parades is unique.

On March 13th, 1964, the Beatles took the first four places with She Loves You, I Want To Hold Your Hand, Please, Please Me, and Twist And Shout. At the 18th In December 1964, they were awarded three gold LPs for 750,000 sold. Even though the album had only been on the English market for two weeks, they were sold out.

Making a movie became a reality too. The Beatles set a record with their first film 'A Hard Day's Night.' It was shot in Liverpool and London. The documentary film features scenes from Beatles appearances and raids through the streets. Anyone may consider this all exaggerated, yet many scenes are recorded and have a newsreel character. A total of 15,000 copies were pulled from the market, so it could be shown simultaneously in 15,000 cinemas around the world. This ad campaign ploy has remained unique in film history until today.

Ringo, George, Paul, and John during the filming of their second film "Help," which began in Austria in March 1965, where Queen Elizabeth II, awarded them the Order of the British Empire at Buckingham Palace on October 26th, 1965 for their services to the English export industry. The Beatles in those four months, where there was hardly a country on earth not selling their records and running charts, or where the Beatles, were not at least, one of the top five. Hardly a day went by in the next few years, when not every newspaper reported on the Beatles, and where these newspapers could not print a special edition.

With the movie 'Help!' Ringo Starr was at the center of the story. He wears the ring of an Indian sect and is to be sacrificed. An exciting chase around the world ensues, as Ringo tries, again and again, to get rid of the ring. This film is nothing more than a cleverly made slapstick film, today it seems boring and superficial. But in 1965 it was a sensation, especially in English cinemas where it ran for months.

Fans, armed with sleeping bags, gathered in front of the cinemas to get a ticket. Meanwhile, boutiques were selling Beatles shoes, jackets and shirts worn by the Beatles, T-shirts, lipsticks, pillows and lollipops with images of the Beatles.

When Queen Elizabeth II gave the Beatles the Order of the British Empire even if she risked the outrage of conservative religious orders. One month later, employees of London's Harrods celebrity luxury department store had to work overtime for two hours, so the Beatles were allowed to shop for Christmas presents after closing time. That would be impossible during regular business hours. Nevertheless, the Beatles decided to end the tour.

The concerts became too frustrating and too dangerous, but even the group sound, which meanwhile had been produced in the record studios, could not be achieved live anymore. In May 1966 they gave their last concert in England. For the fans, it was a concert like any other. After their tour of Germany from 24 to June 26th, with two shows each in Munich, Essen, and Hamburg, they flew to Japan, and on August 12th, 1966, they performed again in America. Their third and last tour began.

It ended on August 29th, 1966 in the Candlestick Park of San Francisco, in the city from which came, just a year later, groups such as Grateful Dead, Jefferson Airplane and the singer Janis Joplin new music. Over 50 years have passed since then, and still, there is something astonishing in this old enthusiasm. When the Beatles record label decided to release 40 early Beatles hits in the spring of 1976 - a single a week - the Beatles again blocked the English hit parade. In April alone, ten of the Beatles were among the first 50 records, just like in the years between 1964 and 1966.

The Millionaires

How much the Beatles have earned can hardly be stated, as the official data differ considerably from one to another. Accordingly, the Beatles, the poor boys from the slums of Liverpool, have come to their millions. Until 1966 there were only the concert fees. Travel and hotel costs, salaries for managers, food, lodging, and transportation ate part of the fee. Often the revenue was confused with the profit or the amount paid to the Beatles did not take into account how much tax still needed to be paid. And this amount is significant in England, for some groups up to 97%. Of $ 200, only $ 3 is remaining. The primary source of income was and is the recordings. The Beatles received about $400,000 from one million LPs sold by 1968. The money went to Brian Epstein, the remainder to John Lennon, Paul McCartney, Ringo Starr, and George Harrison.

In England, Paul and John, as composers and copywriters, receive 6.25% of the retail price of every record sold. How much they receive from other countries varies according to the contract. By January 1968, sales worldwide were estimated at about 225 million records, assuming in 1968 long-playing record as five singles. Double albums count as ten singles. The number of 500 million LPs sold by June 1976 is likely to be realistic. They receive the same percentages when other artists record or perform their songs. Likewise, royalties must be paid to the Beatles when a Beatles song is broadcast or seen on TV. However, this depends on the size of the transmitter and the country. The society for musical performance and mechanical reproduction rights, continually monitors the rights of the authors and deducts the royalties.

Since every day in almost every country in the world a Beatles song is played, this amount is not insignificant. Similarly, royalties must be paid for performances at dances, in cinemas or in jukeboxes. The Beatles get about ten percent of the shop price of the sheet music printed and sold by each Beatles song. A fee is also payable if Beatles texts are quoted or published in a book or magazine. Holdings in other companies, such as NEMS Enterprises, also brought and bring the Beatles profits or losses, depending on the company's business performance. In the box office record of their three films A Hard Day's Night, Help! and Yellow Submarine, the Beatles received their payment. The Beatles made a loss with their entertainment company Apple, which was founded in 1968 as a record label, music publisher, film production and chain of boutiques. Because of poor business policies of this company, only the record company remains. Today, the total income of the Beatles legacy is not known precisely. It is estimated that the surviving member Paul McCartney has alone a net worth of around $1.25 billion.

Confessions of Music

HOMER philosopher and writer from Greek antiquity about the singer:

> All the mortal people of the earth accept the singer's music with respect and awe. The muse teaches the beautiful song and rules over the singers whose song is reaching out and invites the stranger to hear, Where he is not famous because of his arts, As the enlightened seer who pleases us through songs? This invites people in all lands of the earth.

The holy AMBROSIUS of MILAN about power and beauty of the church music:

> Music and poetry are the two wings on which the soul moved by joy, remorse and love is carried up to God. The harmony of heaven and earth is a concert of the universe in which the heavenly powers, the multitudes of the chosen, the whole choir of creatures, and also the waves of the sea participate. The voices of men, women and children resounding in psalms and responsorial resemble the roar of ocean waves. While there is a general murmur among the scriptures, everyone lays himself to silence and sings without disturbance as soon as the psalm is intoned. The songs, which have become so dear, continue to live

outside the church, at home, in the field, on the loom and on the ship, and in this way prove themselves to be a faithful mentor to the dangers of pagan songs.

Magister JUSTINUS on the Knighthood of Count Bernhard zur Lippe 1260:

> Whistles sound, the timpani sings, the flutes sound. See: the funny crowd of men driving is here ... This sings and pleases the heart in a lovely voice, while those in the song raises actions of the heroes. This touches the artificially arranged strings with the fingers; he understands the art of lovely lyre music. Many sounds emanate from a thousand holes in the flutes. The timpani are stirred with tremendous noise.

Martin LUTHER writes to Ludwig Senfl in 1530:

> Grace and peace in Christ! Although my name is so hateful that I must fear that you, my dearest Louis, would hardly be able to receive and read my letter safely, yet such fear has conquered my love of music, with which I gifted and charmed you of my God. This love also makes me hope that my letter will not harm you; because who wants to blame even those in Turkey who does not love this art and praises the artist? At least I even praise your Bavarian dukes, although they are quite averse to me, and honor them high above the others, because they cultivate and honor the music. There are no doubt many seeds of delicious virtues in the hearts, which are gripped by the music; but in which this is not the case, I respect the blocks and stones alike. For we know that music hates the devil and is unbearable. And I am not ashamed to confess openly that according to theology, there is no art which can be put aside for

music. Since, according to theology alone, it can do what otherwise only theology can do, namely make one's mind calm and happy, the obvious testimony that the devil, the author of sad worries and troubled thoughts, escapes almost as much from the voice of music as before the words of theology. That is why the prophets did not practice art like music, by linking their theology not to geometry, arithmetic, astronomy, but to music, so that they spoke the truth in psalms and songs ... Forgive my boldness and my wealth of words. Greetings to your whole choir of singers respectfully! Coburg, October 4, 1530.

SHAKESPEARE about the power of music in what you want:

Flerzog: Make music for me! (some musicians appear)
Good morning, friend
Well then, Cesario, that bit,
the old simple song of last night!
It seems to me, it greatly reduced the grief,
More than wanted word and air wise
From this fast swirl-footed time.
Come! One stanza only!

Johann Sebastian BACH on the basso continuo:

The basso continuo is the most perfect foundation of music, played with both hands in such a way that the left hand plays the prescribed notes, but the right reaches into consonant and dissonances, so that it gives a harmonious harmony to the glory of God and casual delight of the mind and, like all music, including the general bass finis and end, the cause is not to be anything other than God's honor and the recreation of the mind. Where this is not taken into account, there is no actual music but a diabolical babbling and noise.

Wolfgang Amadeus MOZART on the melody:

> Melody is the essence of music. Anyone who invents melodies is compared to a noble racehorse, the mere counterpoint artist with a rented postal dagger.

Friedrich von SCHILLER and Johann Wolfgang von GOETHE about The opera: Schiller to Goethe: Jena, December 29, 1797

> I always had a certain amount of confidence in the opera that made it look like the choruses of the old Bacchus festival the tragedy in a noble shape should unwind. In the opera you really leave those servile imitation of nature, and though only under the name of indulgence, could in this way steal the ideals of the theater. Through the power of music, and through a freer, harmonious stimulation of the sensibility, the opera harmonizes the mind to a more beautiful conception; Here, too, there is a free play in the pathos itself, because the music accompanies it, and the miraculous, which is once tolerated here, would necessarily make one indifferent to the material. Goethe's answer to Schiller: The hope you had of the opera you would have recently met in Don Juan to a high degree. But this piece is also quite isolated and Mozart's death thwarts all hope for something similar.

Johann Wolfgang von GOETHE on music as devotion or dance:

> The sacred is entirely in accordance with its dignity, and here it has the greatest effect on life, which remains the same throughout all times and epochs. The sanctity of church music, the cheerfulness and the mellowness of folk songs are the two hinges around which true music revolves. On both these

points, it always proves an inevitable effect: devotion or dance.

Heinrich von KLEIST on his love of music: August 1811

I feel that there may be many kinds of ups and downs in my mind that are still more and more out of tune with the urge of the disgusting conditions in which I live, and that a very cheerful enjoyment of life, if it ever happened to me, might be easy would dissolve harmoniously. In that case, perhaps I would let the art rest for a year or more and engage in nothing but music, with the exception of some sciences. I regard this art as the root, or rather as the algebraic formula of all the rest. And just as we already have a poet - with whom, by the way, I dare not compare myself - who has all his thoughts on the art he practices, referring to colors (Goethe), so from my earliest youth I have everything universal What I thought about poetry is related to sounds. I believe that the basso continuo contains the most important information about poetry.

Ludwig van BEETHOVEN on his work:

I prefer to write 10,000 notes instead of one letter.

1820 NAPOLEON on the relationship of music to the state:

Of all the arts, music has the most influence on the passions; therefore, a lawgiver should cultivate them most. A deeply felt symphony of the master's hand infallibly moves the mind and has far greater influence than a moral book that convinces reason without affecting habits.

Arthur SCHOPENHAUER on the Beethoven Symphony:

All human passions and affects speak of Beethoven's symphony: joy, sadness, love, hatred, terror, hope, etc., in innumerable nuances, but all, so to speak, only abstractly and without any particularity: it is their mere form here, we see the volitional movements transferred to the realm of mere conception, as which is the exclusive arena of the achievements of all the fine arts, since these absolutely demand the will itself stay tuned and we behave as pure recognizers. Therefore, the affections of the will itself, that is, real pain and real pleasure, should not be excited, but only their substitutes.

Richard WAGNER on dramatic music:

The new form of dramatic music, in turn, as music to form a work of art, must show the unity of the symphonic movement. And this reaches them when, in the most intimate connection with them, it extends over the whole drama, not only over individual, arbitrarily elevated parts of it. This unity gives itself then in the whole work of art passing through fabrics of basic themes, which are similar in the symphonic sentence, complement, re-form, separate and reconnect, except that here the performed dramatic action, the laws of divorces and connections, which were originally taken from the movements of the dance.

Giuseppe VERDI on the future of music: 1875

I could not tell you what to do to find a way out of this crisis of music. One would like to be a melodic like Bellini, the other a harmonist like Meyerbeer; I do not want one or the other, and if it were up to me, a young man who begins to compose should never think of being a melodist, harmonist, realist, idealist, musician of the future, or whatever devil's pedantic forms have invented. Melody and harmony must be in the artist's hand only means to bring about music - and when the day comes when one no longer speaks of melody and harmony, the German and Italian schools, the past and future of music, then the kingdom of art will probably begin. Another evil of the time is that all the works of the young people come from fear. Nobody writes about his heart, but when this youth goes to the letter, it has only the one thought that one does not offend the public and make love with the critics you tell me that I have to thank for my success in uniting both schools. I never thought of anything of the kind. Incidentally, this is an old story, it repeats itself again and again in others and after a certain time. And do not be worried, my dear Arrivabeel The art is not lost on it Depend on it: even the new has already achieved something. (from Giuseppe Verdi, letters, edited by Franz Werfel, Paul Zsolnay Verlag, Vienna 1926)

Hans PFITZNER over the listener:

The audience is part of the art whole, and just as there are good and bad works, good and bad performances, so there is a good and bad public. A good one is above all one with the longing to participate in the great art community, regardless of whether it consists of artists, dilettantes or laymen of all kinds; one that belongs to the work, not to a sensual detail. Just as the creator must be able to create and the performer must reproduce, the recipient must have the ability to receive and enjoy. It is also an art to be an audience. (from Collected Writings Vol. III Dr. Bruno Filser Verlag, Augsburg 1929)

Igor STRAWINSKY and the expression of music:

I believe that music by its very nature is incapable of "expressing" anything, whatever it may be: a feeling, an attitude, a psychological state, a natural phenomenon, or whatever else. "Expression" is never an immanent one property of the music, and in no way does its raison d'être depend on "expression". If, as is almost always the case, the music seems to express something, that is an illusion and not a reality. It is nothing but an external ingredient, a quality that we lend to music in accordance with the ancient tacitly inherited tradition, and with which we provide it as with a label, a formula - in short, it is a garment that we have out of habit or lack of insight All is gradually confused with the being to which we have put it. (from Erinnerungen, Atlantis-Verlag, Zurich-Berlin, 1937)

Paul HINDEMITH on content and form:

Even if the musical creative process in its last heights may always remain inaccessible to human comprehension, like the mysterious source of artistic work in general, yet the point of separation between conscious and unconscious action can be greatly increased. If that were not the case, anyone with this limit still very low could claim to be creating the greatest works of art. There would be no difference between Beethoven and any composer who has laboriously penetrated to a quarter of the human achievable level of artistic achievement and has no suspicion of the three quarters towering above him.

This little man will be reluctant to speak of crafting things, invoking his inspiration, his feeling, his heart, which dictates the way of his actions. Must not this be a tiny inspiration, a meaningless feeling that can be expressed with so little knowledge? Is not a tremendous amount of conscious material mastery and application heard in tones that dictate the heart? Can the mental image of a music that the composer has seen make clear to the receiving counterpart at all, if the power of the sound, the self-glorification of the sound connections, always remain again between the inspiration of the composer and her audible staged form of expression? (from instruction in the composition Bd. I. B. Schott sons, Mainz, 1940)

Wilhelm FURTWÄNGLER about the genius:

It can not be denied that the very term "genius" has become highly suspect to us humans of today. There is a good reason for that. Of course, one defends oneself against a state of dependence on many of the inspirations less; not by the people or - more accurately - by the "public"; this has always been the natural bearer of all genius worship, all genius cult. But on the part of those directly involved in the art world, especially the mediocre artists. If, however, the combined efforts of artists, theoreticians, historians, etc. failed to dethrone the genius, that is essentially only one sign - one of the few signs - that art is still ours & really needed.

Bibliography

The Origin

Anderson, Robert, Salwa El-Shawan Castelo-Branco, and Virginia Danielson. "Egypt, Arab Republic of (Jumhuriyat Misr al-Arabiya)". The New Grove Dictionary of Music and Musicians, second edition, edited by Stanley Sadie and John Tyrrell. London: Macmillan Publishers, 2001

Anon. "Music in Ancient Egypt". Music in Roman Egypt: An Exhibition at the Kelsey Museum of Archaeology 19 March–19 December 1999 (accessed 28 June 2014)

Anon. "Music of Ancient Rome". Georgia Regents University Augusta (2001). Archived from the original on 2013-06-08. Retrieved 2013-05-28

Anon. "Cymbals: UC 33268". University College London website, 2003 (accessed 28 June 2014)

Anon. "Ancient Iraqi Harp Reproduced by Liverpool Engineers". University of Liverpool website (28 July 2005). Archive from 1 July 2010 (Accessed 21 May 2013)

Hickmann, Hans. "Un Zikr Dans le Mastaba de Debhen, Guîzah (IVème Dynastie)." Journal of the International Folk Music Council 9 (1957): 59–62

Hickmann, Hans. "Rythme, mètre et mesure de la musique instrumentale et vocale des anciens Egyptiens." Acta Musicologica 32, no. 1 (January–March 1960)

Kilmer, Anne Draffkorn. "The Strings of Musical Instruments: their Names, Numbers, and Significance". Studies in Honor of Benno Landsberger = Assyriological Studies 16 (1965)

Young Mozart - prodigy

Cairns, David (2006). Mozart and His Operas. Berkeley, CA: University of California Press. ISBN 978-0-520-22898-6. OCLC 62290645

Gutman, Robert (2000). Mozart: A Cultural Biography. London: Harcourt Brace. ISBN 978-0-15-601171-6. OCLC 45485135

Holmes, Edward (2005). The Life of Mozart. New York: Cosimo Classics. ISBN 978-1-59605-147-8. OCLC 62790104

Mozart, Wolfgang (1972). Mersmann, Hans (ed.). Letters of Wolfgang Amadeus Mozart. New York: Dover Publications. ISBN 978-0-486-22859-4. OCLC 753483

"New Mozart Pieces Unveiled (Video)". The Huffington Post. 8 February 2009. Retrieved 29 September 2010

Till, Nicholas (1995). Mozart and the Enlightenment: Truth, Virtue and Beauty in Mozart's Operas. New York City: W.W. Norton & Company. ISBN 978-0-393-31395-6. OCLC 469628809

Mozarts on tour –wizard

Solomon, Maynard (1995). Mozart: A Life (1st ed.). New York City: HarperCollins. ISBN 978-0-06-019046-0. OCLC 31435799

Rosen, Charles (1998). The Classical Style: Haydn, Mozart, Beethoven (2nd ed.). New York City: W.W. Norton & Company. ISBN 978-0-393-31712-1. OCLC 246977555

Mozart's Letters, Mozart's Life: Selected Letters. Translated by Robert Spaethling. W.W. Norton. 2000.

Wolff, Christoph (2012) Mozart at the Gateway to His Fortune: Serving the Emperor, 1788–1791. New York: Norton. ISBN 978-0-393-05070-7

(in German) Haberl, Dieter (2006). "Beethovens erste Reise nach Wien: die Datierung seiner Schülerreise zu W.A. Mozart". Neues Musikwissenschaftliches Jahrbuch (14). OCLC 634798176

Don Giovanni – second to none

Steptoe, Andrew (1990). The Mozart–Da Ponte Operas: The Cultural and Musical Background to Le nozze di Figaro, Don Giovanni, and Così fan tutte. Oxford: Clarendon Press. ISBN 978-0-19-816221-6. OCLC 22895166

Wakin, Daniel J. (24 August 2010). "After Mozart's Death, an Endless Coda". The New York Times. ISSN 0362-4331

Halliwell, Ruth (1998). The Mozart Family: Four Lives in a Social Context. New York City: Clarendon Press. ISBN 978-0-19-816371-8. OCLC 36423516

Einstein, Alfred (1965). Mozart: His Character, His Work. Galaxy Book 162. Arthur Mendel, Nathan Broder (trans.) (6th ed.). New York City: Oxford University Press. ISBN 978-0-304-92483-7. OCLC 456644858.

Da Ponte, Lorenzo. Mozart's Don Giovanni. Dover Publications, New York, 1985. (reviewed in G.S. "Untitled." Music & Letters Vol 19. No. 2 (April 1938)

Rushton, Julian G. (1981). W. A. Mozart: Don Giovanni" Cambridge. (reviewed in Sternfeld, F. W. "Untitled." Music & Letters, Vol. 65, No. 4 (October 1984)

Schünemann, Georg and Soldan, Kurt (translated by Stanley Appelbaum) Don Giovanni: Complete orchestral and vocal score Dover 1974

Folk Music - and folklore

Bronson, Bertrand Harris. The Singing Tradition of Child's Popular Ballads (Princeton: Princeton University Press, 1976).

Czekanowska, Anna. Polish Folk Music: Slavonic Heritage – Polish Tradition – Contemporary Trends. Cambridge Studies in Ethnomusicology, Reissue 2006 (Paperback). ISBN 0-521-02797-7

Cooley, Timothy J. Making Music in the Polish Tatras: Tourists, Ethnographers, and Mountain Musicians. Indiana University Press, 2005 (Hardcover with CD). ISBN 0-253-34489-1

Pegg, Carole (2001). "Folk Music". The New Grove Dictionary of Music and Musicians, edited by Stanley Sadie and John Tyrrell. London: Macmillan.

Cartwright, Garth (2005). Princes Amongst Men: Journeys with Gypsy Musicians. London: Serpent's Tail. ISBN 1-85242-877-5

Ludwig v. Beethoven - eroica

Clive, H.P. (2001). Beethoven and His World: A Biographical Dictionary. Oxford University Press. ISBN 978-0-19-816672-6

Kerman, Joseph; Tyson, Alan; Burnham, Scott G. "Ludwig van Beethoven". In Deane L. Root (ed.). Grove Music Online. Oxford Music Online. Oxford University Press

Lockwood, Lewis (17 January 2005). Beethoven: The Music and the Life. W.W. Norton. ISBN 978-0-393-32638-3

Rosen, Charles. The Classical Style: Haydn, Mozart, Beethoven. Expanded ed. New York: W.W. Norton, 1998. ISBN 0-393-04020-8, 0-393-31712-9

Solomon, Maynard (November 2000). Beethoven (2nd revised ed.). New York: Ingram Pub Services. ISBN 978-0-8256-7163-0

Sullivan, J.W.N., Beethoven: His Spiritual Development New York: Alfred A. Knopf, 1927.

Frederic Chopin - virtuoso

Chopin, Fryderyk (1962). Selected Correspondence of Fryderyk Chopin, coll. B. Sydow, tr. Arthur Hedley. London: Heinemann

Kubba, Adam and Madeleine Young (1998). "The Long Suffering of Frederic Chopin", in Chest, vol. 113 (1998), pp. 210–16. accessed 16 August 2014

Rosen, Charles (1995). The Romantic Generation. Cambridge, Massachusetts: Harvard University Press. ISBN 978-0-674-77933-4

Schumann, Robert (1988), tr. and ed. Henry Pleasants. Schumann on Music: A Selection from the Writings. New York: Dover Publications

Zamoyski, Adam (2010). Chopin: Prince of the Romantics. London: HarperCollins. ISBN 978-0-00-735182-4 (e-book edition)

The Romantics - adventurists

Blume, Friedrich. 1970. Classic and Romantic Music, translated by M. D. Herter Norton from two essays first published in Die Musik in Geschichte und Gegenwart. New York: W. W. Norton.

Cavalletti, Carlo. 2000. Chopin and Romantic Music, translated by Anna Maria Salmeri Pherson. Hauppauge, NY: Barron›s Educational Series. (Hardcover) ISBN 0-7641-5136-3; ISBN 978-0-7641-5136-1

Einstein, Alfred. 1947. Music in the Romantic Era. New York: W. W. Norton.

Encyclopædia Britannica (n.d.). "Romanticism". Britannica.com. Retrieved 2010-08-24

Grout, Donald Jay. 1960. A History of Western Music. New York: W. W. Norton & Company, Inc.

Samson, Jim. 2001. "Romanticism". The New Grove Dictionary of Music and Musicians, second edition, edited by Stanley Sadie and John Tyrrell. London: Macmillan Publishers

Wagner - The monster of genius

Borchmeyer, Dieter (2003), Drama and the World of Richard Wagner, Princeton: Princeton University Press. ISBN 978-0-691-11497-2

Conway, David (2002), "'A Vulture is Almost an Eagle' ... The Jewishness of Richard Wagner", Jewry in Music website, accessed 23 November 2012

Grant, John (1999), "Excalibur: US movie", in John Clute & John Grant (eds.) The Encyclopedia of Fantasy, Orbit, 324. ISBN 1-85723-893-1

Long, Michael (2008), Beautiful monsters: imagining the classic in musical media, Berkeley: University of California Press. ISBN 0-520-25720-0

Spotts, Frederic (1994), Bayreuth: A History of the Wagner Festival, New Haven and London: Yale University Press. ISBN 978-0-300-06665-4

Wagner, Cosima (ed. and tr. Geoffrey Skelton) (1994), Cosima Wagner's Diaries: an Abridgement. London: Pimlico Books. ISBN 978-0-7126-5952-9

Puccini - a problem here?

Berger, William, Puccini Without Excuses: A Refreshing Reassessment of the World's Most Popular Composer, Random House Digital, 2005, ISBN 1-4000-7778-8

Kendell, Colin (2012), The Complete Puccini: The Story of the World's Most Popular Operatic Composer, Stroud, Gloucestershire: Amberley Publishing, 2012. ISBN 9781445604459 ISBN 1-4456-0445-0

Sadie, Stanley (ed.), The New Grove Dictionary of Music and Musicians, London: Macmillan/New York: Grove, 1980, ISBN 1-56159-174-2

Puccini - Opera style

Budden, Julian, Puccini: His Life and Works, Oxford University Press, 2002 ISBN 978-0-19-816468-5

Carner, Mosco (1959). Puccini: A Critical Biography. Alfred Knopf.

Keolker, James, "Last Acts, The Operas of Puccini and His Italian Contemporaries", 2001

Osborne, Charles, The Complete Operas of Puccini: A Critical Guide, De Capo Press, (1982)

Béla Bartók – a Mikro-kosmos

Anon. 1945. "Bela Bartok Dies In Hospital Here". archive.nytimes.com. (27 September).

Einstein, Alfred. 1947. Music in the Romantic Era. New York: W. W. Norton.

Matthews, Peter. 2012. "Bartók in New York". Feast of Music website #1Lib1Ref (accessed 26 September 2018).[unreliable source?]

Rockwell, John. 1982. "Kodaly Was More Than a Composer". The New York Times (12 December).

Stevens, Halsey. 1993. The Life and Music of Béla Bartók, third edition, prepared by Malcolm Gillies. New York: Oxford University Press. ISBN 978-0-19-816349-7

Stevens, Halsey. 2018. "Béla Bartók: Hungarian Composer". Encyclopædia Britannica online (accessed 27 September 2018).

Wilson, Paul. 1992. The Music of Béla Bartók. New Haven: Yale University Press. ISBN 0-300-05111-5

Kurt Weil – Three Penny Opera

Brook, Stephen, ed. (1996). Opera: A Penguin Anthology. London: Penguin Books. ISBN 978-0-14-026073-1.

David Drew. Kurt Weill: A Handbook (Berkeley, Los Angeles, University of California Press, 1987). ISBN 0-520-05839-9

Hinton, Stephen (1990). Kurt Weill: The Threepenny Opera. Cambridge: Cambridge University Press. ISBN 978-0-521-33026-8

Stephen Hinton. "Weill's Musical Theater: Stages of Reform" (University of California Press, 2012) ISBN 978-0520271777

Taruskin, Richard (2010). Music in the Early Twentieth Century. Oxford: Oxford University Press. ISBN 978-0-19-538484-0

Marlene Dietrich – la Chanson

Bach, Steven (2011). Marlene Dietrich: Life and Legend. University of Minnesota Press. ISBN 978-0-8166-7584-5.

Chandler, Charlotte (2011). Marlene Dietrich, a personal biography. Simon & Schuster. ISBN 978-1-4391-8835-4.

O'Connor, Patrick (1991). The Amazing Blonde Woman: Dietrich's Own Style. London: Bloomsbury Publishing. ISBN 978-0-7475-1264-6.

Spoto, Donald (1992). Blue Angel: The Life of Marlene Dietrich Doubleday. ISBN 978-0-385-42553-7.

Walker, Alexander (1984). Dietrich. Harper & Row. ISBN 978-0-06-015319-9

Eric Korngold – Robin Hood

"Erich Wolfgang Korngold Biography". ClassicalConnect.com.

Behlmer, Rudy. The Adventures of Robin Hood, Univ. of Wisconsin Press (1979)

Bernardi, Daniel. Hollywood's Chosen People: The Jewish Experience in American Cinema, Wayne State University Press (2013)

"Korngold Makes Interesting Music Discovery," Los Angeles Times, June 22, 1939 p. 10

Carroll, Brendan G. The New Grove Dictionary of Music and Musicians

Steinberg, Michael, The Concerto, a Listener's Guide (Oxford and New York: Oxford University Press, 1998). ISBN 0-19-510330-0.

"Erich Wolfgang Korngold (1897–1957): The Piano Music: Film Music on the Web CD Reviews November 2003". www.musicweb-international.com. Retrieved 2015-12-02.

On Broadway – the Musical

Bordman, Gerald. American Musical Comedy (Oxford University Press, 1982)

Kenrick, John. "History of The Musical Stage. 1950s I: When Broadway Ruled" musicals101. com, accessed December 2, 2012

Knapp, Raymond. The American Musical and the Formation of National Identity (Princeton University Press, 2005)

Lynne B. Sagalyn (2003). Times Square Roulette: Remaking the City Icon. MIT Press. ISBN 978-0-262-69295-3. Retrieved February 26, 2013.

Snyder, Robert W. *The Encyclopedia of New York City* (New Haven: Yale University Press, 1995), Kenneth T. Jackson, editor, p. 1226.

Stempel, Larry. Showtime: A History of the Broadway Musical Theater (WW Norton, 2010)

Beatles Fever – first rock stars

Epstein, Brian (1964). A Cellarful of Noise. Byron Preiss. ISBN 978-0-671-01196-3. OCLC 39211052.

Frontani, Michael R. (2007). The Beatles: Image and the Media. University Press of Mississippi. ISBN 978-1-57806-965-1.

Kirchherr, Astrid; Voormann, Klaus (1999). Hamburg Days. Guildford, Surrey: Genesis Publications. ISBN 978-0-904351-73-6.

MacDonald, Ian (2005). Revolution in the Head: The Beatles' Records and the Sixties (2nd revised ed.). London: Pimlico. ISBN 978-1-84413-828-9.

Turner, Steve (2005). A Hard Day's Write: The Stories Behind Every Beatles Song (3rd ed.). New York: Harper Paperbacks. ISBN 978-0-06-084409-7.